# SOUTHERN WEALTH

### AND

# NORTHERN PROFITS

# SOUTHERN WEALTH

AND

# NORTHERN PROFITS

AS EXHIBITED IN

STATISTICAL FACTS AND OFFICAL FIGURES:

SHOWING THE

NECESSITY OF UNION TO THE FUTURE PROSPERITY

AND

WELFARE OF THE REPUBLIC.

BY

THOMAS PRENTICE KETTELL,

LATE EDITOR OF THE DEMOCRATIC REVIEW

*Introduction, Bibliography and Index by*
FLETCHER M. GREEN

———

UNIVERSITY OF ALABAMA PRESS

ORIGINAL EDITION:
Entered according to Act of Congress, in the year 1860,
By GEO. W. & JOHN A. WOOD,
In the Clerk's Office of the District Court of the United States for the Southern
District of New York.

0-8173-5012-8 (pbk: alk. paper)
Copyright © 1965 by
UNIVERSITY OF ALABAMA PRESS
Library of Congress Catalog Card Number 65-12246
Manufactured in the United States of America

# CONTENTS.

# INTRODUCTION

## THOMAS PRENTICE KETTELL:

### ECONOMIST, EDITOR, AND HISTORIAN

THOMAS PRENTICE KETTELL was an outstanding spokesman of that group of pre-Civil War Northerners who earnestly believed that it was possible to save their country from the horrors of a sectional conflict, who worked many years to prevent the threatened dissolution of the Union, but zealously supported the national government during the Civil War in the hope that military victory would achieve what thirty years of wrangling, negotiation, and compromise had failed to accomplish—namely the preservation of a united North and South. Most of this Northern group were linked by economic ties to the planters cf the South. As merchants, shippers, and financiers they largely depended upon the cotton trade for much of their prosperity; hence they opposed governmental policies which they believed would disturb their connections with the South and the foundations on which their economic prosperity and well being rested.[1] But the fact that their ideas and position were founded on selfish economic interests did not make their action dishonest or unpatriotic.

Antislavery writers often referred to New York City as the prolongation of the South where "ten thousand cords of interest are linked with the Southern Slaveholder." In fact, New York was a stronghold of Southern sympathizers. Her newspapers

[1] For an excellent treatment of this subject see Philip Sheldon Foner, *The New York Merchants and the Irrepressible Conflict*. See especially vii, 1-5.

ix

regularly carried advertisements addressed specifically to Southerners urging them to visit their stores which specialized in merchandise designed exclusively for the Southern trade. Many of the New York business firms had branches in Southern cities, and some few New York stores were branches of Southern business enterprises.[2] Many New York shipping merchants would have found it almost impossible to carry on a profitable ocean going commerce without cotton, tobacco, and other raw materials produced in the South. They also depended upon Southern products to purchase return cargoes from Europe for, despite the large quantities of Western corn and wheat which poured into New York by canal and railroad, the chief cargo of European bound ocean packets was cotton. Furthermore, since a large part of Southern products was exported from New York City, the coastal vessels were ladened with goods destined for the Southern cities.[3] One contemporary account estimated that New York merchants annually sold merchandise to the five cotton states valued at $131,000,000 and that the total business with the five states was above $200,000,000.[4]

The movement for Southern economic independence which got under way in the 1830's filled the merchants of New York with fear, not because they were worried by the Southern Commercial Conventions but because of the influence of the abolition movement. The merchants feared that, because of the sectional controversy over slavery, *New York* printed on a box of merchandise would symbolize to the Southerners hostility to slavery and Southern Rights. Above all they feared the struggle over slavery would lead to the dissolution of the Union, thereby achieving what direct trade conventions, commercial conventions, and propaganda campaigns could not accomplish. Hence "a vast majority of New York merchants regarded the agitation of the slavery question and the interference with the rights of Southern slave holders as inexpedient, unjust, and pregnant with evils." It was not a question of morals with the merchants but

2 Thomas Prentice Kettell, *The "Southern Trade": An Epitome of Commerce North and South.* See advertisement pages.
3 Robert Greenhalgh Albion, *The Rise of the New York Port, 1815-1860*, 95-96.
4 Stephen Colwell, *The Five Cotton States and New York* (Philadelphia, 1861).

of millions of dollars in Southern trade which would be jeopardized. One of them wrote to Samuel J. May, a New York abolition leader: "We cannot afford, Sir, to let you and your associates endeavor to overthrow slavery. It is not a matter of principle with us. It is a matter of business necessity. . . . we mean, Sir, to put you abolitionists down, by fair means if we can, by foul means if we must."[5]

Thomas Prentice Kettell, son of Thomas Prentice, senior, and his wife Hannah Dawes Pierce Kettell, was born in Boston, Massachusetts, in 1811. His forebears had left England and first settled in Charlestown, Massachusetts, in 1634. Among Thomas' colonial ancestors were architects, merchants, ministers, and soldiers. His father, a merchant, served for twenty-four years in the state senate. Thomas was educated in the Boston schools but as a youth displayed an avid interest in commercial pursuits, and on occasion accompanied his father on trading voyages to the North Atlantic port cities. He was employed for some years in a Boston hardware store, and then went to Europe as a representative of various exporting firms. He visited many of the leading cities of Europe, became acquainted with leading merchants—several of whom he later used as subjects for biographical sketches in American journals—but most important for his future career he studied "the course of general operations of international commerce, with a view to reconcile the practical workings of trade with the general practice of the economists."[6]

Upon his return to the United States in 1837, Kettell settled in New York City where he began his career as a writer, publicist, and editor in the fields of commerce, finance, and industry in which he was to attain not only national but international recognition. In fact, Freeman Hunt in 1849 wrote that Kettell ranked along with McCulloch, Macgregor, Taylor, Tucker, and Carey as the leading authorities in the field of economics.[7]

James Gordon Bennett, founder and editor of the New York *Herald,* had in 1835 begun a series of articles dealing with

5 Foner, 13-14.

6 "Commercial Sketches with Pen and Pencil. Thomas Prentice Kettell," *Hunt's Merchants' Magazine,* XX (June, 1849), 618-627. Portrait facing page 576.

7 Freeman Hunt, "The Editor to His Friends and Patrons," *Hunt's Merchants' Magazine,* XXI (July, 1849), 143-144.

economic conditions. He employed Kettell in 1837 to do a series titled "Money Articles" which "became famous throughout the commercial and financial circles of Europe and the United States, and the public, those with money to invest as well as the Bulls and Bears, . . . derived great benefit in having the financial affairs of the world daily spread before them."[8] Prior to 1837 the public press had not systematically followed commercial events nor exerted itself in the advocacy of economic measures distinct from party politics. Kettell changed this. He determined to expose pernicious conditions and practices in commercial and financial matters and to suggest judicious issues. His articles were penetrating and informative and soon attracted general attention throughout the United States and in the major financial and commercial cities of Europe. From 1837 to 1843, during which period the series regularly appeared, "they acquired an almost oracular authority."[9]

The press generally was high in its praise of the "Money Articles." The Boston *Courier* printed with approval the statement of a leading merchant of that city that Kettell was a "man of extensive knowledge of the mercantile affairs of the country, and a mind of uncommon shrewdness in observation." Frank P. Blair of the Washington *Globe* in 1841 characterized Kettell as a "man of principle, of judgment, of information. His views of the Exchequer scheme are characterized by honesty and patriotism, and by the judicious and practical considerations which have given so much deserved weight to his notices of the monetary concerns of the country." The Hartford (Connecticut) *Times* declared, "These articles are among the best, if not the very best that are written for the American Press, on the monetary affairs, public or private, of the country. The author is not . . . a blind partisan, but a clear headed, honest, and most able collector and disseminator of facts." Complimentary

8 Frederick Hudson, *Journalism in the United States, from 1690 to 1872* (New York: Harper and Brothers, 1873), 434. There is a controversy over the authorship of the articles. Hudson claims that Bennett was the author but modern authorities recognize Kettell as the author of the "Money Articles." See Alfred D. Chandler, Jr., *Henry Varnum Poor: Business Editor, Analyst, and Reformer*, 335, n. 37, who says Kettell even originated the Bennett series.

9 *Ibid.*, 101.

reports came in also from abroad. The *Times* (London) wrote: "The New York *Herald* has been one of the most powerful instruments in the United States in exposing the frauds, bubbles, and stock-gambling machinery which our fund managers had organized in America for robbing the land and labor of that country, as they have robbed this since the days of Walpole. For correctness of detail, research, industry, sound political economy and decided talent . . . [the] Money Articles have not yet been equalled on this side of the Water."

Members of both houses of Congress—one contemporary writer said "nearly every member of the Senate"—publicly acknowledged Kettell's ability to expose the evils of the financial system. They spoke of "the clearness of his style, the perfect mastery of his subject . . . the fullness and accuracy of his information, and the soundness of his judgment." William Allen, Senator from Ohio, remarked in 1842 "that for a year or two past they ["Money Articles"] have, in general, displayed a very uncommon industry and ability, and greatly aided in displacing error and exposing frauds and corruption with which the country has been so long afflicted through its corporations, its currency, its stock jobbers and paper [stock] mongers." And Thomas W. Bagley, a Representative from Virginia, declared that the "Money Articles were written with an ability which the whole country acknowledged."[10]

Possessed of vigorous intellect, clear perception and rare sagacity, Kettell grasped the essence of a problem and presented it with a force and clearness that carried conviction. His "Money Articles" constitute a valuable commentary upon the stirring economic and financial problems of the late thirties and forties and gave him a reputation as one of the ablest and soundest economists of that day. Freeman Hunt declared that Kettell was "one of the most forceful writers on political economy in the Country," that he had "done more to impart a respectable character to the tone of the press on that subject than any other," and that he was entitled to a high rank among the economic reformers of the day; a class of men whose labors effect a world of good, while the laborers are scarcely known even by name to those who profit most by their exertions."[11]

10 "Commercial Sketches," 624-627.
11 Hunt, "The Editor to His Friends," 143-144.

The reputation and fame he gained by the "Money Articles" opened for Kettell a wider field of activity. In January 1846 he was appointed editor of the *United States Magazine and Democratic Review*, the semi-official organ of the Democratic Party and the spokesman of the expansionists or "Young America" element of that party in the 1840's and 1850's. He held the post until December 1851. He contributed four signed articles to the *Review* during that period, three of which were concerned primarily with the South. These were "Stability of the Union," "The South," and "The Methodist Church Property Case."

The theme of "Stability of the Union," based on official United States data, was that the industrial and material well being of the North depended largely upon the production of raw materials in the South which in turn depended upon slave labor. Kettell maintained that the South produced the greater part of the national wealth of the Union and that the North gained, through the influence of her capital and the operation of federal laws, bounties, tariffs, etc., a large proportion of that wealth. He also criticized the abolition attacks upon slavery.[12]

In "The South" Kettell claimed that his first article had made a strong impression on the North and had resulted in "a manifest subsidence in the suicidal cry against Southern institutions." His study of commerce, capital, and industry had convinced Kettell "of the criminal folly of attempting to disturb the only conditions upon which a society may almost be said to exist." He declared that the chief articles of American trade and commerce were the raw materials produced by slave labor in the South. In return for their servitude "the Africans receive civilization and Christianity in addition to physical support." Without their servitude the "Negro slaves would still be Pagan cannibals." And if "civilization and Christianity are things of value" they should not "be left out of the account of black remuneration for service by those [the Northern abolitionists] who profess to hold the precepts of Scripture, as they understand it, to be the highest law of our government."[13] This

12 Kettell, "Stability of the Union," *United States Magazine and Democratic Review*, XXVI (January, 1850), 1-16.
13 Kettell, "The South," *United States and Democratic Review*, XXVIII (February, 1851), 139-147.

defense of slavery and criticism of the abolitionists was highly pleasing to Southern slaveholders.

Kettell's view of the attempt of the Methodist Episcopal Church [North] to deny the Methodist Episcopal Church South its share of the property held by the parent church before the division in 1845 may be summed up in his statement that "the thieving spirit of philanthropy which bred this scism for the sake of robbing the South . . . was stimulated and nurtured by English Methodists."[14] He is bitter in his condemnation but ignores the fact that the Reverend Orange Scott who first seceded from the church was a native New Englander not an English Methodist.

Relinquishing his post as editor of the *United States Magazine and Democratic Review,* Kettell became owner and editor of the *United States Economist* in 1852. He patterned his magazine after the London *Economist* and adopted as a subtitle "A weekly journal devoted to political economy, finance, commerce, manufactures, and agriculture." He gave to the *United States Economist* a reputation unequaled by that of any of its competitors and established an editorial policy that remained with the *Economist* for nearly thirty years. His financial and business analyses often surpassed those of his chief competitor, *Hunt's Merchants' Magazine.* He also gave his readers general political and foreign news, and his broad knowledge, good sense, and sound judgment assured his readers of his reliability.[15]

In the field of transportation and especially railroads Kettell's *Economist* was the major competitor of Henry Varnum Poor's *Railway Journal.* Kettell's articles were more general and not always accurate but they were always suggestive and cleverly written. Kettell furnished the American people much information on railroads during the 1850's and sponsored the Illinois Central which was of much interest to Southerners because of its tie up with the Mobile and Ohio road in the first federal land grant to railroads. The *Economist* also provided its readers with valuable information on political as well as economic problems. In fact its editorials carried almost as much weight

[14] Kettell, "The Methodist Church Property Case, U.S. Circuit Court, Southern District of New York, 1851," *United States and Democratic Review,* XXIX (October, 1851), 382-383.

[15] David P. Forsyth, *The Business Press in America, 1750-1865* (Philadelphia: Chilton Books, 1964), 86.

on business conditions both here and abroad as did the London *Times*.[16]

Kettell began to write for Freeman *Hunt's Merchants' Magazine* in 1845 when he published an article on "British Commercial Policy." It was soon followed by "A Hamburg Merchant in His Counting House" and "Commercial Treaties of the United States: With Reference to the Progress of Commercial Freedom." All three of these articles grew out of travel and studies in Europe, supplemented of course by research in America. In November, 1847, Kettell began his great series on "State Debts of Europe and America." Twelve chapters were published (1847-1858) covering all of the Eastern and Midwestern states. Maryland was the only Southern state studied. In some 155 pages Kettell gave a thorough and exhaustive treatment of this question, delving into the financial burdens, and the significance of state debts for the people. The articles are noted for the research and ability that went into them, and they constitute the most comprehensive and reliable account of the debts, finance, and resources of the several states studied. As such they are a most valuable storehouse of data for the historian.

When Hunt died on March 2, 1858, he was succeeded as editor by Kettell who also continued to edit the *United States Economist* until he sold it in 1859. Kettell edited *Hunt's Merchants' Magazine* until 1861. While editor of the *United States and Democratic Review*, Kettell had begun to write for James Dunwoody Brownson DeBow's *Commercial Review of the South and West*, published in New Orleans.

Between September 1847 and September 1856 Kettell contributed eight articles to *DeBow's Review*. In the two articles on "Progress of American Commerce, Agriculture, and Manufactures," Kettell analyzed the credit system and warehouse exchanges, discussed banks, imports, and exports, especially Southern commodities, and concluded that these gave to the South and nation "promise of greater and more lasting prosperity than perhaps any which the commercial world has heretofore witnessed."[17] In "The Money of Commerce" and "Cur-

16 Chandler, 33, 101, 221.

17 The two articles appear in *DeBow's Review*, IV (September, 1847), 85-95, and (November, 1847), 326-337. The quotation is found on page 85.

rency and Banks," Kettell emphasized the importance of private
capital and the banks of New Orleans. He related the Southern
export trade to the Bank of England and the French banking
practices. He dealt also with state banking policies and warned
of the injurious effects of state financial legislation.[18] In "The
Commercial Growth and Greatness of New York," Kettell described the growth and significance of the port and its role in
the shipping, commercial, and financial life of the South.[19] In
"The Industry of the South" Kettell discussed recent develop-
ments in manufacturing and, basing his interpretations on the
abundance of raw materials, labor, capital, and markets, pre-
dicted a bright future for textiles, lumber, and tobacco.[20]
"Stability of the Union," a reprint from the *United States and
Democratic Review* and analyzed above, was probably Kettell's
most significant contribution to *DeBow's Review*.[21] But "The
Future of the South" was the most pleasing to his Southern
readers. It is primarily a discussion and defense of the institution of slavery as it existed in the South. Kettell declared that
the cotton which had "enveloped the commercial world, and
bound the fortunes of American slaves so firmly to human
progress, that civilization may also be said to depend upon the
continual servitude of the blacks in America." The cotton textile industry formed an indissoluble cord, "binding the black
who was threatened to be cut off [from] human progress," for
"the black race . . . has made no progress whatsoever [in
Africa]. They were without invention, almost without language,
and destitute of the faculties or the wish to advance." Kettell
further argued that American wealth and power were largely
based upon the culture of cotton which in turn depended upon
slave labor. Northern shipping was basically in Southern commodities which in turn paid the duties on imports. In fact the
economic prosperity of both North and South depended upon
Southern staples. Truly cotton was King! The only trouble
was that the textile industry was located too far from the source
of cotton. But that would change. England had had the advantage prior to 1830 because of her control of the ocean. New

18 *Ibid.*, VI (October, 1848), 243-264, and IX (October, 1850),
412-416.
19 *Ibid.*, V (June, 1848), 30-44.
20 *Ibid.*, XII (February, 1852), 169-181.
21 *Ibid.*, VIII (April, 1850), 348-363.

England now dominated the industry but she was losing and control would soon shift to the South. Kettell concluded: "There are conditions which shadow forth the greatness and power of the South, and as she rises in power and wealth she will elevate the black race with her. She will have, however, to encounter the zealous hatred of rivals whose philanthropy will be developed as her prosperity increases. It is, however, through the long lesson of industry taught by white surveillance, that the great work of regeneration of the black race can be accomplished."[22] However far from truth or reality these views may have been, Kettell's words were as sweet music to his Southern readers.

Three of the articles discussed above, with slight changes in titles, were reprinted in DeBow's, *Industrial Resources of the Southern and Western States,* 3 volumes (New Orleans: De-Bow's Review, 1852, 1853). They were "New York," "Union— Its Stability," and "The Future of the South."[23]

A sequel to Kettell's article "The Stability of the Union," which as already noted was published in three periodicals, was his "Strength of Union—Magic of Cooperation" which appeared in 1860. The editor of *The Southern Trade,* in which "Strength of Union" was published, introduced it with the statement that Kettell had presented "facts and figures . . . in a clear and concise manner, showing the all-pervading influence of Southern productions on the commerce and wealth of the country and exposing the fallacies sought to be imposed on the credulous, by the fabrications of 'Helper's Impending Crisis.'" The editor hoped, in vain as time was to tell, that the article "would commend itself to the calm reflection of every thinking man."[24]

Kettell developed his argument historically. England was the first of the great nations to reap the benefits of the commercial

---

22 *DeBow's Review,* XXI (September, 1856), 308-323.

23 See Vol. II (1853), 154-164; Vol. III (1853), 357-367 and 37-45.

24 Kettell, "Strength of Union—Magic of Cooperation," *The Southern Trade. An Epitome of Commerce North and South, Etc., with a Directory of Prominent New York Houses Interested in Southern Trade,* No. 2 (May, 1860). Kettell's article begins on page 5, moves to even numbered pages 6 to 26 and is continuous on pages 28-32. I have been unable to locate but one copy, that in Widener Library, Harvard University.

and industrial revolution of the last half of the eighteenth century. She did this through her exploitation of India and the development of the continental and West Indian colonies through forced labor of more than two and one half million Negro slaves. In the nineteenth century the United States forged ahead through prosperity based upon profits drawn from the compulsory labor of other races of men. The North supplied manufactured goods to the South and in return received raw materials produced by slave labor. The North exchanged manufactured goods—hardware, drygoods, shoes, groceries, and so on—for the raw materials of the South. In other words the South had the wealth, while the North acquired the profits. And every person in the North shared in these profits. Nevertheless, some Northerners—abolitionists—had begun to quarrel with the manners and customs of the South and attempted "to force upon them a new system of morality." In doing so they were driving a wedge between the two sections which neither really desired. If the North "should supinely permit a few unscrupulous politicians, clerical agitators, and reprobate parsons to hasten, . . . [their] most wanton attacks upon the institutions of their best customers" piety would be their only "reward and their crown of martyrdom" might be, in fact, "an idiot's cup."

In conclusion, Kettell maintained that the North had already suffered economically because of the abolition attacks upon slavery. "This state of things cannot but be of pecuniary injury to the North, even when the present distrust shall have passed away, and the loyalty of the whole people for the Union, its compromises, its duties and obligations shall have manifested itself so strongly as to bury forever in oblivion those politicians who seek advancement by agitating purely sectional issues." And he earnestly pleaded with Northerners to cease their attacks upon the South "before any further serious difficulties grew out of . . . [the disturbed] state of the public mind."[25]

Kettell's supreme and final effort to convince the Northern people that it was to their best interests to cease their attacks upon the South and her institutions, especially slavery, in order to preserve the Union was the publication of *Southern Wealth and Northern Profits, as Exhibited in Statistical Facts and*

[25] *Ibid.,* 24, 26, 32.

*Official Figures: Showing the Necessity of Union to the Future Prosperity and Welfare of the Republic.* As the title indicates his approach was entirely economic. There was no attempt to meet the moral argument of the abolitionists. This was his strength and his weakness. Exaggerated, and even false his arguments might be, yet they were widely accepted in some circles; but they were of no weight to those who found slavery a great moral issue. Hence there was no hope of bringing the two groups together. Furthermore by 1860 Kettell had himself reached the stage where he would not listen to those who disagreed with him. Too long had he repeated his own arguments. He was immovable. He castigated his opponents in extremely abusive language. If they did not agree with him, they were corrupt, unscrupulous, slanderers, prevaricators, and reprobate parsons.

The publisher's blurb, probably written by Kettell himself for it has the tone and phraseology as well as the substance and ideas of his earlier writings, is a forthright statement of the author's views and purpose. It reads:

This able work addresses itself peculiarly to the *patriotism* and *interests* of the *American people,* at this juncture, when it has become the duty of every good citizen, whatever may be his political creed, to aid in spreading the light of that truth which alone is depended upon to "combat error where the press is free." The press and the pulpit have stirred up domestic strife by broadcast misrepresentations of the South and her institutions, and the greatest exertions have been made to create a belief in Southern decrepitude and distress as a result of slavery. In the present volume the official figures are concisely produced and analyzed, exploding those INCONCEIVABLY ERRONE-OUS ASSUMPTIONS and FABRICATIONS of "Helper's Crisis," which tend to irritate the South, mislead the North, and create sectional dissensions, for the sole benefit of unscrupulous politicians.

The immense WEALTH PRODUCED AT THE SOUTH is clearly demonstrated, and the expenditure and ACCUMULA-TION of that WEALTH AT THE NORTH, where it stimulates industry, employs shipping, constructs palaces, builds railroads, occupies land, raises rents, impels trade, conferring affluence upon many and competence upon all, are clearly traced and made vividly manifest.

The welfare of this Union, the existence of the American nation, and the industry of Western Europe, are DEPENDENT upon the APPRENTICESHIP of the BLACK race to useful industry. They are working out, by an indispensable servitude, their passage from the brute condition to a semblance of manhood. The Deity has manifestly appointed the white race to drag forth, through the operation of servitude, those black savages from their cannibal lair in the African wilds into the light of the Gospel and the knowledge of the true God.

By the same operation, MODERN CIVILIZATION, which takes date from the ORIGIN of the SLAVE TRADE, has reached its present development. This glorious progress is sought to be arrested by clerical agitators, unprincipled office seekers, and CORRUPT FABRICATORS of SLANDERS upon SISTER STATES. These despise the best gifts of the Almighty, and reject his organization of creation; and, seeking fellowship with an inferior race, strive to plunge back into that slough of barbarism whence it has required three centuries to escape.

The simple truth alone is requisite to stem the torrent of disunion, strife, desolation, and bloodshed thus let loose, and the pages now offered contain that truth in a concise and clear form.[26]

*Southern Wealth and Northern Profits* was favorably received in the South where Kettell's free trade principles, sympathetic attitude toward slavery, and his interest in Southern economic development had long been known. Moderate Southerners hoped the book might be helpful toward a compromise that would prevent secession, whereas radicals hoped it would further the cause of secession.

James D. B. DeBow devoted seventeen pages to an analysis and review of the book. He spoke of Kettell as "one of the ablest political and statistical writers, who has for nearly thirty years, in various publications, illustrated the industrial conditions of the Union, and sustained, by incontrovertible facts, their mutual dependence, demonstrating the wealth, resources, and self sustaining power of the Southern States." He declared the book deserved a place upon every table for it was an important campaign document in "the struggle between the adherents of law and the Constitution and the powerful body of disorganizers which, under the banner of Lincoln, Seward, and Sumner, threaten the existence of the government and even of republican institutions." He closed his review with the statement that the book would, in the hands of the conservative men of the North,

26 This copy is taken from the outside back cover of the 1860 paper back printing.

"prove an engine of tremendous power against the black and treasonable designs of Seward and Lincoln."[27]   The wish was father to the thought but alas for DeBow, Hinton Rowan Helper's *The Impending Crisis of the South: How to Meet It,* which Kettell had attacked, was much the more influential in the election.

*The Southern Literary Messenger,* reviewing Kettell's book after the election and the organization of the Confederate States of America, used Kettell's arguments to bolster secession rather than to try to prevent it as DeBow had done.   It declared that if every newspaper, south of the Mason and Dixon line, would get a copy of Kettell's book, "it would have at hand a vast treasury of facts and figures with which to abolish at once, and forever, those pernicious sheets which are playing traitor to their own section by copying the infamously false statements of the northern press, and thus alarm our people with the preposterous idea that, when the worst comes to the worst, the Abolitionists can easily subjugate the South."[28]

As was to be expected, Northerners vigorously attacked *Southern Wealth and Northern Profits.*   Newspapers and periodicals generally condemned it, and at least one individual, Samuel Powell of Pennsylvania, published a thirty-one page reply under the title *Notes on Southern Wealth and Northern Profits.*[29]   Emphasizing Kettell's Southern bias Powell refers to his work as "the very text-book of the mad movement [Secession] of the hour . . . [which] cannot fail to provoke the most stern indignation."   He characterized Kettell's statement that slave labor was more advantageous than free as a "fatal error."   He found Kettell in error also in regard to the quantity and value of Southern products, that "slaves were well fed and well clothed," and that the North benefited unduly from protective tariffs and fishing bounties.   He was especially bitter because of Kettell's strictures on abolitionists; he in turn castigated the Southern secessionists who, with "subtile cunning . . . intentionally sow the seeds of sectional hatred, to ripen

27 *DeBow's Review,* XXIX (August, 1860), 197-213.

28 *Southern Literary Messenger,* XXXII (February, 1861), 159-160.

29 [Samuel Powell], *Notes on "Southern Wealth and Northern Profits"* (Philadelphia: C. Sherman and Son, 1861).

into the poison fruit of treason and national destruction." It is clearly evident that he had Kettell in mind when he wrote the above statement. In fact, he charged that Kettell deliberately held up to his readers the idea of "the annihilation of the North . . . its fields grown with weeds, its ships rotten, its factories and towns in ruins, their people departed. . . ." Powell admitted that Kettell's book was full of facts but charged that the author was "incapable of developing a single important truth from the whole of them."

The reader of the reviews of *Southern Wealth and Northern Profits* inevitably comes to the conclusion that the book had little or no influence on its readers in 1860-1861. It only confirmed them in the views they already held in regard to slavery and the sectional controversy.

## EPILOGUE

Kettell had been sincere in his efforts to persuade the North that her interests both economic and political would be best served by recognizing the constitutional guarantees of slavery but when secession and war came he loyally supported the United States government. He found himself at loose ends, however, for his connection with *Hunt's Merchants' Magazine* was abruptly ended in January 1861. His economic views and political philosophy were no longer acceptable to his Northern readers, and he turned during the war years to historical writing.

In 1862 Kettell published a *History of the Great Rebellion* in which he traced the sectional controversy over secession; discussed the formation of the Confederate States' government, the raising of armies and the immense financial resources of the United States; and praised the patriotism, enthusiasm, and loyalty of the Northern people. A second volume appeared in 1863. In the preface Kettell said that in giving "the views of leading opponents" he had avoided "tracing their present position . . . to remote causes operating in past years." He further explains that the "Introduction and Chapter I" were written by some one other than himself; hence, "by this means were introduced sentiments that may appear to the reader far more partisan than historical." For these reasons Kettell "dis-

claims all responsibility." He further explains that his own
narrative was "written from a Union point of view." For that
he "neither desires to apologize nor expects an apology will be
required." At least he had recanted and hoped to get a
favorable Northern hearing.

A revised and complete *History of the Great Rebellion* was
published in 1865. In this edition Kettell wrote that "Passion
must become cool, prejudices be softened, and the light of truth
illumine many passages at present obscure, before efforts can
be traced to their proper causes, and such history be written
as will bear the unmistakable imprint of accuracy and im-
partiality." Evidently he was not yet ready to yield entirely
on the views he had expressed about sectionalism and slavery
in the years before the war.

Kettell's next works were more nearly in line with his pre
Civil War interests. In 1866 he published *The History of the
War Debt of England; the History of the War Debt of the
United States, and the Two Compared.* This was followed by
*Eighty Years' Progress of the United States,* a co-operative work
treating the economic and industrial growth of the nation.
Kettell contributed three chapters on colonial trade and manufacturing, three on transportation, three on cotton textiles, two
each on paper and woolens, and one each on shoes and firearms.
Kettell avoided sectional issues and comparisons of Northern
and Southern development. Only once did he express his views
on the sectional issue of slavery in such manner as to criticize
the North. That had to do with the abolition of the foreign
slave trade in 1808.

Kettell also attempted to re-establish himself in the publication
field. He left New York City for San Francisco, where he
for a short time edited the *Alta California.* He also attempted
to re-establish himself in trade publications, and in August 1867
became editor of the San Francisco *Mercantile Gazette and
Prices Current Shipping List and Register.* But despite his
great reputation and long experience this trade journal failed
and ceased publication on October 16, 1867.[30]

When and where Thomas Prentice Kettell died I have been
unable to learn. Strange as it may seem I have found no obitu-
ary notice, nor does he appear in any of the biographical dic-

[30] Forsyth, 80.

tionaries. The only biographical sketch located was that printed in *Hunt's Merchants' Magazine* in 1849. One can only surmise that his championship of the South and slavery caused Kettell to become the forgotten man of his generation. Even so, it is difficult to explain how a man who contributed so much to American life and was toasted by the press during his lifetime as "one of America's most brilliant editors," "the major spokesman of American bankers and merchants on issues of political and economic interest," and as "the writer on political economy who did more to impart respectable character to the tone of the press on that subject than any other man," could have dropped totally out of sight.

# SOUTHERN WEALTH

### AND

# NORTHERN PROFITS

# PREFACE.

THE Emperor of the French has said, that "France is the only nation that goes to war for an idea." With more truth may it be said, that "the United States is the only nation that goes to destruction for an idea." This appears, however, to be the settled policy of a party at the North. The United States, at the age of seventy years, have exhibited a degree of success in working out the "experiment" of self-government, that has baffled the sagacity, while it has excited the admiration, of the most far-seeing statesmen of the Old World. This great success manifests itself in the international peace that the country enjoys, its rapid increase in numbers, the general wealth of the people, and the vast aggregate which that wealth presents.

At the close of the War of Independence, the country was composed of exhausted Colonies, having a population of 3,172,464 whites. The government was heavily in debt and without credit, the channels of trade flooded with irredeemable and depreciated paper that had driven away specie, national bankruptcy and individual insolvency were the rule. The people were destitute of capital and manufactures; the employment of the shipping apparently destroyed, and the future presenting but little hope. There were 751,363 black slaves, who were without employment that would earn their own support, and their fate and that of their masters gave ample cause of uneasiness, as well to statesmen as to owners. To abandon the blacks to their fate, under the plea of philanthropy, suggested itself to many. The employment of Northern ships was mostly the slave-trade, while the South, having daily less employment for the blacks, was determined to stop their arrival,—a measure which the North regarded as depriving it of its legitimate business. Thus growing jealousy was added to other evils. The lapse of seventy years has changed all that. The North has come to rival the mother

3

country in manufactures—her shipping is the first in the world—
capital of every description has become redundant—the Federal
debt is nominal, and local wealth superior in Massachusetts to
that of any community of like numbers in the world. The condition of the South has changed to one of the most brilliant
promise. From a desponding position, in the possession of
600,000 idle blacks, she has 4,000,000, whose labor is inadequate
to the production of that staple which the civilized world demands from her fertile soil. The blacks themselves have been
gradually elevated in material comforts and religious sentiment—not only far above those of any other country, but
greatly and progressively above their own former condition.
And this is comprehended in the material fact, that their value,
which was $200 by assessment in 1790, is $550 in 1858. From a
market value of $250, they have risen to $1500 and $2000. This
simple fact alone would show not only the great value that
their labor is to the Christian world, but that their owners have
thus, as it were, come under bonds in the sum of $1200 and
$1800 each hand, to give them the best moral and material care.
That rise in the value of the blacks is also the index to the rise
in the aggregate property of the Union, which has become as
follows, showing the official assessed valuation:

|  | 1850 | 1858 |
|---|---|---|
| North | $3,095,833,338 | $ 3,426,180,318 |
| West | 1,022,948,262 | 2,111,233,345 |
| South | 2,947,781,366 | 4,620,617,564 |
| Total | $7,066,562,966 | $10,158,031,127 |

The valuation for 1850 is that of the census, and that of 1858
is from each State census. In 1800, the whole valuation for the
levy of a Federal tax was 619 millions. There has then been an
increase of property valuation of 6,447 millions up to 1850,
and of 3,072 millions from 1850 to 1858. How strong a contrast
does this present to the condition of affairs in 1790! This
immense property has been developed under the harmonious
working of the Federal Constitution, and the country has become
the asylum and admiration of the Old World, from the political
contests of which it has remained aloof.

We have endeavored, in the following **pages, to** trace the gradual development of this great wealth, to show its sources, the course of the resulting trade, and the great profits derived from sectional intercourse, harmony, and dependence. The mutual benefit will be found to be large; and that, on the other hand, the disasters of disunion would be only the more terrible for the greatness of former success. In the midst of this prosperity, a wanton attack, by political and clerical agitators, is made upon sister States, a new idea of morality is conjured up as a means of stirring up domestic strife, and wantonly destroying the source of all this material good. Historians record with surprise the amazing folly of George the Third and his ministers, who drove the colonies into rebellion for a system! But they wanted revenue. What will the future historian say of the North, which destroyed its source of profit for a more trivial pretence! The monkey that persisted in sawing off the limb between himself and the tree, seems to be the model of modern sagacity. We are told that there is no intention of destroying the institutions of the States—that the design is only to exclude the institution from territory where it would have been long since had nature permitted. There is here, then, nothing practical—a mere pretence of agitating the popular mind and engendering animosities, for the mere sake of those animosities. The national prosperity, the domestic peace, the safety of life and property, the very existence of the nation, are jeopardized for an idea, admitted by the agitators to be fruitless. The agitation has at the North no one practical application whatever; while at the South, it has in the background servile insurrection, bloodshed, and annihilation of person and property, involving ultimately the ruin of the North.

This Republican hobby, so violently ridden, has at best but a feeble constitution. The idea of non-intervention where slavery exists, and of intervention where it cannot exist, is certainly but a thing of straw; yet this is the very head of the pretence, while the popular contempt for slavery is stimulated by such assertion as the following:

"The annual hay crop of the Free States is worth considerably more, in dollars and cents, than all the cotton, tobacco, rice, hay, hemp, and cane-sugar annually produced in the fifteen Slave States."

When we find that the South keeps 3,000,000 head of cattle

more than the North, without this vast expense for haymaking, the absurdity of this proposition in a partisan tale becomes apparent, and we recognize the hobby of the nursery,

"His head was made of peas-straw,
His tail was made of hay."

Europe looks on in surprise, to see this "model Republic,".this successful "exponent of self-government," this "eyesore to aristocrats," this "asylum of the oppressed," this "paradise of industry, and demonstration of human equality," voluntarily casting behind it all claim for human supremacy, all prospect of advancement, and seeking self-destruction, for the sake of wallowing in the kennel with an inferior race. The philosopher demands if the persons who commit this monstrous outrage upon human dignity are really entitled to those godlike qualities that are generally ascribed to the intellect of man. Is man, after all, no better than a brute, that he should libel his Creator for making distinctions between his creatures, and pretend to correct the errors of the Deity by voluntarily resigning his rank in the scale of creation? The statesman asks, if really the "most intelligent" people of the world are so besotted as to take seriously the political clap-traps of Europe, to pretend that they are no better than negroes, and destroy themselves for a sentiment? That Europe, through her large interest in American States, has been alarmed lest this should really be so, is manifest in the London "Times," which, from a virulent assailant, has lately become the efficient defender of American institutions, which were capital staples for abuse while there was no danger of losing them, but they really cannot afford to have the thing taken seriously.

The South views the matter in the spirit of Patrick Henry. "The object is now, indeed, small, but the shadow is large enough to darken all this fair land." They can have no faith in men who profess what they think a great moral principle, and deny that they intend to act upon it. It was the principle of taxation without representation that the colonies resisted, and it is the principle of the "irrepressible conflict," based avowedly on a "higher law," that the South resists. She is now in the position of the Colonies eighty-four years ago, and is adopting the same measures that they adopted, viz., non-intercourse. These are now derided as they were then, and this even while the effects of the preliminary movements are falling heavily upon the Northern workmen. A prompt retreat from this dangerous agitation within the shadow of the Constitution, is the only means of realizing the rich future, which will be the reward only of harmony, good faith, and loyalty to the Constitution.

T. P. K.

NEW YORK, *March* 6, 1860.

# CHAPTER I.

THE fact that labor is the source of all wealth, has long been demonstrated by all schools of economists; so also have they shown that what is called capital, in whatever shape it exists, is the surplus of production over consumption. These are very plain propositions, but there is another quite as manifest: it is, that the unaided labor of a man can produce for him very little more than his own requirements. An individual in the occupation of a farm soon finds that unless he can procure other labor than his own, no matter how fruitful may be the earth, he will have very little surplus at the end of the year, after satisfying his own wants. In the early ages of the world, when, as is supposed, there were fewer labor-saving machines than now, this insufficiency of individual labor was the more marked. A man's wealth was then increased in proportion to the number of sons he possessed, and who were then, as they are to this day, legal slaves until the age of 21. Very soon the idea possessed a strong family to compel others to work for them. It was speedily discovered that numbers of persons had no disposition to labor at all if they could help it. It was equally obvious that if they did not produce they must still exist at the expense of those who did produce. As this could not in justice be permitted, the remedy was to force them to labor. The production was thus increased, and the surplus enhanced by taking care that those slaves should consume less than they earned. That system of slavery, with many modifications, has prevailed down to the present time; and all the wealth or capital existing has been the result of slave-labor, or of the working of capital originally derived from slave-labor. The history of the wealth and power of nations is but a record of slave products. The monuments of antiquity, the magnificence of the modern world, the power of states; the position of nobles and the fortunes of individuals, are the results of slave-labor—the accumulations from forced servitude. In a free state each individual enjoys as much as he produces, and it is only when men are compelled to work much, and enjoy comparatively but little of the proceeds of their labor, that the task-master of many accumulates wealth in proportion to the skill with which he directs their services. The possessor of many slaves must have a lucrative mode of employing them, or he will be ruined by the expense of maintaining them. The ancient world was maintained by slaves and enjoyed by patricians. In modern Europe, serf-labor, under the feudal system, was universal, and if the nobles have now ceased to have an ownership in the man, they do not the less surely exact from him his earnings through the credit system which has replaced feudality. The soil of Europe and of England was, however, unfitted to slave-labor. If it was everywhere owned by the nobles, it yielded but little under the unintelligent cultivation of the serfs, and capital was of very slow growth, notwithstanding that the condition of the mass of people was miserable in the extreme.

It was soon discovered, in the progress of civilization, that intelligent white men would produce more in a state of freedom than as serfs; that the rewards of industry were a sufficient stimulus to them to labor; while tithes, taxes, and rents were the ready means of exacting more of the proceeds of labor from the freeman than could be obtained from the serfs. The restraints upon individuals were then gradually relaxed, while the most severe means were taken to compel idlers to work. "Sturdy beggars" were not only visited with the severe penalties of the law, but those who harbored and relieved them were punished; while "work-houses" were the recipients of those arrested and those who required alms.

The slave system gradually faded out,—the sovereigns, as they wanted money from time to time, selling freedom to the slaves. The last record of transactions of this nature was in 1574, by Queen Elizabeth. Sixty years previously, "Bluff King Hal," being short of funds, had "made a raise" on the freedom of some of his slaves. As this is a curious fact, but little known, we transcribe the law.

A manumission granted by Henry VIII., to two persons, ran as follows:

" *Whereas*, originally, God created all men free; but afterward the laws and customs of nations subjected some under the yoke of servitude, we think it pious and meritorious with God, to make certain persons absolutely free from servitude who are at present under villenage to us ; wherefore we do now accordingly manumit and free from yoke of servitude Henry Knight, a tailor, and John Erle, a husbandman, our slaves, as being born in our manor of Stoke Clymmy Slande, in our county of Cornwall; together with all their issue born or hereafter to be born, so as the said two persons, with their issue, shall henceforth be deemed by us and our heirs free and of free condition."— *Fœdera*, V., xiii., p. 470.

This wonderfully pious prince became suddenly "republican," it appears, when he found that Henry Knight would pay for such an exercise of piety. It is a pity that this devout mood should not have lasted 20 years later, to save the head of Anne Boleyn from forfeiture for too much alleged freedom. Sixty years later, the "Good Queen Bess," being sorely impecunious, bethought her of the profitable piety of old Hal, and directed a commission to her Lord Treasurer Burghley and Sir Walter Mildmay, Chancellor of her Exchequer, for inquiring into the condition of all her bondmen and bondwomen in the counties of Cornwall, Devon, Somerset, and Gloucester, or such as were by "birth of slavish condition," by being born in any of her manors ; and to compound with such bondmen and bondwomen in those counties for their manumission, and to enjoy their chattels, &c., as freemen. By this exhibition of republicanism the respectable old spinster raised a considerable sum of money for her own enjoyment. Those bondmen, however, fared worse than "black brothers" 260 years later, since they had to pay for their freedom, and the "darkies" were discharged and "hired over again at better wages."

It is a little remarkable that the preamble of the law of Henry VIII. begins with almost the identical phrase that heads the Declaration of American Independence. It is to be supposed that Mr. Jefferson had diligently followed the slow course of human emancipation in England, and was duly impressed with the fact announced by the king in respect of *men;* but the idea does not seem to have occurred to either that before the emancipation of " men" should have become perfected, zealots would have descended a grade in the scale of creation to embrace an inferior race in a common right of freedom.  As " Revolutions never go backward," race after race of animals may expect their turn of emancipation, since the same argument, that all are born free, applies to all.  Naturally, all were born free ; but it was to serve the common end of creation that they are made useful to man by domestication.  In his free state, amid the wilds of Africa, the negro, to this day, is no more useful to man than the gorilla, the gorilla than the orangoutang, the latter than the chimpanzee, and so down to the little ape, which obeys the law of creation in being domesticated to the service of the Savoyard organists.  The discovery of the usefulness of the negro was made at about the date in which the respectable Elizabeth sold freedom to her white slaves.  The use which England made of that discovery was to prosecute it during 274 years, in the course of which 5,000,000 negroes were caught and put to labor.  Nearly all the *commercial wealth of England at this day is due to those negroes.* But that was not the only cause of the rapid increase of British wealth in the last century.  During countless ages there had existed 200,000,000 laborious and frugal slaves to local despots in India, when Clive, with the vanguard of the English, burst in upon them, in 1756.  Those people had accumulated fabulous wealth ; and the instant the English took possession, the transfer of that wealth to England commenced.  Numberless individuals were sent thither to be enriched, and they returned to England in great numbers, with vast fortunes.  The property so transferred has been estimated, on data afforded by the India trade, at 2000 millions of dollars, from the battle of Plassy, 1757, to 1830.  The mere operations of the India Company were as nothing compared with the wealth acquired by England in this transfer of private fortunes.  This process was simultaneous with the vigorous prosecution of the slave-trade, which gave such vast capital to the British Islands.

In the year 1561, Sir John Hawkins fitted out three vessels, of 40, 60, and 120 tons, with English goods, for Guinea, where he exchanged the goods for negroes, sold the latter in Hispaniola, and brought home hides, sugar, and ginger.  This was the origin of that immense trade which England prosecuted with such success during 274 years.  The profits in 1689 were already so large, and the trade had so extended the English marine, that a convention was held in London, by which England undertook to supply the Spanish West Indies with slaves. From that time the trade took large dimensions. In 1713 the South Sea Company contracted to supply 4800 negroes per annum, for 30 years. The enormous development of the trade may be estimated from an official letter of General O'Hara, Governor of Senegambia, in 1760. It states that for 50 years past there had been shipped from the country "70,000 negroes per annum of its prime inhabitants," whence he concludes the great population of the continent. In the year 1768, a British report gives the number shipped for that year, from the west coast of Africa, between Cape Blanco and Rio Congo, at 97,100, of which 53,100 were by British, and 6,700 by American vessels.

Under the convention with Spain the Island of Jamaica became a great depot, and the island progressed as follows:

| | NEGROES. | | POPULATION. | |
|---|---|---|---|---|
| | *Imported.* | *Exported.* | *White.* | *Black.* |
| 1702............ | ....... | ...... | 7,644 | ....... |
| to 1752............ | 152,328 | ...... | ...... | ........ |
| " 1762............ | 229,443 | 45,705 | 15,000 | 146,464 |
| " 1774............ | 497,736 | 137,114 | 16,000 | 220,000 |
| " 1787............ | 609,241 | 166,076 | 23,000 | 256,000 |
| " 1791............ | 708,318 | ...... | ...... | ...... |
| " 1807............ | 1,128,400 | ...... | 37,152 | 373,405 |

These figures are from various British official reports. In 1719 a duty of 5*s.* per head was laid on the import into Jamaica; in 1720 it was raised to 10*s.*, and 20*s.* on exportation. In 1774 the number of blacks in the island had become alarmingly large, and there was imposed a duty of £2 10*s.*, and raised to £5 before the close of the year. This excited the opposition of the English slave-traders, and on their appeal to Parliament the duty was abrogated. That movement, however, caused an inquiry by Parliament into the slave-trade, and the movement, gathering force and strength by the example of the United States, in prohibiting the slave-trade after 1808, finally resulted in its prohibition by Parliament, in 1807. Thus ended the traffic that had been begun by the British in 1561. The results of this traffic upon British wealth are easily estimated. As seen above, there were imported into Jamaica, in the 18th century, 1,128,400 blacks, selling at an average, by official tables, of £30 each. The number imported in the 140 years up to the 18th century is put at 600,000, and into all other colonies at 1,000,000; making, together, 2,728,400 negroes; which, at £30 each, realized £81,852,000, or $450,000,000: but if each black produced, during his life, but 8 times his own cost, the amount of wealth sent to England was 3600 millions of dollars, or a sum exceeding the present national debt. In estimating the value of the island in 1788, the commercial export value was put down at £5,400,000; and 12 years' purchase gave £64,600,000 as the value of the island. That rate, for 100 years, gives £540,000,000, and at half the rate for the previous 170 years, the aggregate would be £810,000,000, or 4000 millions dollars. We have, then, the following results of the India and slave operations of the 18th century:

| | |
|---|---:|
| Realized from India............................... | $2,000,000,000 |
| "      "      slaves and islands................... | 3,600,000,000 |
| Total capital............................... | $5,600,000,000 |

This vast capital poured into the lap of England was the source of its greatness and of the sudden development of power and wealth which took date from the middle of the 18th century.

The effects of this capital become surprising when we turn to the British population tables.

*Population of England and Wales.*

| Year. | Population. | Year. | Population. |
|---|---|---|---|
| 1086............. | 1,000,000 | 1770............. | 7,227,586 |
| 1670............. | 6,000,000 | 1790............. | 8,540,738 |
| 1695............. | 8,000,000 | 1800............. | 8,894,536 |
| 1700............. | 5,134,516 | 1850............. | 17,907,409 |
| 1750............. | 6,039,684 | | |

The population, for 1086, is that of Doomsday book; that of 1695 is by d'Avenant. The figures for the 18th century are in " Porter's Progress," vol. i., page 14. The result is, that up to the close of the 18th century, the population of England and Wales was stationary. It required 700 years to rise from one to five millions, showing the severe struggles for life the people had, until the wealth we have pointed out flowed in upon them. That wealth stimulated industry of all kinds, and, aided by inventions, has so improved the condition of the people, that the population gained more in the first 50 years of the present century, 15 of them of war, than in the previous 800 years.

Although England discontinued the slave-trade in 1807, it was not until 30 years later that slavery was abolished. The islands had become stocked with laborers, and the false principle was assumed, that, as the whites had become more industrious and productive in a state of freedom than in a state of slavery, the blacks would do so also, and thus develop a large market for goods. This idea, in connection with the fact that the British system of slavery was enormously expensive for the suppression of insurrection, brought about emancipation. After enslaving negroes for 274 years, they discovered that the black was a "man and a brother." They freed him, petted him, encouraged him; the papers and preachers lied for him. They said, if he did not work, it was only the natural rest that one generation wanted, after the fatigues of their progenitors. A singularly long rest, certainly, and a new generation has shown a disposition to prolong the rest, while ruin stares them in the face. At last, after 25 years' experience, the *London Times*, which worked so hard to bring about abolition, finally breaks down as follows:

"There is no blinking the truth. Years of bitter experience; years of hope deferred; of self-devotion unrequited; of poverty; of humiliation; of prayers unanswered; of sufferings derided; of insults unresented; of contumely patiently endured, have convinced us of the truth. It must be spoken out loudly and energetically, despite the wild mockings of 'howling cant.' The freed West India slave will not till the soil for wages; the free son of the ex-slave is as obstinate as his sire. He will not cultivate lands which he has not bought for his own. Yams, mangoes, and plantains—those satisfy his wants; he cares not for yours. Cotton, sugar, coffee, and tobacco, he cares but little for. And what matters it to him that the Englishman has sunk his thousands and tens of thousands on mills, machinery, and plants, which now totter on the languishing estate that for years has only returned beggary and debt. He eats his yams, and sniggers at 'Buckra.'

"We know not why this should be, but it is so. The negro has been bought with a price—the price of English taxation and English toil. He has been redeemed from bondage by the sweat and travail of some millions of hard-working Englishmen. Twenty millions of pounds sterling—one hundred millions of dollars—have been distilled from the brains and muscles of the free English laborer, of every degree, to fashion the West India negro into a 'free, independent laborer.' 'Free and independent' enough he has become, God knows, but laborer he is not; and, so far as we can see, never will be. He will sing hymns and quote texts, but honest, steady industry he not only detests, but despises. We wish to Heaven that some people in England—neither government people, nor parsons, nor clergymen, but some just-minded, honest-hearted, and clear-sighted men—would go out to some of the islands (say Jamaica, Dominica, or Antigua),—not for a month, or three months, but for a year, would watch the precious *protégé* of English philanthropy, the freed negro, in his daily habits; would watch him as he lazily plants his little squatting; would see him as he proudly rejects agricultural or domestic services, or accepts it only at wages ludicrously disproportionate to the value of his work. We wish, too, they would watch him, while, with a hide thicker than a hippopotamus, and a body to which fervid heat is a comfort rather than an annoyance, he droningly lounges over the prescribed task, over which the intrepid Englishman, uninured to the burning sun, consumes his impatient energy, and too often sacrifices his life. We wish they would go out and view the negro in all the blazonry of his idleness, his pride, his ingratitude, contemptuously sneering at the industry of that race which made him free, and then come home and teach the memorable lesson of their experience to the fanatics who have perverted him into what he is."

The great wealth acquired by England from slavery and India enabled her to carry through the wars with Napoleon, and to put in motion the vast machinery which now manufactures clothing for the world. It will be observed that simultaneously with the receipts of the slave and India money began the credit system. The fortunes so derived were loaned to the government, and William began the national debt. That debt was for the most part spent in England, employing labor, but creating a moneyed aristocracy which draws $150,000,000 yearly from the people.

The supplies of blacks in the colonies were large, at a time when there was no work like that of the cotton culture to give unlimited expansion to their labor, and they were becoming a burden. The cessation of the slave-trade caused a reaction, and the demand for more labor has since increased to a positive inconvenience. When British philanthropy, taking a lesson from " old Hal" and " Bess," adopted the idea of investing in negro freedom, it simultaneously set to work to operate upon the northern classes, in New England, and that in the true Jesuit style. That sagacious body of men always educated youth in the principles they meant to spread. The Exeter Hall Jesuits did not neglect that mode. The religious sentiment of New England caused Sunday-schools to become very popular in that section, and through those Exeter Hall operated. Teachers were found, who, by tracts, precepts, lectures, readings, and inculcations of all sorts, impressed the youthful mind of the North with those sentiments, which they foresaw would, at no distant day, produce fruits. The leaders of British aristocracy are foremost in recognizing the first budding of that stem, which, if it produces only an apple of discord in this detested Republic, will have repaid the care in planting. Until party politics discovered the use which could be made of the sentiment thus long and laboriously sown and nurtured, it was harmless. Singularly enough, however, that Providence which formed the black slave and his white master, and which so strangely interposes at times for the salvation of the Union, has caused to be demonstrated the slave nature of the black, through the experiment of England, at the very moment their machinations have brought the Union into danger.

We have seen how rapidly the population and wealth of England, 'after slumbering for 700 years, began to develop itself under the influence of slave-acquired capital. The American Union presents a similar marvel, and from a similar cause. The bands of pilgrims who made settlements in different parts of the country, early in the 17th century, had slowly multiplied their numbers up to the era of Independence. In 170 years, up to 1790, the Pilgrims of New England had increased to 1,000,823 souls; and in the same period—that is, from the settlement of the colonies to the settlement of the federal compact—the number in all the colonies had reached only to 3,331,730 white souls, and the blacks, under the active supply kept up by the British merchants, had only reached 617,817. The capital of the country had hardly increased even in the slow ratio of the population; on the other hand, the colonies came out of the war exhausted. The moment the separation took place, however, New England became, to the South and slave-labor, what Britain had been. The population and wealth of the country have since advanced in a ratio which, in 50 years, has made the former equal to that of England, while, if the wealth is not so great in the aggregate, it is better distributed, because a greater number of manufacturers participate in the profits of slave-labor.

The North American colonies were supplied with slaves by England, who drew thence the produce of their labor. While 600,000 slaves were at work raising produce to send to England, she did not permit manufactories, and the colonies, after

200 years of servitude, presented the same aspect as the West Indies. An enormous wealth had been produced here, but it was conveyed to England, leaving the place of production as poor as ever. It is urged, sometimes, that emancipation did not injure Jamaica, since it was ruined before that event. That is no doubt true. It had been used only as an *instrument*, and, after 200 years' labor, it still retained only worn-out land and negroes. The North American colonies were in the same position. The wealth they had produced, ornaments London and gilds St. James's. The dilapidated towns of Jamaica shelter idle negroes, who live on the spontaneous products of the earth, while they relapse into barbarism. The American colonies were equally exhausted after 200 years of industry, but the 600,000 blacks have since been made steadily to produce an increasing ratio of wealth, even as their numbers have swollen to 4,000,000; and, instead of ruin, they vie with the mother country in prosperity. The American colonies had insisted upon a cessation of the slave-trade, because they were overrun with blacks for whom they had no adequate employment. The crown refused. The separation took place, and from that moment the New England States assumed the position, in regard to slavery, which Great Britain had previously occupied. The New England States owned the shipping, and enjoyed the slave-trade. They accumulated capital in both; and when the convention met to frame the Constitution, it was as a concession to New England interests that the trade was continued to 1808. The Duke de Rochefoucault Liancourt, travelling in the United States in 1795, remarks:

" Nearly 20 vessels from the harbors of the northern States are employed in the importation of negroes to Georgia and the West India isles. The merchants of Rhode Island are the conductors of this accursed traffic, which they are determined to persevere in until the year 1808, the period fixed for its final termination. They ship one negro for every ton burden."

The fisheries, the export of lumber and fish to the West Indies in exchange for sugar and molasses, the carrying of tobacco, indigo, &c., from the South to England, thence to Africa, and home with a cargo of slaves, were the chief means of employing the shipping of the New England and the Middle States, which were owners of nearly all the shipping of the Union. If the French wars, by throwing the carrying trade into the hands of neutrals, were a great benefit to the ship-owners as well as to the farmers of the middle States, the difficulties that led to the embargo of 1809, and subsequently the war of 1812, were felt only the more severely by that interest, since both the slave-trade and the carrying trade were lost together, and the war was denounced as the cause of all the difficulties that resulted. It followed that the large capital that had been accumulated in that trade, thus forcibly driven from commerce, betook itself to manufacturing, and the "free traders" of New England became clamorous for "protection." Since then the capital earned in commerce and in the slave-trade has enjoyed a monopoly of navigating, importing, and manufacturing for the South, getting large pay, swollen by protective duties, in the proceeds of slave-labor. In the mean time, if the South had ceased to employ northern shipping for the importation of negroes, it began to furnish a much more extensive employment for it in the exportation of cotton.

## CHAPTER II.

### COTTON CULTURE AND MANUFACTURE.

We have seen that England, in the course of her colonial system, had, by furnishing goods and slaves, and enjoying the carrying trade of her dependencies, acquired a vast capital, while the colonies that produced that wealth had accumulated nothing—they had, in fact, become poorer. The operation was the same as if an individual, owning a town-house and a farm of perhaps 200 acres, should employ persons to work the latter, and draw from it all its proceeds for the use of his town-house. If the farm should give $600 per annum, in ten years he would have added $6000 to the value of his city mansion; but at the end of that time the farm would simply be exhausted, its land and implements worn out. It was thus with Jamaica and the West Indies at the date of emancipation, and with the North American colonies at the date of the separation. At that date, however, three events occurred which were to change the face of the world. These were the inventions of the steam-engine, the cotton-jenny, and the cotton-gin. The two former gave employment to the vast capital of England in manufactures;

and the latter, while it supplied the material of that manufacture, opened a new future to the United States, and laid out for the blacks work which has ever since increased before them. The blacks, numerous as they were at the South, had no employment that paid their support; cotton was indeed grown, but the difficulty of cleaning it from the seed was so great that a man could prepare but one pound per day for market. In 1793, Eli Whitney invented a cotton-gin which would clean 350 lbs. per day. From that moment the cotton culture was established, and work was laid out for not only the 600,000 negroes then on hand, but for more than all the increase since in their number; at the same moment, nearly, a demand for the cotton was created by the inventions of Watt, Arkwright, and Hargraves, which furnished employment for the capital of England, and a large portion of her population, in manufacturing clothing for the world, and in employing her shipping in exchanging that clothing for the products of all nations. The state of affairs that existed at the South at the moment of those inventions, is well described by Judge Johnson, in his charge in a suit brought by Whitney in Savannah, in 1807, to make good his patent.

"The whole of the interior," said Judge Johnson, "was languishing, and its inhabitants were emigrating, for want of some object to engage their attention and employ their industry, when the invention of this machine at once opened views to them which set the whole country in active motion. From childhood to age, it has presented to us a lucrative employment. Individuals who were depressed with poverty and sunk in idleness, have suddenly risen to wealth and respectability. Our débts have been paid off, our capitals have increased, and our lands trebled in value. We cannot express the weight of obligation which the country owes to this invention. The extent of it cannot now be seen."

This clearly indicates the exhausted state in which 200 years of colonial dependence had left the colonies, and also foreshadows a future which, as we shall see, has been more than justified in the event.

It was the gloomy state of affairs then existing which caused the fathers of the Revolution to take so desponding a view of the future of slavery. They did not foresee the brilliant future which cotton was to draw from that service. With the operation of the cotton-gin the culture began to extend, but with its extension the price suffered a decline, for the reason that down to within ten years the supply rather exceeded the demand. Nevertheless, the increase in value has been enormous.

The value of cotton has always been much influenced by the state of the crops in Europe. When food is dear, as a general thing, in a manufacturing country dependent upon foreign supplies of bread, a short harvest causes such a rise in its price as to absorb the earnings of the mass of people for its purchase. It results from this that the purchases of clothing are much lessened, the raw material is less in demand, and its price falls. Naturally this decline acts upon wages, and there is less employment, at lower rates. Thus the end of dear food is the cause of less means to buy it; a double distress is thus produced, which tells powerfully upon the price of cotton, as well as of other raw materials. The column of prices follows this rule. In 1845, the first famine year, the rate was 5.9 cents, and, as the price of bread fell, it rose to 12.1 in 1851, and again fell as food rose during the Crimean war, and has since well maintained its rate.

The following table shows the crops, distinguishing the Atlantic from the Gulf States, the exported quantity and value, the price per pound, and the number of blacks at each census.

*Product and Export of Cotton.*

| | CROP—BALES | | | EXPORT. | EXPORT. | PRICE. |
|---|---|---|---|---|---|---|
| Year. | Atlantic. | Gulf. | Total. | lbs. | Value. | U. States. |
| 1800.... | ........ | ........ | 35,000 | 19,000,000 | 5,726,000 | .... |
| 1824.... | 333,253 | 175,905 | 509,158 | 142,369,663 | 21,947,401 | 15.4 |
| 1830.... | 522,062 | 348,353 | 870,415 | 298,459,102 | 29,674,883 | 9.9 |
| 1835.... | 493,405 | 760,923 | 1,254,328 | 387,358,992 | 64,961,302 | 16.8 |
| 1840.... | 642,287 | 1,535,654 | 2,177,532 | 743,941.061 | 63,870,307 | 8.5 |
| 1845.... | 769,948 | 1,635,015 | 2,394,503 | 872,905,996 | 51,739,643 | 5.92 |
| 1850.... | 751,271 | 1,345,435 | 2,796,706 | 635,381,604 | 71,984,616 | 11.3 |
| 1851.... | 742,846 | 1,612,411 | 2,355,257 | 927,237,089 | 112,315,317 | 12.11 |
| 1852.... | 839,625 | 2,175,404 | 3,015,029 | 1,093,230,639 | 87,965,732 | 8.05 |
| 1853.... | 871,712 | 2,391,170 | 3,262,882 | 1,111,570,370 | 109,456,404 | 9.85 |
| 1854.... | 788,649 | 2,151,378 | 2,930,027 | 987,833,106 | 93,596,220 | 9.47 |
| 1855.... | 942,766 | 1,904,573 | 2,847,339 | 1,008,424,601 | 88,143,844 | 8.74 |
| 1856.... | 910,192 | 2,617,653 | 3,527,841 | 1,351,431,701 | 128,382,351 | 9.49 |
| 1857.... | 775,116 | 2,164,403 | 2,939,519 | 1,048,282,475 | 131,575,859 | 12.55 |
| 1858.... | 746,562 | 2,367,900 | 3,113,962 | 1,118,624,012 | 131,386,661 | 11.70 |
| 1859.... | 1,111,954 | 2,739,427 | 3,851,481 | 1,386,468,542 | 161,434,923 | 11.40 |
| 1860.... | 1,480,000 | 2,920,000 | 4,300,000 | 1,165,600,000 | 184,400,000 | 11.5 |

The value here given is the export value, according to the official returns of the Treasury department; the value of the whole crop runs much higher. That of this year, 1860, will reach 4,300,000 bales—3,200,000 having already been received, and sold at a value of $54 per bale. At the same valuation, the whole will be worth $232,000,000, or $60 for every black hand. This value has grown up, as we shall see, in addition to all other agricultural produce, and in face of the constant decline in price. The war of 1812 affected prices much, producing a great difference in value between Liverpool and the United States. That "perturbation" was the source of some immense northern fortunes, by enabling those with means to buy and hold for the peace, with the return of which the culture resumed its course, and the quantity, which had reached 509,158 bales in 1824, was doubled in 1831. In the ten years ending with 1840 it had again doubled in quantity, involving a very great decline in price. The discovery in those years that the bottom lands of the valley of the Mississippi could raise cotton much cheaper than the Atlantic States, caused a great speculative excitement, which was fostered by the struggle that took place between the late National Bank and the federal government. The planters, many of them young, with gangs of hands from the paternal estates, migrated to the new lands and entered upon the culture, through bank aid. The lands and the hands being mortgaged, these mortgages were constituted bank capital under State charters, and State loans were issued in aid of them. The loans were to a considerable extent negotiated through the United States Bank, and it is somewhat curious that the bank-charter mortgages upon negroes by *name* found ready negotiation in London " at a price," notwithstanding the anti-slavery furor which was then there in its zenith. Loans upon American slaves were " as easy" as the loan to free the West India blacks. The money thus borrowed was loaned out to the planters, whose cotton was pledged to the lenders. The extent of this operation may be estimated by the figures furnished by the census and Treasury returns. The following table gives the number of blacks and whites in the cotton States, the crops of cotton, distinguishing the Gulf from the Atlantic States, and the bank capital of the Gulf States.

In the table, the population of the four Atlantic States increased regularly up to 1830, as did also that of the six western States. Florida gave a return first in 1830, and Texas not until 1850, although before its admission into the Union that State was a large recipient of blacks and whites, following the revulsion of 1839. From 1830 to 1840, the four Atlantic States scarcely increased at all, either in blacks or whites. In the corresponding period, the western States increased 70 per cent. in slaves, and 40 per cent. in whites.

The speculation subsided in 1840, leaving a very healthy state of affairs; but it will be observed that the production did not increase very rapidly in the ten years to 1850, although the value gradually improved. In the last ten years, however, an immense progress has been made in the production and value of cotton. Not only has the increased number of hands added to the production, but the number of bales per hand that can be raised has risen from 4 and 5, to 8 and 10 per hand in some localities—while, as a whole, the South has been free from speculation, but has accumulated a large capital.

*Population, Bank Loans, and Crop of the Cotton States.*

| | 1820. | | 1830. | |
|---|---|---|---|---|
| | *White.* | *Black.* | *White.* | *Black.* |
| Virginia................ | 6o3,074 | 425,153 | 694,3oo | 469,757 |
| North Carolina......... | 419,200 | 205,017 | 472,843 | 245,6o1 |
| South Carolina......... | 237,440 | 258,475 | 257,863 | 315,401 |
| Georgia................ | 189,566 | 149,656 | 296,8o6 | 217,531 |
| | 1,449,280 | 1,038,3o1 | 1,721,812 | 1,248,290 |
| Florida................. | ...... | ...... | 18,385 | 15,5o1 |
| Alabama............... | 96,245 | 47,439 | 190,406 | 117,549 |
| Mississippi............. | 42,176 | 32,814 | 70,443 | 65,659 |
| Louisiana.............. | 73,383 | 69,o64 | 89,441 | 109,588 |
| Arkansas.............. | 12,579 | 1,617 | 25,671 | 4,576 |
| Tennessee............. | 339,927 | 80,107 | 535,746 | 141,6o3 |
| Kentucky.............. | 434,644 | 126,732 | 517,787 | 165,213 |
| | 998,954 | 357,773 | 1,447,879 | 619,689 |

| | 1840. | | 1850. | |
|---|---|---|---|---|
| | *White.* | *Black.* | *White.* | *Black.* |
| Virginia................ | 740,968 | 448,987 | 894,800 | 472,528 |
| North Carolina......... | 484,870 | 245,817 | 553,028 | 288,548 |
| South Carolina......... | 259,084 | 327,o38 | 274,563 | 384,984 |
| Georgia................ | 407,695 | 280,944 | 521,572 | 381,682 |
| | 1,892,617 | 1,3o2,786 | 2,243,963 | 1,527,742 |
| Florida................. | 27,943 | 25,717 | 47,2o3 | 39,31o |
| Alabama............... | 335,185 | 253,532 | 426,514 | 342,844 |
| Mississippi............. | 179,070 | 195,211 | 295,711 | 3o9,878 |
| Louisiana.............. | 158,457 | 168,452 | 255,491 | 244,8o9 |
| Texas................. | ...... | ...... | 154,o34 | 58.161 |
| Arkansas.............. | 77,174 | 19,935 | 162,189 | 47,100 |
| Tennessee............. | 640,627 | 183,o59 | 756,836 | 239,459 |
| Kentucky.............. | 590,253 | 182,258 | 761,413 | 210,981 |
| | 2,008,709 | 1,028,164 | 2,859,391 | 1,492,542 |

| | 1830. | 1840. | 1850. |
|---|---|---|---|
| Bank capital............ | $3,756,643 | $13,214,025 | $28,707,341 |
| Gulf cotton crop......... | 348,353 | 1,535,654 | 1,345,431 |
| Total .................. | 870,415 | 2,177,831 | 2,096,206 |

When the cotton-gin of Whitney laid out the future work of the blacks, the steam-engine of Watt, and the jenny of Hargraves, with the improvements of Arkwright and Crompton, laid out the future manufacturing industry of England and the mode of employing her capital.

The old mode of preparing the cleaned cotton for spinning

was by carding it between two flat cards in the hands of an individual, in order to straighten out the fibres as much as possible. The material so carded was spun by a wheel worked with one hand to give velocity to a single spindle that spun a thread from the cotton held upon a distaff in the left hand of the operator. The thread thus produced was irregular, and served only as a woof for linen warp. By a new invention the cards were placed upon a revolving drum, which operated against several rollers also covered with cards. The action of these rollers distributed the cotton in a fleecy web upon the surface. This was removed from the last roller by an instrument which caused the cotton to come off in long rolls ready for spinning. Arkwright added rollers that were to "draw" these rolls as they were carded, so as, by making the fibres of cotton more parallel to each other, to increase the fineness and regularity of the thread. The invention of Hargraves, in 1764, was to put 8 spindles in a frame, and draw the ends in a clasp held by the operator. The number was soon raised to 80 spindles. Samuel Crompton, in 1779, added the "mule spinner." The effect of all these inventions was, that, whereas one man could clean 1 lb. of cotton, another card it, and another work one spindle, one man might now clean 360 lbs., another card it, and the third work 2200 spindles instead of one.

These English inventions were previous to the American invention of the gin, and their utility depended altogether upon the latter. The anxiety then took possession of the mind of the English manufacturer in relation to a supply of material, which now, after 70 years, is as active as ever. Hitherto the demand has, as we have seen, developed black industry.

From that moment, the accumulated capital of England, New and Old, became engaged in the gigantic operation of clothing the world with cotton. Hand-loom goods were everywhere to be supplanted by those formed on the new principle. When Watt started his engine, mechanical genius seemed to have sprung suddenly into life, and each subsequent year witnessed some improvement in machinery, by which the texture of cloth has been improved, and its cost diminished. Chemistry has as rapidly multiplied the number and richness of colors. The art of applying them, by steel dies and copper cylinders, has improved, until 16 colors are imparted at one impression, more perfectly than was one 40 years ago; and the perfection of the designs is equalled only by the excellence of the execution. With each improvement in texture and design and colors, the fabric is produced at less cost, because a class of persons who formerly did not produce at all, are now the chief manufacturers. Steam-engines and young females clothe the world.

The export of cotton goods from Great Britain, in 1800, was valued at £3,602,488, official value. Since 1814, the accounts have been kept in "declared" or real value, as well as in the official value, which was fixed a century or more since. The official value expresses more quantity than value, and a comparison of the official with the declared shows the decline in prices. The progress of the trade has been as follows :

| | Official. | Declared. | Liverpool price of Upland cotton. |
|---|---|---|---|
| 1814................... | £17,655,378 | £20,133,132 | 30d. |
| 1820................... | 22,531,279 | 16,516,758 | 11¹/₂ |
| 1830................... | 41,050,969 | 19,335,971 | 6⁷/₈ |
| 1840................... | 73,124,730 | 24,668,618 | 6 |
| 1850................... | 113,718,401 | 28,257,401 | 7¹/₄ |
| 1856..... .......... | 163,887,196 | 38,232,741 | 6 |
| 1858................... | 169,201,107 | 42,797,000 | 7¹/₂ |

In 1814 the real was in excess of the official value. In 1856 the latter had increased nearly tenfold, while the real was only 24 per cent. of it. This indicates a progressive decline of 76 per cent. in the price of the goods.

The mode in which the manufacturers progress was thus stated in a paper read recently by Mr. David Chadwick, before the London Statistical Society :

"In 1859 the average rate of wages of a spinner on a pair of unimproved mules, of 400 spindles each, in producing No. 70's yarn, are 5s. 1d. per 20 lbs.; his gross weekly earnings, 41s.; and deducting piecer's wages, 16s., the spinner's net wages are 25s. The same workman, with a pair of 'double-deckers,' with 1600 spindles, and more piecers, earns 3s. 11¼d. per 20 lbs., 50s. 10d. per week ; or, deducting 20s. for piecers' wages, a net amount of 30s. 10d. weekly. Of the 3046 cotton factories in England and Wales, in 1856, 1480 were situated in Lancashire: 23 new mills are now in course of erection in Blackburn and its neighborhood, and, notwithstanding various restrictions on the employment of young persons, and the reduction of the hours of labor for adults (by the Ten Hours Act of June, 1847), from 69 to 60 hours weekly, the import of raw cotton increased from 646,000,000 lbs., in 1844, to 1,034,060,000 lbs. in 1858; while the value of exports of cotton manufactured goods, and cotton twist and yarns, increased from 26 millions sterling in 1844, to 43 millions sterling in 1858,—an extension of one branch of trade in 14 years unparalleled in the history of any country in the world."

While the British cotton trade has thus been developed, that of the United States and Europe has increased, also, until its magnitude last year may be seen in the following table:

*Cotton Manufactures of Europe and the United States.*

|  | No. of factories. | Hands employed. | Spindles. | Lbs. cotton used. |
|---|---|---|---|---|
| Great Britain | 3,046 | 650,000 | 21,000,000 | 990,000,000 |
| France | 2,600 | 274,830 | 5,500,000 | 140,000,000 |
| Switzerland | 132 | 51,908 | 1,112,303 | 30,000,000 |
| Zollverein | 208 | 110,190 | 2,018,536 | 65,000,000 |
| Austria | 99 | 32,010 | 655,000 | 25,000,000 |
| Belgium | 28 | 28,000 | 510,000 | 31,000,000 |
| Lombardy | 33 | 29,000 | 140,000 | 10,000,000 |
| Sardinia | 17 | 14,000 | 210,000 | 17,000,000 |
| Russia | 55 | 60,000 | 1,100,000 | 63,000,000 |
| United States | 90 | 101,000 | 6,000,000 | 426,719,000 |
|  |  | 1,350,938 | 38,245,829 | 1,797,719,000 |

This number of hands embraces only those directly employed in the manufacture, and is exclusive of all those who are engaged in transporting the material to the spinners; in distributing the goods produced, through all the gradations of trade, to the hands of the consumers; and also in the movement of the produce and merchandise received in exchange for the goods; also all the banking, exchange, and insurance business which grows out of this movement.

The quantity of cotton so consumed was nearly 300,000,000 lbs. in excess of the United States' production, yet the Southern States are the *sole* dependence of England, Europe, and the United States for a supply of cotton clothing. The question of future cotton supply is one that, as the above figures indicate, may well occupy the minds of the manufacturers. There are many sources of supply, but the *United States alone furnish more than they consume*, and alone produce the requisite quality. In order to understand this, we give the following paper upon the subject, read by J. B. Smith, Esq., member for Stockport, before the Society of Arts.

"Every one seems adequately impressed with the desirableness, not to say the necessity, of extending and multiplying to the utmost possible extent, the sources whence we derive the supply of this raw material of our greatest national manufacture. But one branch of the question, though a most essential one, appears to have been nearly overlooked. We need not only a large supply and a cheap supply, but a supply of a peculiar kind and quality.

" For practical purposes, and to facilitate the comprehension of the subject by non-professional readers, we may state in general terms that the cotton required for the trade of Great Britain may be classified into three divisions—the long-staple, the medium-staple, and the short-staple.

" 1. The long-staple (or long-fibre) cotton is used for making the warp, as it is technically called ; i. e., the longitudinal threads of the woven tissue. These threads, when of the finer sorts—for all numbers, say above 50's—must be made of long staple-cotton ; for numbers below 50's, they may be made of it, and would be so made were it as cheap as the lower qualities of the raw material. No other quality of cotton is strong enough or long enough either to spin into the higher and finer numbers, or to sustain the tension and friction to which the threads are exposed in the loom.

" 2. The medium-staple cotton, on the contrary, is used partly for the lower numbers of the warp (and, as such, enters largely into the production of the vast quantities of ' cotton yarn' and sewing-thread exported), but mainly for the weft, or transverse threads of the woven tissue. It is softer and silkier than the quality spoken of above, makes a fuller and rounder thread, and fills up the fabric better. The long-staple article is never used for this purpose, and could not, however cheap, be so used with advantage ; it is ordinarily too harsh. For the warp, strength and length of fibre is required ; for the weft, softness and fulness. Now, as the lower numbers of ' yarn' require a far larger amount of raw cotton for their production than the higher, and constitute the chief portion (in weight) both of our export and consumption, and as, moreover, every yard of calico or cotton woven fabric, technically called cloth, is composed of from two to five times as much weft as warp, it is obvious that we need a far larger supply of this peculiar character of cotton, the medium-staple, than of any other.

" 3. The short-staple cotton is used almost exclusively for weft (except a little taken for candle-wicks), or for the very lowest numbers of warp, say 10's and under. But it is different in character from the second description, as well as shorter in fibre ; it is drier, fuzzier, more like rough wool ; and cannot be substituted for it without impoverishing the nature of the cloth, and making it, especially after washing or bleaching, look thinner and more meagre ; and for the same reason it can only be blended with it with much caution, and in very moderate proportions. But its color is usually good ; and its comparative cheapness is its great recommendation.

" It will be seen, therefore, that while we require for the purposes of our manufacture a limited quantity of the first and third qualities of raw cotton, we need and can consume an almost unlimited supply of the second quality. In this fact lies our real difficulty ; for, while several quarters of the world supply the first sort, and India could supply enormous quantities of the third sort, the United States of America alone have hitherto produced the second and most necessary kind.

" 1. The finest long cotton in the world is called the ' Sea Island.' It is grown on the low-lying lands and small islands on the coast of Georgia. The quantity is small, and the price very high. It is used mostly for muslin thread, and the very finest numbers of yarn—say 100's and upwards ; and price, in fact, is of little moment to the manufacturers who purchase it. It usually sells at about two shillings per pound. A quality much resembling it, and almost if not quite as good, has been grown, as a sample article, in Australia. But of this denomination of cotton the consumption is very small. Another species— long, strong, fine, and yellowish—is grown in Egypt, and imported in considerable quantities. An inferior quality—coarse, harsh, bright in color, but strong—is imported from Brazil, and a very small quantity from the West Indies. Doubtless if the price were adequate, and the demand here very great and steady, the supply from many of these quarters might be largely augmented. But it is not of this sort that we need any considerable increase, nor could we afford the price which probably alone would remunerate the grower.

" 2. Our great consumption and demand is for the soft, white, silky, moderately long cotton of America—the quality usually called ' Uplands,' ' Bowed Georgia,' and ' New Orleans.' This used to be sold at prices varying from 3*d*. to 6*d*. per pound (it is now from 6*d*. to 8*d*.) : it can be consumed in any quantity ; for it is available not only for weft but for warp, except for the finer numbers. We need and consume nine bags of this cotton for one bag of all other qualities put together.

" 3. It is the insufficient supply, or the higher price of this cotton, that has driven our manufacturers upon the short-stapled native article of India, commonly called Surat. If the price of the two were equal, scarcely a bag of Surat would be employed. When the price of American cotton rises, owing to an inadequate supply, that of East India cotton follows it at a considerable interval—the usual ratio being two to three—and the import of the latter is greatly stimulated. It is always grown in India in large quantities, and with improved means of communication and more careful preparation, might be supplied in time in indefinite and probably ample quantities. But it is its quality that is in fault ; and, as far as the past is a guide, it would seem incurably in fault. Many attempts to amend the character of this cotton have been made. American planters and American "saw-gins" have been sent over, and American seed has been planted; and the result has been a sensible amelioration in cleanliness and color, and some slight increase in length of fibre, but scarcely any change in specific character. The dry, fuzzy, woolly characteristics remain. Sometimes the first year's samples nearly resemble the American article, but the resemblance never becomes permanent. Hitherto (we believe we are correct in stating), either from the peculiarity of the soil or of the climate, or as some say, from adulteration by the air-borne pollen of the inferior native plant, the improved and altered character of the cotton has never been kept up.

" We are far from saying that this difficulty may not be overcome, and American cotton be naturalized in our East Indian possessions; but certainly the results of our past efforts have not been of favorable augury. So far as our own observation and experience have gone, only from two other parts of the world have we seen samples of cotton analogous in character to that of the United States, and equally available for our purposes : one of these was the west coast of Africa, where we understand there is a considerable native growth, which doubtless our commerce might encourage and increase ; the other is the opposite side of the continent, where Port Natal has exported some very hopeful samples, soft and silky, but not clean nor of a very good color, but still decidedly American in quality.

" The point we have to bear in mind, then, is this : our desideratum is not simply more cotton, but more cotton of the same character and price as that now imported from the States. If India were to send us twò millions of bales of Surat cotton per annum, the desideratum would not be supplied, and our perilous problem would be still unsolved. We should be almost as dependent on America as ever."

In accordance with this idea of procuring a supply of cotton, the attention of English statesmen, manufacturers, travellers, and commercial men has been directed to all countries where cotton may be grown, and false hopes are continually raised only to be disappointed. The present sources of British supply are as follows :

*Receipts of Cotton into Great Britain.*

|  | **1835.** | **1841.** | **1845.** | **1850.** | **1857.** |
|---|---|---|---|---|---|
| United States....... | 282,855,880 | 336,647,798 | 626,650,412 | 493,153,112 | 654,758,048 |
| Brazil.............. | 27,530,300 | 15,388,974 | 20,157,633 | 30,299,982 | 29,910,832 |
| Egyptian........... | 11,917,208 | 11,162,336 | 14,614,699 | 18,931,414 | 24,882,144 |
| West Indies........ | 2,518,836 | 10,759,840 | 88,394,448 | 228,913 | 1,443,568 |
| East Indies......... | 43,876,820 | 100,104,510 | 58,437,426 | 118,872,742 | 250,338,144 |
| All other........... | ... ...... | .......... | 725,336 | 2,090,698 | 7,986,160 |
| Total lbs....... | 368,698,544 | 474,063,453 | 721,979,953 | 669,576,861 | 969,318,896 |

The influences at work in India, in Egypt, and the West Indies, favored by the rise in prices, developed the supply. In 1841, the quantity shipped by India rose to a high point, because the China war turned much of it from its usual destination. After that event the supply fell to a low figure from that source. Of late it has steadily increased under the rising value of the article, seemingly justifying the hopes of those who looked to India as a source of supply. There has arisen, however, another feature, which, as far as the markets of the world go, entirely neutralizes that Indian supply. It is to be found in the fact, that step by step as the shipment of raw cotton from India has increased, the demand there for goods has improved. In fact, this demand has outrun the supply of the material, and India is every year becoming more important as a cotton consumer. The following table will show the quantity of cotton goods sent from England to India, with the equivalent weight in raw cotton, together with the weight of cotton received thence:

*Cotton Exports from England to India.*

|  | Yarn. lbs. | Calicoes. yards. | Aggregate raw cotton to India. lbs. | Raw cotton imported from India. |
|---|---|---|---|---|
| 1835 | 5,305,212 | 54,227,084 | 16,000,000 | 43,876 820 |
| 1841 | 13,639,562 | 126,003,400 | 43,000,000 | 100,104,510 |
| 1845 | 14,116,237 | 193,029,703 | 60,000,000 | 58,437,426 |
| 1857 | 20,027,859 | 469,958,011 | 130,000,000 | 250,338,146 |
| 1858 | 36,889,583 | 791,537,041 | 223,000,000 | 132,722,575 |

The year 1857 was an exceptional year for imports of cotton from India. In the year 1858 it appears 91,000,000 pounds more cotton have been sent to India than was received thence. If we were to include China in the calculation the result would be still more remarkable, since China took in 1857, 121,000,000 yards of cloth. And as China derives a great deal of raw cotton from India, if that article is sent to England for manufacture, and then sent to China in the shape of goods instead of as raw material, the result may be beneficial to English workshops, but it does not increase the European supply of cotton.

If we turn to Egypt and Turkey, we find that in 1858 there were derived thence 38,248,112 pounds of raw cotton, and there were sent thither 10,389,353 pounds yarn, and 257,567,351 yards cloth; together equal to 62,000,000 pounds of raw cotton, 23,700,000 pounds more than was received. The fact is the same in relation to South America. The United States alone afford a net surplus of cotton above the weight of goods they buy back. This process seems to be on the increase, since all those distant nations, as they progress in wealth, demand machine goods. These are supplanting, apparently, the rude hand-loom goods of China and India; and where the clothing of 200,000,000 is liable to undergo this change, the prospect is that, how great 'soever may be the increased production of cotton, it cannot keep pace with the demand for goods.

The French Emperor now proposes to follow the example of England and Germany, and remove the duty on cotton, as a bonus to its manufacturers, in compensation of a reduction in protective duties. This cannot fail to give a new impulse to the cotton demand.

In the late debate in the House of Lords on the subject of slave-grown cotton, great glorification was raised over the production of cotton in Africa, and Lord Wodehouse read from Dr. Livingstone a letter, dated May 12, 1859, as follows:

" Cotton is cultivated largely, and the further we went the crop appeared to be of the greater importance. The women alone were well clothed with the produce, the men being content with goat-skins and cloth made of bark of certain trees. Every one spins and weaves cotton. Even chiefs may be seen with the spindle and bag, which serves as a distaff. The process of manufacturing is the most rude and tedious that can be conceived. The cotton goes through five processes with the fingers before it comes to the loom. Time is of no value. They possess two varieties of the plant. One, indigenous, yields cotton more like wool than that of other countries. It is strong, and feels rough in the hand. The other variety is from imported seed, yielding a cotton that renders it unnecessary to furnish the people with American seed. A point in its culture worth noticing is, the time of planting has been selected so that the plants remain in the ground during winter, and five months or so after sowing they come to maturity, before the rains begin or insects come forth to damage the crop."

If it were admitted that those blacks could raise and get to market a considerable quantity of cotton—and the matter is hardly possible—what would be the result? Why, that all the laboriously hand-made goods now used by them would be superseded by machine goods, and the demand for these would still exceed the supply of cotton.

The consumption of cotton in the three countries where it is most used is as follows:

| | Population. | lbs. used. | Per head. |
|---|---|---|---|
| France....................... | 36,039,364 | 140,000,000 | 4 |
| Great Britain .............. | 28,416,508 | 253,000,000 | 9 |
| United States.............. | 30,000,000 | 368,000,000 | 12 |
| Rest of Europe............. | 213,476,424 ⎱ | | |
| Asia........................ | 775,000,000 ⎰ | 1,096,719,000 | 1 |
| Rest of America............ | 29,411,000 ⎱ | | |
| Africa ..................... | 200,000,000 | ............ | .. |
| Total................ | 1,217,887,424 | 1,797,719,000 | |

These figures show the quantities that are consumed of machine goods. As the use of the goods extends in Europe, to bring the rate per head up to the consumption of France will require 900 million pounds more of American cotton. To raise the consumption in Asia to that of France will require more than double the present supply, and to take Africa into the account, there will be still 800 millions more added. Thus there is a prospective demand for 4700 million pounds more cotton than is now grown, even to reach the French rate of consumption.

These results follow: 1. That while the use of cotton clothing is rapidly extending throughout the world, the *U. States alone furnish more than they use.* 2d. That the extension of the cotton manufacture in the South is taking proportions that will soon enable her to refuse cotton at all except in the shape of goods. The South is master of the position.

As an indication of the extension of the British cotton trade, the following table, from official sources, shows the destination of cotton cloths:

*Exports of Plain and Dyed Goods from Great Britain, in yards.*

| | **1846.** | **1858.** |
|---|---|---|
| Hanse Towns.................... | 42,364,421 | 52,116,151 |
| Holland ........................ | 29,520,699 | 30,289,562 |
| Portugal........................ | 38,068,792 | 56,234,370 |
| Turkey, &c..................... | 76,702,784 | 243,875,534 |
| Egypt.......................... | 7,530,289 | 63,970,305 |
| United States................... | 24,196,724 | 154,818,134 |
| Foreign West Indies............. | 34,959,583 | 52,843,406 |
| Brazil.......................... | 108,900,770 | 124,922,834 |
| Buenos Ayres.................... | 2,660,178 | 28,657,209 |
| Chili and Peru.................. | 46,373,072 | 65,578,796 |
| China .......................... | 73,561,889 | 138,488,957 |
| Java ........................... | ............ | 37,737,234 |
| Gibraltar ...................... | 17,491,264 | 29,311,554 |
| British North America .......... | 28,556,318 | 27,910,772 |
| British West Indies.............. | 35,524,218 | 43,019,274 |
| British East Indies.............. | 196,140,790 | 791,537,041 |
| Australia....................... | ............ | 29,115,064 |
| Other countries ................ | 193,472,277 | 352,352,519 |
| Total yards............... | 885,923,978 | 2,322,780,716 |

The increase in this period has been nearly 200 per cent. The progress of the trade has been mostly to the countries which furnish raw material in payment. Europe has taken but a small proportion of the increase. The countries of the East are those which present the largest outlet. If we now look at the number of bales of cotton taken for consumption on the continent of Europe last year, we shall have results as follows:

*Bales of Cotton taken for Consumption in Europe in* 1859.

| | U. States. | Brasil. | W. Ind. | E. Ind. | Egypt. | Totals. |
|---|---|---|---|---|---|---|
| Great Britain .............. | 1,907,000 | 105,000 | 6,000 | 177,000 | 99,000 | 2,294,000 |
| France .................... | 452,000 | 5,000 | 17,000 | 15,000 | 36,000 | 525,000 |
| Belgium................... | 38,000 | ...... | 1,000 | 25,000 | ...... | 64,000 |
| Holland .................. | 62,000 | ...... | 3,000 | 59,000 | 1,000 | 125,000 |
| Germany ................. | 146,000 | ...... | 5,000 | 61,000 | ...... | 212,000 |
| Trieste ................... | 31,000 | ...... | ..... | 14,000 | 21,000 | 66,000 |
| Genoá..................... | 41,000 | ...... | ..... | 11,000 | 1,000 | 53,000 |
| Spain...................... | 109,000 | 8,000 | ..... | 1,000 | ...... | 118,000 |
| Surplus of export—G. Britain | 94,000 | 6,000 | ..... | 79,000 | 15,000 | 194,000 |
| Total deliveries...... | 2,880,000 | 124,000 | 32,000 | 442,000 | 173,000 | 3,651,000 |

Of 3,651,000 bales delivered for consumption in 1859, the United States supplied 2,880,000 bales, and with those large deliveries, the stock on hand at the close of the year did not increase. Under these circumstances there is little surprise that the question of cotton supply should become so anxiously discussed. The "London cotton-supply reporter" of Feb. 3, remarks:

"Upwards of 500,000 workers are now employed in our cotton factories, and it has been estimated that at least 4,000,000 persons in the country are dependent upon the cotton trade for subsistence. A century ago Lancashire contained a population of only 300,000 persons; it now numbers 2,300,000. In the same period of time, this enormous increase exceeds that on any other equal surface of the globe, and is entirely owing to the development of the cotton trade. In 1856 there were, in the United Kingdom, 2,210 factories, running 28,000,000 spindles and 209,000 looms, by 97,000 horse-power. Since that period a considerable number of new mills have been erected, and extensive additions have been made to the spinning and weaving machinery of those previously in existence.

"The amount of actual capital invested in the cotton trade of this kingdom is estimated to be between £60,000,000 and £70,000,000 sterling.

"The quantity of cotton imported into this country in 1859 was 1,181¾ million pounds' weight, the value of which at 6*d.* per lb. is equal to £30,000,000 sterling. Out of 2,829,110 bales of cotton imported into Great Britain, America has supplied us with 2,086,341—that is, 5-7ths of the whole. In other words, out of every 7 lbs. imported from all countries into Great Britain, America has supplied 5 lbs., India has sent us about 500,000 bales, Egypt about 100,000, South America, 124,000, and other countries between 8,000 and 9,000 bales. In 1859 the total value of the exports from Great Britain amounted to £130,513,185, of which £47,020,920 consisted of cotton goods and yarns. Thus, more than one-third, or £1 out of every £3 of our entire exports, consists of cotton. Add to this the proportion of cotton which forms part of £12,000,000 more exported in the shape of mixed woollens, haberdashery, millinery, silks, apparel, and slops. Great Britain alone consumes annually £24,000,000 worth of cotton goods. Two conclusions, therefore, may safely be drawn from the facts and figures now cited : first, that the interests of every cotton-worker are bound up with a gigantic trade which keeps in motion an enormous mass of capital, and this capital, machinery, and labor depend for five-sevenths of its employment upon the slave States of America for prosperity and continuance; secondly, that if a war should at any time break out between England and America, a general insurrection take place among the slaves, disease sweep off those slaves by death, or the cotton crop fall short in quantity, whether from severe frosts, disease of the plant, or other possible causes, our mills would be stopped for want of cotton, employers would be ruined, and famine would stalk abroad among the hundreds and thousands of work-people who are at present fortunately well employed.

"Calculate the consequences for yourself. Imagine a dearth of cotton, and you may picture the horrors of such a calamity from the scenes you may possibly have witnessed when the mills have only run on "short time." Count up all the trades that are kept going out of the wages of the working classes, independent of builders, mechanics, engineers, colliers, &c., employed by the mill-owners. Railways would cease to pay, and our ships would lie rotting in their ports, should a scarcity of the raw material for manufacture overtake us."

The Manchester Chamber of Commerce, at about the same date, discussed the same question, and the chairman, in addressing the meeting, drew the attention of the members to the state of the cotton trade itself; to the amazing increase in the trade during the last year; and to the necessity there was for forethought for seeing where they stood. "He had made, at some trouble, a calculation of the probable exports for the present year. These would very nearly amount to £46,000,000, which would be nearly an increase of £3,000,000 on last year, and of £5,000,000 upon the year previous. That was a startling increase; but on coming to look whence it arose, it would be seen that it was due solely to one portion of the world— India and China. Looking at the whole state of the cotton trade, we *had not yet recovered from the depreciation before* 1857. If it had not been for the increase of the exports to India, the cotton trade would not have stood in as good a position as it was previous to the crisis. The cause of the great increase in the demand for goods for India arose in the amazing increase in the capital sent out to that country, which, during the last three years, would not amount to less than £60,000,000. We must not consider the present state of the cotton trade as the normal one, for unless these loans were continued we should not find the increase of exports continue to the East. If so, the state of our cotton trade would be much changed in twelve months. The export to India this year would amount to upwards of £17,000,000, and from this it would be seen that the proportion of our cotton exports to the East was £17,000,000 out of £46,000,000. If our cotton trade was to be increased it must probably be with the East, and this brought him to the question of the policy of the Indian government. The report stated that they had sent a resolution protesting against any increased duties on manufactures to the East. There was a rumor afloat that these duties were to be increased, and if they were they would materially affect our prosperity. Nothing could be more unsound in policy than increased duties on manufactured goods, going into a part really of our own country. It was burning the candle at both ends, so to speak; taxing ourselves for exports from India, and for the imports of these same cotton goods again."

This condition of the Indian trade is no doubt correctly stated. The system of transferring capital to England had nearly exhausted the country, and the question presented itself of abandoning the country, or endeavoring to restore its activity. Capital had become cheap in England, and dear in India; following the law of trade, therefore, it returns, and with its return revives the demand for goods, which thus far outruns the production of cotton. As the prosperity of India increases, the demand for goods will become still more considerable. The discussion in the House of Lords, Jan. 27, was to the same effect.

"Lord Brougham, in rising to move, according to notice, for returns relating to the importation of cotton, said he understood there would be no objection on the part of the government to granting them. He thought it would be most satisfactory to all to know, that since the repeal of the duty upon cotton there had been such an enormous increase in the importation of cotton, from 63,000,000 lbs. to 1,024,000,000 lbs., an increase of sixteen-fold, and the importations from the United States alone had risen from 23,000,000 lbs. to 830,000,000 lbs., or an increase of thirty-two-fold. This enormous increase in the importation of cotton—so advantageous to our manufacturers and the community generally—had been accomplished at the trifling cost of £500,000, which was the amount of the duty upon cotton previous to its remission. He hoped the fact would be an encouragement to us to repeal duties without any regard to what was called the reciprocity system, but to repeal them simply because we wished to get rid of the burden imposed upon us by those duties. There were now no less than 480 articles upon which excise or customs duties were levied, to the great discomfort of trade, and the injury of those who dealt in those articles, while the total product to the revenue was under £1,000,000; indeed, he believed it was only about £630,000. He rejoiced in the benefits which had resulted to the people of the United States from our repeal of the duty on raw cotton; but it should not be forgotten that some of our own colonies presented great facilities for the growth of cotton, and he hoped that in British Guiana, Jamaica, and in Africa, every encouragement would be afforded by the government to the cultivation of this most important material. Above all, he trusted that a trade in cotton would be opened up on the coast of Africa, in the districts explored by Dr. Livingstone, for upon the high land of that country cotton to any amount, and of the best quality, might, with a slight encouragement, be raised. He was told that a capital of £20,000, judiciously directed there, would be sufficient to secure this very great advantage; and he did hope that if it were inexpedient for the government to interfere in such matters, his wealthy friends at Manchester and Liverpool would lend a hand to raise that sum of money."

After much vituperation of the United States on the part of the noble lord—

"The Bishop of Oxford had heard with satisfaction what had fallen from the noble duke. It was quite true that it was not the custom of the British government to engage in direct speculations to promote the trade in any article, but with regard to the growth of cotton, the British government had rendered great assistance in another way—namely, by making the highways of the great continent of Africa—the rivers—accessible to English merchants, so that cotton might be cultivated on each side of them, and the traders have a safe passage up and down. The difficulty which was experienced in other countries, of obtaining free labor to produce cotton, did not exist in Africa, where there was an abundant native population, whose cultivation of cotton would be attended with the additional advantage of introducing a wholesome and lawful commerce, which would absolutely destroy the slave-trade ; for the only way by which that trade could be ultimately destroyed was by *teaching the African chiefs that the employment of their dependent people in the production of the raw material of cotton, would be more advantageous than the selling them into slavery for transportation to other parts of the world.* He therefore earnestly trusted that the attention of the government would be directed to the maintenance and even to the increase of efforts for opening the great rivers in Africa, especially the Zambesi, the opening of which he believed the government was about to aid, and the Niger, which for years the government had assisted in opening. (Hear, hear.)

" Lord Overstone believed that a question of more importance than that relating to the extension of the source for the supply of the raw material of cotton could not be brought under the consideration of the Legislature. (Hear, hear.) He had therefore heard with satisfaction the statement of the noble duke, that the attention of the government was directed to this subject, and that every encouragement consistent with sound principles would be afforded to extend the supply of cotton. (Hear, hear.) The noble and learned lord had stated that within a short period the importation of cotton had multiplied thirty-two-fold in this country, and when their lordships considered how extensive was the demand for cotton goods throughout the world, they would at once perceive that it was a serious matter to have for the supply of the raw material only a single source, liable to be affected by the uncertainties of climate, to say nothing of the obstacles which any unfortunate state of politi-

cal relations might raise up in the way of our merchants applying to that source. (Hear, hear.) He trusted that no efforts
would be omitted by the people of this country to promote
every rational enterprise for the supply of cotton in every
quarter where it could be obtained, and that all the encouragement which the government could legitimately give would be
afforded. (Hear, hear.)"

The coolness with which the Bishop of Oxford states that
cotton could be made by "free labor" if the "African chiefs
would *employ their dependent people*," instead of "selling them
into slavery," is amusing. If, instead of selling the man, or
eating him, he compelled him to grow cotton, the bishop, it
appears, would be satisfied with the progress of freedom. The
discussion was narrowed down to hopes that Africa might
grow cotton. If we reflect that the supply of other materials
for clothing increases much less than cotton, the importance
of the question will appear to be greater.

The five chief materials for human clothing are hemp, flax,
silk, wool, and cotton. These have been imported into England as follows:

*Imports of Raw Materials for Textile Fabrics into Great Britain.*

| | Hemp. | Flax. | Silk. | Wool. | Total four articles. | Cotton. |
|---|---|---|---|---|---|---|
| 1835.*lbs.* | 72,352,200 | 81,916,100 | 4,027,649 | 41,718,514 | 160,014,463 | 326,407,692 |
| 1840... | 82,971,700 | 139,301,600 | 3,860,980 | 50,002,976 | 276,137,256 | 531,197,817 |
| 1845... | 103,416,400 | 159,562,300 | 4,866,528 | 76,813,855 | 344,258,785 | 721,979.953 |
| 1850... | 119,462,100 | 204,928,900 | 5,411,934 | 74,326,778 | 404,137,912 | 714,502,600 |
| 1855... | 136,270,912 | 145,511,437 | 7,548,659 | 99,300,446 | 388,631,454 | 891,751,962 |
| 1856... | 142,613,525 | 189,792,112 | 8,236,685 | 116,211,392 | 456,863,714 | 1,023,886,304 |
| 1857... | 169,004,562 | 209,953,125 | 12,718,867 | 129,749,898 | 521,426,452 | 969,318,896 |
| 1858... | 184,316,000 | 144,439,332 | 6,635,845 | 127,216,973 | 462,608,150 | 1,076,519,800 |

*Price of Upland Cotton in Liverpool.*—In 1835, 10¹/₄d.; 1840, 6d.; 1845, 4¹/₂d.; 1850,
4¹/₄d.; 1855, 5³/₄d.; 1856, 6d.; 1857, 7¹/₄d.; 1858, 7¹/₄d.

This table gives in pounds weight the quantities of raw material imported into Great Britain from all countries in each
year. It does not include the wool used of home growth, or
the increasing supply of Irish flax, but it indicates the demand
that England has annually made upon the countries that produce raw materials for the means of supplying the large demands made upon her factories for goods. The stimulus everywhere given to the production of exchangeable values, and the
diminished cost of transportation, as well as the more liberal
policy of governments, has left to the producer a larger share
of the products of his own industry, and this has shown itself
in a demand for clothing. It is to be observed in the table,

that up to 1850 the proportion of the four other articles increased faster than cotton.

Since that date the cotton demand has again become larger, and the value of all raw materials has risen in an important degree. The future increase of supply in human clothing must come altogether from cotton, and every effort to increase the supply of that article ends only in a despairing appeal to the United States. The discussion of the question draws that fact, and practical English sense shows itself strongly in the following rebuke, contained in the London Times, to Lord Brougham and his confreres:

" The importation of cotton into this country has, since the import duty was abolished, increased sixteen-fold. Having been 63,000,000 pounds, it is now 1,000,000,000 pounds. This is one of those giant facts which stand head and shoulders higher than the crowd—so high and so broad that we can neither overlook it nor affect not to see it. It proves the existence of a thousand smaller facts that must stand under its shadow. It tells of sixteen times as many mills, sixteen times as many English families living by working those mills, sixteen times as much profit derived from sixteen times as much capital engaged in this manufacture. It carries after it sequences of increased quantity of freights and insurances, and necessities for sixteen times the amount of customers to consume, to our profit, the immense amount of produce we are turning out. There are not many such facts as these, arising in the quiet routine of industrial history. It is so large and so steady that we can steer our national policy by it; it is so important to us, that we should be reduced to embarrassment if it were suddenly to disappear. It teaches us to persevere in a policy which has produced so wonderful a result; its beneficent operation makes it essential to us to deal carefully with it now we have got it. Some years ago an island arose in the Mediterranean, and we were all discussing it, and quarrelling about it, and keeping up a brisk fire of diplomatic notes over it, when one fine morning the disgusted island suddenly went down again, and ships sent out to survey it sailed over the site it had occupied. We must not do any thing to disgust this huge lump of profitable work which has suddenly arisen among us. We are inclined to look at it with a respectful and superstitious tenderness, rather as a gambler does upon a run of luck at cards, hoping it may last forever.

" Lord Brougham and the veterans of the old Anti-Slavery Society do not, we fear, share our delight at this great increase in the employment of our home population. Their minds are still seared by those horrible stories which were burnt in upon them in their youth when England was not only a slave-owning, but even a slave-trading state. Their remorse is so great, that the ghost of a black man is always before them. They are benevolent and excellent people; but if a black man happened to have broken his shin, and a white man were in danger of drowning, we much fear that a real anti-slavery zealot would bind up the black man's leg before he would draw the white man out of the water. It is not an inconsistency, therefore, that while we see only cause of congratulation in this wonderful increase of trade, Lord Brougham sees in it the exaggeration of an evil he never ceases to deplore. We, and such as we, who are content to look upon society as Providence allows it to exist—to mend it when we can, but not to distress ourselves immoderately for evils which are not of our creation—we see only the free and intelligent English families who thrive upon the wages which these cotton bales produce. Lord Brougham sees only the black laborers who, on the other side of the Atlantic, pick the cotton pods in slavery. Lord Brougham deplores that in this tremendous importation of a thousand millions of pounds of cotton the lion's share of the profit goes to the United States, and has been produced by slave-labor. Instead of twenty-three millions, the United States now send us eight hundred and thirty millions, and this is all cultivated by slaves. It is very sad that this should be so, but we do not see our way to a remedy. There seems to be rather a chance of its becoming worse. If France, who is already moving onwards in a restless, purblind state, should open her eyes wide, should give herself fair play by accepting our coals, iron, and machinery, and, under the stimulus of a wholesome competition, should take to manufacturing upon a large scale, then these three millions will not be enough. France will be competing with us in the foreign cotton markets, stimulating still further the produce of Georgia and South Carolina. The jump which the consumption of cotton in England has just made is but a single leap, which may be repeated indefinitely. There are a thousand millions of mankind upon the globe, all of whom can be most comfortably clad in cotton. Every year new tribes and new nations are added to the category of cotton wearers. There is every reason to believe that the supply of this universal necessity will for many years yet to come fail to keep pace with the demand, and, in the interest of that large class of our countrymen to whom cotton is bread, we must continue to hope that the United States will be able to supply us in years to come with twice as much as we bought of them in years past.

" ' Let us raise up another market,' says the anti-slavery people. So say we all. We know very well that the possibility of growing cotton is not confined to the New World. The plains of Bengal grew cotton before Columbus was born, and we, with our mechanical advantages, can actually afford to take the Bengal cotton from the growers and send it back to them in yarns and pieces cheaper than they can make it up. So, also, thousands of square miles in China are covered by the cotton plant; and some day we may perhaps repeat the same process there. Africa, too, promises us cotton. Dr. Livingstone found a country in which the growth was indigenous, and where the chiefs were very anxious to be taught how to cultivate it for a European market. There is no lack of lands and climate where cotton could be produced. It is said of gold that no substance in nature is more widely diffused and more omnipresent; but, unfortunately, it is diffused under conditions which make it seldom possible to win it with a profit. So it is of cotton. The conditions under which it becomes available for our markets are not often present in the wild cotton which our travellers discover; nor are they to be immediately supplied. Remember the efforts which the French have made to produce cotton in Algeria, the enormous prizes they offered, the prices at which they bought up all the produce, the care with which fabrics were prepared from these cottons at Rouen and exhibited at the Paris Exhibition, and then note the miserable result after so many years of artificial protection. It will come eventually; as the cotton wants of the world press heavily and more heavily, it must come. We shall have cotton from India, from China, and from Africa; we would advocate every means within reasonable limits to quicken the development. We would not even ask whether to introduce cotton culture upon a large scale into Africa, would be to secure that African cotton would not be raised by slave-labor. But even Lord Brougham would not ask us to believe that there is any proximate hope that the free cotton raised in Africa will, within any reasonable time, drive out of culture the slave-grown cotton of America. If this be so, of what use can it be to make irritating speeches in the House of Lords against a state of things by which we are content to profit? Lord Brougham and Lord Grey are not men of such illogical minds as to be incapable of understanding that it is the demand of the English manufacturers which stimulates the produce of slave-grown American cotton. They are neither of them, we apprehend, so reckless or so wicked as to wish to close our factories and throw some two millions of our manufacturing population out of bread. Why, then, these inconsequent and these irritating denunciations? Let us create new fields of produce if we can; but, meanwhile, it is neither just nor dignified to buy this raw material from the Americans, and to revile them for producing it."

---

## CHAPTER III.

### GENERAL AGRICULTURE.

THE New England States, from the first, were mostly engaged in navigation and manufactures. It was there that capital first accumulated from application to those employments. Agriculture spread in two directions, viz., across the mountains to the west, and southwest from the south Atlantic States. These two agricultural branches divided naturally into free and slave labor, and both sections held the same position to New England as all the colonies had before held to the mother country. The manufacturing and navigating States, as a matter of course, accumulated the wealth which the other sections produced, each in proportion to its productions. To estimate correctly the effects of slave-labor, therefore, it is not to be compared to a manufacturing section, but to a free agricultural section; it is in the same employment that the relative results of free and slave labor are to be justly compared. We shall find that the latter has largely the advantage over the former—that the productions of the individual free man is not greater than that of the slave; but his wants and necessities are greater. He consumes more, while his labor lacks that concentration of co-operation that marks slave-labor. This result is very much opposed to the common idea, which supposes the South to produce cotton only. The great prominence of that article in a manner overshadows other products, which come in a degree to be overlooked. Thus the following remarks, and similar ones, are frequently encountered in the daily press:

"Such is the mutual dependence of the South and the North, that, were it not that the latter supplies to the former its provisions, clothing, and agricultural implements, the South would not be able to supply any cotton for export, but could scarcely supply the home demand."

The fallacy of this idea may be at once demonstrated by an inspection of the census returns, which show a larger quantity of food per head produced in the South than elsewhere, and from its abundance it furnishes food to the North. To form a just comparison between the three sections, a table is formed from the national census returns of 1850, in which the quantities produced in each section are given in separate columns, with the area and population of each section. The " North" is composed of *New England, New York, New Jersey, Pennsylvania.* The " West" of *Ohio, Michigan, Illinois, Indiana, Wisconsin, Iowa, California, Minnesota,* and the *Territories.* The " South," of *Maryland, Delaware, District of Columbia, Virginia, North Carolina, South Carolina, Georgia, Alabama, Louisiana, Florida, Texas, Missouri, Mississippi, Kentucky, Tennessee,* and *Arkansas,* making, together, all the States and Territories. To the quantities, transcribed from the national census, in aggregates for each section, we have appended the values, as given by Professor Tucker in his " Progress of the Nation," as exhibited in the national census, from 1790 to 1850. The value is useful in arriving at the aggregate relative value produced, but the quantity of food per head is an important point.

*Area, Population, and Live-stock of the Union.*

|  | SOUTH. | WEST. | NORTH. |
|---|---|---|---|
| Area—Acres | 871,458 | 1,417,991 | 160,747 |
| Population | 9,664,656 | 4,900,369 | 8,626,852 |
| Horses | 2,044,377 | 1,220,703 | 1,073,639 |
| Asses and mules | 517,224 | 34,454 | 7,653 |
| Milch cows | 2,963,237 | 1,363,253 | 2,058,604 |
| Oxen | 2,835,358 | 341,883 | 494,280 |
| Other cattle | 5,632,717 | 2,236,056 | 1,834,297 |
| Sheep | 6,821,871 | 7,396,331 | 7.505,018 |
| Swine | 20,008,964 | 6,874,796 | 3,468,469 |
| Total head of stock | 40,823,748 | 19,967,176 | 16,441,958 |
| Value of stock | $253,795,330 | $112,563,851 | $173,812,690 |

*Agricultural Productions of the United States, per official Census of* 1850, *distinguishing the South, North, and West.*

| | SOUTH. | | WEST. | | NORTH. | |
|---|---|---|---|---|---|---|
| | *Quantities.* | *Value.* | *Quantities.* | *Value.* | *Quantities.* | *Value.* |
| Wheat..*bush.* | 27,878,815 | 25,090,933 | 41,394,545 | 37,255,088 | 30,761,941 | 27,685,746 |
| Oats......... | 49,882,979 | 17,459,035 | 37,122,774 | 12,992,971 | 59,477,597 | 20,817,175 |
| Corn......... | 349,057,501 | 219,534,500 | 186,384.139 | 111,830,483 | 56,234,511 | 33,740,706 |
| Potatoes..... | 44,878,403 | 17,951,371 | 14,416,390 | 5,766,556 | 44,616,780 | 17,846,712 |
| Rye......... | 1,608,200 | 1,608,200 | 774,555 | 774,555 | 11,800,068 | 11,800,068 |
| Barley ...... | 161,907 | 145,716 | 842,402 | 754,161 | 4,166,611 | 3,747,650 |
| Buckwheat.. | 405,357 | 202,678 | 1,578,578 | 789,289 | 6,971,667 | 3,485,833 |
| Beans and peas. | 7,637,227 | 13,365,147 | 313,278 | 548,237 | 1,229,017 | 2,150,778 |
| Clover, &c., seed. | 123,517 | 370,551 | 142,764 | 428,292 | ₁ 619,501 | 1,858,503 |
| Flaxseed .... | 203,484 | 254,355 | 240,219 | 300,273 | 118,704 | 148,374 |
| Value garden | ........ | 1,377,260 | 664,303 | 664,303 | ........ | 3,050,302 |
| " orchard | ........ | 1,355,827 | 1,640,028 | 1,640,028 | ........ | 5,692,886 |
| Rice .....*lbs.* | 215,313,497 | 8,612,539 | ........ | ........ | | |
| | | $307,328,112 | | $173,744,236 | | $132,024,727 |
| Tobacco..*lbs.* | 185,023,906 | 18,505,390 | 12,358,879 | 1,236,888 | 2,383,208 | 238,320 |
| Wool ....... | 12,797,829 | 3,839,348 | 17,675,129 | 5,302,538 | 21,972,082 | 6,591,624 |
| Butter .... Cheese .... | 68,634,224 | 6,863,422 | 98,266,884 | 9,826,688 | 251,593,899 | 25,159,389 |
| Hay ....*tons.* | 1,137,784 | 11,377,846 | 3,227,253 | 32,272,530 | 9,473,605 | 94,736,050 |
| Hops....*lbs.* | 33,780 | 5,067 | 194,961 | 29,244 | 3,268,215 | 490,232 |
| Hemp...*tons.* | 34,673 | 3,883,376 | 150 | 7 | 443,370 | 22,178 |
| Flax.....*lbs.* | 4,768,198 | 476,619 | 1,330,859 | 133,085 | 1,717,419 | 171,742 |
| Cocoons..... | 5,374 | 53,740 | 2,340 | 23,400 | 3,129 | 31,290 |
| Maple sugar. | 2,088,687 | 104,434 | 10,889,722 | 544,486 | 21,272,077 | 1,061,603 |
| Honey and wax. | 7,964,760 | 1,194,714 | 3,401,078 | 510,140 | 3,487,290 | 523,093 |
| | | $46,303,950 | | $49,879,006 | | $129,025,521 |
| Value slaughtered animals. | | 54,398,015 | | 22,473,786 | | 34,516,451 |
| | | $408,030,077 | | $246,097,028 | | $295,566,699 |
| Per head of population...... | | $42 | | $50.25 | | $34.26 |

From this table we learn that of those grains which constitute food, and are common to all sections, the South raised in value equal to about $30 per head of its whole population, including the slaves. The value raised in the northern section was equal only to $15 per head, a quantity unequal to the support of life, but the large manufacturing interests of that section enable it to command food from the West and South in exchange for merchandise. The product of food at the West is equal to $35½ per head. If we were to include the whites only, the quantity per head at the South would reach $48 per head, a quantity in excess of their wants, and of which they indeed export largely. The quantity of corn alone raised per head is 37 bushels, or the same as at the West. The wheat product at the South gives 4½ bushels per head of the white population, a quantity more than sufficient for its service, and it exports of the surplus largely to the New England States. The aggregate of agricultural productions, it appears, is \$42 at the South, embracing the same articles which at the West give \$50.25 per head, and at the North \$34.26 per head. The South, however, produced in addition, in the year 1849, 978,311,690 lbs. of cotton, which was sold in 1850 at 11 cents per lb., according to the United States Treasury reports, making \$101,834,616. It also produced 237,133,000 lbs. of sugar, valued at \$16,599,310; and, in addition, naval stores to the value of \$2,107,100.

The aggregate results are as follows:

|  | SOUTH. | WEST. | NORTH. | Total. |
|---|---|---|---|---|
| Slaughtered animals.... | \$54,398,015 | \$22,473,786 | \$34,516,451 | \$111,388,252 |
| Grains................ | 307,328,112 | 173,744,236 | 132,026,727 | 613,099,075 |
| Other................. | 46,303,950 | 49,879,006 | 129,025,521 | 225,208,477 |
| Cotton, 978,311,600 *lbs*... | 101,834,616 | .......... | .......... | .......... |
| Sugar, 237,133,000 " .. | 16,599,310 | .......... | .......... | .......... |
| Naval stores........... | 2,107,100 | .......... | .......... | .......... |
| Total............ | \$528,571,103 | \$246,097,028 | \$495,568,699 | \$1,070,236,830 |
| Per head.............. | \$54 | \$50 | \$34 |  |
| Value of live stock..... | \$253,795,330 | \$112,563,851 | \$173,812,690 | \$538,171,871 |

If now—supposing that the black laborers raise the cotton, sugar, rice, and naval stores—we compare the aggregate agricultural products in the above table with the number of white persons employed in agriculture, according to the same census, we have the relative production as follows:

|  | No. employed in agriculture. | Value produced. | Per hand. |
|---|---|---|---|
| North .................... | 823,171 | \$295,568,699 | \$359 |
| South.................... | 849,285 | 409,030,077 | 481 |
| West .................... | 728,127 | 246,097,028 | 335 |
| Total .............. | 2,400,583 | \$950,695,804 |  |

This gives the absolute fact that the West, a peculiarly agricultural section, with very prolific soil, produces a value per hand employed, less than even the comparatively sterile soil of the North and East. This strongly illustrates the fact to which we have previously alluded, viz., that free-labor, even with the fruitful soil of the West, unaided by machinery, can produce no surplus. These figures unexplained, however, embrace a fallacy, and one which has attracted much attention of late. It is, that the Northern and Eastern section has included in its aggregate \$94,736,000 worth of hay, which article, if deducted from all the accounts, would leave the Eastern production less per hand than any other section. This crop of hay

has, however, been vaunted as a crop of great value, even as
" rivalling cotton" in magnitude, and offsetting that crop in its
importance as a national product.   This view of the subject is
more specious than real, however.   The object of making hay
is to cure the grass so that it can be transported to cover, and
feed cattle through those rigorous Northern winters, which
prevent the cattle from seeking their own food in its natural
state.   Where those winters do not exist, that necessity does
not arise, but the cattle have not the less food.   The making
of hay is, then, not a valuable labor, but an expense in the
keeping of cattle, imposed by climate.   Accordingly we find,
as we proceed South, the winters being shorter, less hay is
made in proportion to the number of cattle kept.   In Maine,
755,889 tons of hay were made, and there were 385,115 head
of cattle and horses to feed.   This is a ratio of nearly two tons
per head.   In Illinois, 601,952 tons of hay were made, but
1,190,264 head of cattle were kept, or rather more than half a
ton per head.   In Alabama, 32,685 tons of hay were made,
and 915,911 head of cattle kept, or about one ton to 30 head
of cattle.   In the aggregate, the hay-crop of the country, and
the number of cattle kept, was as follows :

|  | No. of cattle. | Tons hay cut. | lbs. per head. |
|---|---|---|---|
| North..................... | 5,460,820 | 9,473,605 | 3,460 |
| West..................... | 5,161,895 | 3,227,253 | 1,260 |
| South..................... | 13,475,689 | 1,137,784 | 170 |
| Total.............. | 24,098,404 | 13.838,642 | |

This crop of hay, therefore, is a tax upon the labor of the
Northern farmer, proportioned to the number of cattle he seeks
to winter, and the rigor of the winter he has to provide for.
To count this expense among the advantages of free-labor, is
certainly a very fallacious mode of convincing the laborer of
its blessings, and would leave the inference that free-labor in
Maine is much more profitable than in other free States.   The
advantages of the Southern climate are, that not only is natural fodder more abundant, enabling the same land to support
more cattle, but the labor which at the North is applied to
making that fodder available, is at the South applied to other
productions.   The labor which at the North will give 100 millions of hay, will at the South, not being needed for that purpose, give 100 millions of cotton, while the cattle are feeding
themselves.   It is for this, among other reasons, that the aggregate productions of the South are so much more per hand

than at the North and West. The chief reason is, however, that the labor at the South is collective, while the free-labor at the West depends upon its own resources, and is not able to hire the needful help in sowing and harvest seasons. Improvements in machinery have been a great help in that respect, enabling the farmer to get more into, and more off the ground, than his unassisted labor could effect.

As an example of the productions of hands employed in the South, we take the sugar product and number of slaves in each sugar county of Louisiana:

*Louisiana Production of Sugar, Corn, and Rice.*

|  | hhds. | Slaves. | Corn. bush. | Rice. lbs. |
|---|---|---|---|---|
| Rapides | 17,133 | 11,340 | 357,480 | 4,500 |
| Avoyelles | 6,413 | 5,161 | 310,985 | 291,350 |
| West Feliciana | 6,471 | 10,666 | 360,585 | 8,000 |
| Pointe Coupee | 18,213 | 7,811 | 199,790 | 16,840 |
| East Feliciana | 1,570 | 9,514 | 391,789 | 42,670 |
| West Baton Rouge | 21,683 | 4,350 | 226,942 | 900 |
| East Baton Rouge | 12,255 | 6,351 | 151,750 | 4,009 |
| Iberville | 38,876 | 8,606 | 371,065 | ...... |
| Ascension | 28,444 | 7,266 | 368,500 | 35,500 |
| St. James | 27,302 | 7,751 | 334,480 | 68,500 |
| St. John the Baptist | 11,271 | 4,540 | 188,390 | 314,200 |
| St. Charles | 9,146 | 4,132 | 178,980 | 619,000 |
| Jefferson | 3.143 | 6,196 | 197,849 | 122,000 |
| Orleans and St. Bernard | 6,566 | 20,391 | 32,180 | 40,000 |
| Plaquemines | 12,433 | 4,779 | 149,090 | 1,536,740 |
| Assumption, Bayou Lafourche | 32,725 | 5,341 | 564,302 | 99,770 |
| Lafourche Interior | 8,866 | 4,368 | 227,015 | 231,980 |
| Terrebonne | 22,815 | 4.328 | 187,420 | 466,900 |
| St. Mary, Attakapas | 44,634 | 9,850 | 305,290 | 140 |
| St. Martin, Attakapas | 13,548 | 6,489 | 517,401 | 3,700 |
| Vermillion, Lafayette | 862 | 1,067 | 46,061 | 1,664 |
| Lafayette | 1,286 | 3,170 | 288,358 | 2,168 |
| St. Landry, Opelousas | 7,388 | 10,871 | 372,180 | 6,144 |
| Cistern bottoms | 9,252 | ...... | ....... | ....... |
| Total | 362,296 | 162,018 | 6,327,882 | 4,911,680 |

| | |
|---|---|
| Value of sugar | $24,998,424 |
| Value of molasses | 6,470.817 |
| Total | $31,399,241 |

The result is $200, in average value of sugar, for each hand. In some sections the product is immense. In St. Mary, the sugar was worth $3,000,000, without counting molasses, or over $300 to each hand. The labor of the slave in this employment is greatly aided by machinery. The number of slaves is the total for the counties, which, however, produce a great agricultural wealth in addition to their sugar. Thus their slaves produce 40 bushels corn per head, and 30 lbs. rice per head. The cash value of these two crops was $5,000,000. It follows, from these facts, that the South has a far larger surplus to export than any other section, and that the value of that surplus per hand annually increases. It supplies the wants of the North in naval stores, rice, tobacco, sugar, hides, wool, cotton, and annually swells the aggregate exports of the Union to foreign countries. The surplus which has thus poured out of the country manifests itself in the following table, which is compiled from the annual reports of the Secretary of the Treasury:

*Southern Exports from the United States, Number of Slaves, and Value per Hand.*

| Year. | Naval Stores. | Rice. | Tobacco. | Sugar. | Cotton. | Total. | No. of slaves. | Prod. per hand. |
|---|---|---|---|---|---|---|---|---|
| 1800.. | 460,000 | 2,455,000 | 6,220,000 | ........ | 5,250,000 | 14,385,000 | 893,041 | 16.10 |
| 1810.. | 473,000 | 2,626,000 | 5,048,000 | ........ | 15,108,000 | 23,255,000 | 1,191,364 | 19.50 |
| 1820.. | 292,000 | 1,714,923 | 8,118,188 | 1,500,000 | 26,300,000 | 37,934,111 | 1,543,688 | 24.63 |
| 1830.. | 321,019 | 1,986,824 | 8,833,112 | 3,000,000 | 44,058,025 | 48,225,838 | 2,009,053 | 29.11 |
| 1840.. | 602,520 | 1,942,076 | 9,883,957 | 5,200,000 | 74,640,307 | 92,292,260 | 2,487,355 | 37.11 |
| 1850.. | 1,142,713 | 2,631,557 | 9,951,023 | 14,796,150 | 101,834,616 | 130,556,050 | 3,179,509 | 43.51 |
| 1851.. | 1,063,842 | 2,170,927 | 9,219,351 | 15,385,185 | 137,315,317 | 165,034,517 | 3,200,000 | 51.90 |
| 1859.. | 3,695,474 | 2,207,148 | 21,074,038 | 31,455,241 | 204,128,493 | 262,560,394 | 4,000,000 | 65.64 |

These figures for naval stores, tobacco, and rice, are the official export values. The figures for cotton are the crop valued at the export rate in official returns. Those for sugar and molasses are those of the New Orleans prices current. As all these products are the results of slave-labor, in addition to what supplies food for consumption, they are very nearly the exchangeable values produced per hand, and the increase has been in regular progression. The exportable value per hand that was $16.10 in 1800, has risen to $65.64 in 1859, and was $43.51 per hand in 1850, the date of the census, when, as seen in the above table, the food production in that section equalled that of the West, which had no other production. This large value, amounting to $262,560,374, is remitted to the North, either in the shape of sterling bills drawn against that portion sent directly in Northern ships to Europe, or in produce sent to the North. The value of the raw cotton taken by Northern spinners in 1859, was 760,000 bales, worth $40,000,000. There are, unfortunately, no statistics for all the produce sent north from the South, but much may be gathered from the statistics of the several cities. Thus, Louisiana sent north in 1859, 280,000 hhds. sugar, valued at $19,000,000. The city of Richmond sent north $4,000,000 worth of tobacco. Savannah, a large value in lumber, &c. The *Boston Post* remarks in relation to the Southern trade of that city—

"What does New England buy of the South to keep her cotton and woollen mills in operation—to supply her lack of corn and flour, to furnish her with sugar, rice, tobacco, lumber, etc.? Boston alone received from the Slave States in 1859, cotton valued at $22,000,000; wool worth $1,000,000; hides valued at $1,000,000; lumber $1,000,000; flour $2,500,000; corn $1,200,000; rice $500,000; tobacco estimated at $2,000,000. We thus have $31,200,000 in value, only considering eight articles of consumption. Nor have we reckoned the large amounts of portions or all of these articles which arrived at Providence, New Haven, Hartford, Portland, and other places. Nor have we reckoned the value of other articles that arrive at Boston, very considerable though it be, such as molasses, naval stores, beef, pork, lard, and other animal produce, hemp, early vegetables, oysters and other shell-fish, game, peaches, etc. May we not estimate then, with good reason, that New England buys of the South her raw materials and other products to the amount of $50,000,000 annually? In 1858, about one-third of all the flour sold in Boston was received from the commercial ports of the Southern States, and in the same year seven-fifths of all the corn sold in this city was received direct from the States of Delaware, Maryland, and Virginia. The value of the product of sugar and molasses, principally produced in Louisiana, in 1858 was about $33,000,000; and though but a small portion of it came to New England, nearly one-half the crop is consumed in the Northern States, reaching the points of consumption by the Mississippi river."

The cities of Philadelphia, New York, Cincinnati, Pittsburgh, and of the Ohio and Mississippi rivers, receive quantities that swell the figures to $200,000,000, independently of the articles mentioned in the above table, which, being added, makes an aggregate as follows :

| | |
|---|---|
| Sent North in bills and raw materials..................... | $262,560,394 |
| Sent North in other produce............................. | 200,000,000 |
| Total to the credit of the South, per annum......... | $462,560,394 |

This is probably an under-valuation of the amount of means sent North by Southern owners and producers. The produce and the bills drawn against foreign shipments form the credits against which the Southern banks draw, and these credits form an important item of deposits in all the Northern banks, but particularly in those of New York city, where the " balance due banks " swells from 17 millions to frequently 35 millions in the summer, when the crops are mostly realized. The vast movement of produce also gives premiums to the Northern Insurance Companies, whose swelling dividends and premium-shares have been so tempting of late. If the South produces this vast wealth, she does little of her own transportation, banking, insuring, brokering, but pays liberally on those accounts to the Northern capital employed in those occupations. Those who visit the North in the summer months, crowd the hotels and watering-places, and scatter the proceeds of Southern labor broadcast among shopkeepers and trades-people in return for manufactured articles.

In the last few years of speculative excitement at the West, whence such floods of bonds have been sent to New York for negotiation, the presence of the proceeds of Southern crops lying in the New York banks, and by them used to sustain the stock-market, has been a great aid in the negotiation of those Western credits, which were applied to the construction of railroads. That large expenditure reflected upon the Western trade, producing an unusual demand for goods, which disappeared when the railroad expenditures ceased. A very considerable portion of the capital created at the South was applied to the consumption of Western produce, since the thousands of men who were employed in building railroads at the West caused a large local demand for that produce on one hand, while they increased the demand for goods on the other. There has doubtless been a large amount expended for railroad construction at the South, but this has not been speculative. We shall in a future chapter see that although there are as many miles of railroad in operation at the South as at the West, they have cost hardly more than half the money per mile, and their influence in developing local resources has been immense. We shall see that more than 20 per cent. of Western railroad obligations is dishonored, while none of the Southern roads have failed to pay. The reason is, the superior cheapness of the latter. It is also a peculiar feature of the Southern roads, that their stocks and liabilities are nearly all owned at home. The dividends and interest do not therefore form a drain upon Southern resources, while at the West that drain has reached a very serious extent, and must lead to the breaking up of numerous companies.

The employment of such numbers of men at the South as are requisite to work 9058 miles of railroad, is, of itself, an important item of expenditure, and affords a local market for produce not previously enjoyed, while they have a great influence in swelling the surplus delivered at the seaboard for exportation. The extension of manufactures also at the South imparts an increasing demand for local produce. The census gave 163,904 persons engaged in manufacturing at the South, and the progress of that industry is, as we shall see in a succeeding chapter, rapid. These are causes which would naturally tend to diminish the quantity of produce the South would have to send North, unless the production was proportionately increased. This appears to be the case, and the supplies that go forward by steamboat are continually increasing. An interesting branch of this subject is the quantities of farm produce received early and late in the year, in the Northern markets, by steamboats from the South. New York, particularly, owes nearly all its supplies of early and late vegetables and fruits to the Southern slave productions received by steam. The tables of the rich, and those ample boards spread by the hotels, famed throughout the world for the profusion and variety of their bills of fare, are indebted to the farm labor of the South for the enjoyment of those luxuries; and these items amount to many millions per annum. It is a little curious that while New York draws so largely upon the slave-labor of the South for the supply of the table, it also furnishes the same articles, to some extent, to free negro Jamaica, in exchange for the spontaneous products of that fertile island; and Northern vessels do the carrying trade at a profit. The South has, nevertheless, prospered in the trade, and has taken in exchange a large quantity of hats, shoes, clothing, &c., that are manufactured by the artisans in New York, and who would severely feel the want of such a demand should it by any untoward event be cut off. In the nature of things, manufacturing must grow rapidly at the South, for the reason that the mere expense of transportation will, of itself, be an inducement, when the capital shall have been acquired, to prosecute these undertakings. The unfortunate difficulties that have recently sprung up have given a great spur to the attempts of manufacturers at the South.

The progress of these, with the operation of the railroads in employing thousands of hands, is the first step towards accumulating capital at the South, where so much is produced.

# CHAPTER IV.

### MANUFACTURES.

THE Northern or New England States are endowed by nature with a mountainous and sterile soil, which but poorly rewards the labor of the husbandman.  However, its wooded slopes, and tumbling streams, which fall into commodious harbors, early pointed out to the restless energy of the first settlers the direction in which their industry was to be employed. Ship-building and navigation at once became the leading industry, bringing with it more or less wealth.  The harsh rule of the mother country forbade a manufacturing development, and that branch of industry had never got a footing in the colonies.  The act of independence which opened up that field of employment, also provided, by freedom of intercourse, a large market for the sale of manufactures to the agricultural laborers of the more fertile fields of the Middle and Southern States. The genius of Northern industry was not slow in applying the capital earned in commerce to the prosecution of this branch of labor, and with every increase in numbers, and every extension of national territory, the New England States have had only a larger market for their wares, while the foreign competing supply has been restricted by high duties on imports.  The mountain torrents of New England have become motors, by which annually improving machinery has been driven.  These machines require only the attendance of females, but a few years since a non-producing class, to turn out immense quantities of textile fabrics.  In the hands of the male population, other branches of industry have multiplied, in a manner which shows the stimulant of an ever-increasing effective demand.

At about the time that New England became free to manufacture, the discoveries in navigation wrought that singular change in commerce by which Charleston, S. C., was no longer regarded as the nearest port to Europe, and New York assumed its proper position, as the central marine point.  The commerce of the Middle States rapidly increased, and with that increase a larger demand for the manufactures of New England was created.  When population spread west of the Alleghanies, and the annexation of Louisiana opened the Mississippi river to a market for Western produce, thus putting an end to that Western discontent, which had made separation from the East, and consolidation with the lower countries of the Mississippi for the sake of an outlet, imminent, a new demand for New England manufactures was felt, and this was further enhanced by the opening of the Erie canal. In later years, the vast foreign immigration, pouring over new lands opened up by railroads, has given a further stimulus to consumption; more, however, through the enormous sums of money sent in that direction to build railroads, than by any legitimate development of Western wealth. The South, in the mean time, has progressed regularly and solidly, not by help of borrowed capital, but by means of the actual sale of its swelling crops, at still rising prices. It is to be supposed, that although New England was the original source of manufactures, yet, with the progress of the national wealth, those manufactures would gradually spread towards the markets of consumption, and this in proportion to the wealth and enterprise in localities.

The extraordinary hallucinations that exist in relation to the Southern population, and the self-glorification with which Northern writers dwell upon Northern industry, are somewhat surprising. Thus the *Tribune* of Feb. 13 bestowed two columns upon its readers ; and the basis of the homily were the following assertions :

"We were apprised, by the official returns of 1850, that the lands of the South were held by a small number of proprietors, and the residue of the white citizens were without property, and therefore were in a serfdom, or, I might say, more than that, for the serfs in European countries are at least the cultivators of the soil, and have certain inherent privileges attached thereto; in other words, they are '*adscripti glebæ*'—the tenants of the soil; but the white population of the South, other than the great land proprietors, have no interest in the soil, nor does it appear what proprietary interest they have in any sort of property. Manufactories scarcely exist at the South; mechanical industry, distinct from agriculture, has hardly any existence."

This is the sort of declamation with which, for political purposes, the Northern ear is dinned. It is probable that the writer never saw the census returns; but, like candidates for the most responsible offices of the government, when confronted with their signatures affixed to treasonable documents, excuse themselves by saying they "signed without reading," because some "power behind the throne" required them to do so. We find, on examining the census for ourselves, that all such statements are without foundation in truth.

In illustration of the progress of manufactures in the whole Union, we take aggregates from official returns. In March, 1855, the Honorable James Guthrie, Secretary of the Treasury, appointed Messrs. R. C. Morgan and W. A. Shannon to report the manufactures of each State from 1790 to 1850. From page 87 of that report to the Secretary of the Treasury, June 30, 1855, we extract the following table of the cotton manufactures of each section at four periods, and the aggregate of all manufactures for 1840.

| | | COTTON. | | | Total manufac's. |
|---|---|---|---|---|---|
| | **1820.** | **1830.** | **1840.** | **1850.** | **1840.** |
| Texas............ | ........ | ........ | ........ | ........ | ........ |
| Alabama.......... | ........ | ........ | 17,547 | 382,260 | 4,236,000 |
| Arkansas.......... | ........ | ........ | ........ | 16,637 | 1,473,715 |
| Columbia, D. C.... | ........ | ........ | ........ | 100,000 | 1,431,020 |
| Delaware.......... | 151,266 | 310,000 | 332,272 | 538,439 | 2,563,218 |
| Florida........... | ........ | ........ | ........ | 49,920 | 587,167 |
| Georgia.......... | 101,232 | ........ | 304,342 | 2,135.044 | 4,631,191 |
| Kentucky........ | 197,925 | ........ | 329,380 | 273,439 | 12,182,786 |
| Louisiana........ | ........ | ........ | 18,900 | ........ | 8,641,439 |
| Maryland........ | 274,031 | ........ | 1,150,580 | 2,120,504 | 12,430,866 |
| Mississippi........ | ........ | ........ | 1,744 | 30,500 | 2,386,857 |
| Missouri........ | ........ | ........ | ........ | 142,900 | 4,505,186 |
| North Carolina.... | 17,222 | ........ | 438.900 | 831,342 | 6,824,303 |
| South Carolina ... | 4,666 | ........ | 350,000 | 748,338 | 4,111,247 |
| Tennessee........ | 125,266 | ........ | 325,719 | 510,624 | 8,089,992 |
| Virginia.......... | 14,000 | ........ | 446,063 | 1,486,384 | 19,317,214 |
| Total.......... | $885,608 | ........ | $3,724,447 | $9,367,331 | $93,362,202 |
| Population ........ | 4,502,224 | 5,848,303 | 7,334,434 | 9,664,656 | ........ |
| Connecticut........ | 243,268 | 1,853,296 | 2,715,964 | 4,257,522 | 19,971,228 |
| Maine............ | 35,750 | 612,636 | 970.397 | 2,596,356 | 13,792,150 |
| Massachusetts ..... | 735,512 | 7,754,803 | 16,553,423 | 19,712,461 | 71,010,703 |
| New Hampshire ... | 154,547 | 2,447,634 | 4,142,304 | 8,830,619 | 10.052,598 |
| New Jersey ....... | 190,915 | 1,879,180 | 2,086,104 | 1,109,524 | 18,479,444 |
| New York........ | 738,140 | 2,706,920 | 3,640,237 | 3,501,989 | 88,594.350 |
| Pennsylvania...... | 555,673 | 2,099,715 | 5,013.007 | 5,322,262 | 59,140,480 |
| Rhode Island...... | 988,157 | 2,645,081 | 7,116,792 | 6,447,120 | 13,428,287 |
| Vermont ......... | 49,882 | 225,550 | 113,000 | 196,100 | 6,579,086 |
| Total goods.... | $3,991,834 | $22,224,815 | $42,351,230 | $52,062,953 | $301,028,326 |
| Total population... | 4,359,553 | 5,442,381 | 6,761,082 | 8,626,852 | ........ |
| Illinois............ | ........ | ........ | ........ | ........ | 5,956,327 |
| Indiana .......... | 5,400 | ........ | 135,400 | 44,200 | 8,138,274 |
| Iowa............. | ........ | ........ | ........ | ........ | 347,713 |
| Michigan.......... | ........ | ........ | ........ | ........ | 3,327,671 |
| Ohio ............. | 51,315 | ........ | 139,378 | 394,700 | 27,681,570 |
| Wisconsin......... | ........ | ........ | ........ | ........ | 1,468,723 |
| Minnesota......... | ........ | ........ | ........ | ........ | ........ |
| New Mexico....... | ........ | ........ | ........ | ........ | ........ |
| Oregon............ | ........ | ........ | ........ | ........ | ........ |
| Utah.............. | ........ | ........ | ........ | ........ | ........ |
| Total ......... | $56,715 | ........ | $274,778 | $438,900 | $46,920,286 |
| Total population... | 772,819. | 1,575,336 | 2,953,737 | 4,903,368 | ........ |

It is to be remarked, in relation to this cotton manufacture, that in the early part of the century nearly all clothing was home-spun, or made in families. As the art of manufacturing progressed, and cotton became abundant, the quantities of all kinds of clothing made in families gradually diminished, being supplanted by the machine or power-loom goods, until the quantity so made in 1850 had become unimportant. The cotton manufactures of the West did not prosper up to 1850, when the population of that section was equal to that of the South in 1820. On the other hand, the cotton manufacture in the South had taken a long stride in the ten years ending with 1850. The product was about $1 per head of the population : a larger ratio than that of the North in 1820. There are no official returns of the progress of the cotton manufacture since then ; but it is shown that in 1859 the spinners of that section took 98,000 bales of cotton, or an increase of 50 per cent. over the quantity used in 1850. At the same rate of valuation for cloth, the manufacture in 1859 would be valued at $14,000,000. The rate of progression was far greater than in the North and East, where the increase was 25 per cent. only, from 1840 to 1850. The manufacture thus shows a strong affinity for the neighborhood of the raw material and the market for the goods. " Producers and consumers" attract each other.

According to the census returns, the quantity of cotton purchased by the Northern spinners in 1840 was 82,077,200 pounds ; again, in 1850, it was 518,039 bales, of 400 pounds each. The quantity was therefore 207,215,600 pounds ; and the price of the year averaged 6½ cents, according to the treasury returns of exports, making a value of $13,469,000. This year the quantity taken by the same interest was 760,218 bales, which, at 460 pounds to the bale, gives 349,701,280 pounds, which, at 11 cents average, makes $38,467,140. If we take the cloth produced at 4 yards to the pound, at the average of 10 cents per yard, the results are as follows :

|  | Lbs. used. | Value. | Goods produced. | Excess of goods. |
|---|---|---|---|---|
| 1840 | 82,077,200 | 6,976,562 | 40,350,453 | 39,373,891 |
| 1850 | 207,215,600 | 13,469,000 | 58,369,185 | 38,467,424 |
| 1859 | 349,701,280 | 38,467,140 | 140,000,000 | 101,532,860 |

Thus the profits actually fell in this period (1840 to 1850), but since then there has been a general improvement. In relation to the latter circumstance the above official returns give the following facts :

### Value of Goods Produced in certain States.

| | SOUTHERN. | | | NORTHERN. | |
|---|---|---|---|---|---|
| | **1840.** | **1850.** | | **1840.** | **1850.** |
| Delaware ....... | $332,272 | $538,439 | Indiana......... | $135,400 | $44,200 |
| Georgia ........ | 304,302 | 2,135,044 | New Jersey..... | 2,086,104 | 1,109,524 |
| Maryland ....... | 1,150,580 | 2,120,504 | New York ..... | 3,640,247 | 3,591,989 |
| Missouri........ | ........ | 142,900 | Rhode Island.... | 7,116,792 | 6,447,120 |
| North Carolina.. | 438,900 | 831,342 | Kentucky ....... | 329,380 | 273,493 |
| South Carolina.. | 359,000 | 748,338 | | | |
| Tennessee ...... | 329,715 | 510,624 | | | |
| Virginia ........ | 446,063 | 1,486,384 | | | |
| Alabama........ | 17,547 | 382,260 | | | |
| Total....... | $3,378,379 | $8,895,835 | | $13,307,923 | $11,466,326 |
| Increase .................. | | 5,517,466 | | | |
| Decrease........................................................ | | | | | $1,841,597 |

This is a singular result, and shows that the cotton manufacture does not increase in the Middle and Western States, but increases North and South.  In the following states the highest increase has taken place :

| | **1840.** | **1850.** | *Increase.* |
|---|---|---|---|
| Connecticut ...................... | $2,715,964 | $4,257,522 | $1,541,558 |
| Maine............................ | 970,397 | 2,596,356 | 1,625,959 |
| Massachusetts .................... | 16,553,423 | 19,712,461 | 3 159,038 |
| New Hampshire................... | 4,142,304 | 8,830,619 | 4,688,315 |
| Vermont......................... | 113,000 | 196,100 | 83,100 |
| Total New England.......... | $24,495,088 | $35,593,058 | $11,097,790 |
| "     South ................. | 3,378,379 | 8,895,835 | 5,517,466 |
| "     other States........... | 18,476,986 | 17,380,291 | |
| | $46,350,453 | $61,869,184 | |

The cost of the cotton is found by adding to the market price the value of the waste in spinning ; and the difference between the value and the selling price of the goods per pound shows the margin out of which is to be paid "profit," labor, interest, and other expenses of production.  Thus the cost of cotton has been as follows :

| | **1853.** | **1854.** | **1855.** | **1856.** | **1857.** |
|---|---|---|---|---|---|
| Fair, per lb....................... | 6.30 | 6.18 | 5.97 | 6.61 | 7.78 |
| Waste, $\frac{1}{8}$th....................... | .78 | .77 | .82 | .95 | .97 |
| Cost to trade..................... | 7.09 | 6.95 | 6.72 | 7.43 | 8.75 |
| 39 inch domestics—26½ lb......... | 9.53 | 9.45 | 9.41 | 9.52 | 10.25 |
| Margin ................ | 2.44 | 2.49 | 2.69 | 2.08 | 1.40 |

Thus, in 1854, the margin was $2\frac{1}{2}d$. per pound, and this year less than $1\frac{1}{8}d$. per pound.    If the profits of 1854 were $1d$. per pound, then the mills must, in the year 1857, have been running at a loss of $\frac{1}{10}d$. per pound, and were consequently compelled to work short time. The state of affairs so adverse in Great Britain is the same in this country, and affects more particularly those coarser descriptions which require more cotton. In those years when money and labor is cheap, and the material dear, the factories save themselves by running on the fine numbers, and the reverse in years when cotton is cheap and money and labor dear. In the Southern States, the choice of fresher material direct from plantation, less the cost of expensive transportation, gives great advantages, and is materially drawing—with the aid of steam—the mills to the neighborhood of plantations, where the supply and choice of the best cottons are at hand. The long-stapled Sea Island cotton—indispensable for numbers above 50—is grown nowhere but in Georgia; but the soft, silky fibre of New Orleans descriptions is suitable for all descriptions of work below 50, and this cotton is grown nowhere but in the United States. The South has developed a capacity for manufacturing that cannot be denied; and while the progress of the coarse numbers is to the South, the capital and skill of the North is progressing in the finer business.

If now we take the aggregate of all manufactures, we find the results as follows.

The statistics of manufactures of the Union, as completed under the direction of Jos. E. G. Kennedy, Esq., results in the following abstract report of the Secretary of the Interior to Congress, January 21, 1859. If we compare the aggregates with the population of each section, we have results as follows:

| SOUTH. | | NORTH. | | WEST. | |
|---|---|---|---|---|---|
| *Population.* | *Value.* | *Population.* | *Value.* | *Population.* | *Value.* |
| 1840.... 7,334,434 | $93,362,202 | 6,761,082 | $301,028,526 | 2,953,737 | $46,920,286 |
| 1850.... 9,664,656 | 164,579,937 | 8,626,852 | 715,846,142 | 4,900,368 | 138,780,537 |

| | **1840.** | **1850.** |
|---|---|---|
| Total population............... | 17,069,453 | 23,191,876 |
| Total value................. | $23,191,876 | $1,019,106,616 |

The South, it appears, is not so entirely destitute of manufactures as the popular mind has been led to believe.

## Manufactures of the United States.

| South. States. | Establish-ments. | Capital. | Cost of raw materials. | Male hands. | Female hands. | Cost of labor. | Value of product. |
|---|---|---|---|---|---|---|---|
| Alabama..... | 1,026 | $3,450,606 | $2,224,960 | 4,397 | 539 | $1,105,834 | $4,528,876 |
| Arkansas .... | 261 | 305,015 | 215,789 | 812 | 30 | 158,676 | 537,908 |
| Maryland .... | 3,726 | 14,764,450 | 17,394,436 | 22,678 | 7,483 | 7,385,832 | 32,591,892 |
| Delaware .... | 531 | 2,978,945 | 2,864,607 | 3,237 | 651 | 936,684 | 4,649,296 |
| D. of Colum.. | 403 | 1,001,575 | 1,405,871 | 2,036 | 534 | 757,584 | 2,690,258 |
| Florida ...... | 103 | 547,060 | 220,611 | 876 | 115 | 199,452 | 668,335 |
| Georgia...... | 1,522 | 5,456,482 | 3,404,917 | 6,650 | 1,718 | 1,709,664 | 7,082,075 |
| Kentucky.... | 3,609 | 11,810,462 | 12,165,075 | 19,576 | 1,900 | 5,106,048 | 21,710,212 |
| Louisiana .... | 1,008 | 5,032,424 | 2,459,508 | 5,458 | 759 | 2,033,928 | 6,779,418 |
| Mississippi .. | 947 | 1,815,820 | 1,275,771 | 3,046 | 108 | 771,528 | 2,912,068 |
| Missouri ..... | 2,923 | 8,576,607 | 12,798,351 | 14,880 | 928 | 4,692,648 | 24,324,418 |
| N. Carolina.. | 2,587 | 7,221,745 | 4,602,501 | 10,630 | 1,704 | 1,784,604 | 8,861,025 |
| S. Carolina... | 1,429 | 6,053,265 | 2,787,534 | 5,992 | 1,074 | 1,127,712 | 7,045,477 |
| Tennessee ... | 2,887 | 6,527,729 | 5,116,886 | 11,080 | 954 | 2,247,492 | 9,725,608 |
| Texas........ | 309 | 539,290 | 394,642 | 1,042 | 24 | 322,368 | 1,165,538 |
| Virginia ..... | 4,740 | 18,109,143 | 18,101,131 | 25,790 | 3,320 | 5,434,476 | 29,602,507 |
| Total .... | 27,087 | 94,995,674 | 87,779,090 | 129,672 | 22,272 | 35,692,812 | 164,579,937 |

| Western States. | | | | | | | |
|---|---|---|---|---|---|---|---|
| Illinois....... | 3,162 | $6,217,765 | $8,959,327 | 10,066 | 493 | $3,132,336 | $16,534,272 |
| Indiana...... | 4,392 | 7,750,402 | 10,369,700 | 13,748 | 692 | 3,728,844 | 18,725,423 |
| Iowa......... | 522 | 1,292,875 | 2,356,681 | 1,687 | 20 | 473,016 | 3,551,783 |
| Ohio ........ | 10,622 | 29,019,538 | 34,678,019 | 47,054 | 4,437 | 13,467,156 | 62,691,270 |
| California.... | 1,003 | 1,006,197 | 1,201,154 | 3,964 | .... | 3,717,180 | 12,862,522 |
| Michigan..... | 2,023 | 6,563,660 | 6,136,328 | 8,990 | 354 | 2,716,124 | 11,169,002 |
| Wisconsin ... | 1,262 | 3,382.148 | 5,414,931 | 5,798 | 291 | 1,912,490 | 9,293,068 |
| Minnesota.... | 5 | 94,000 | 24,300 | 63 | .... | 18,540 | 58,300 |
| N. Mexico ... | 23 | 68,300 | 110,220 | 81 | .... | 20,772 | 249,010 |
| Oregon ...... | 52 | 843,600 | 809,560 | 285 | .... | 388,620 | 2,236,640 |
| Utah......... | 14 | 44,400 | 337,381 | 51 | .... | 9,984 | 291,220 |
| Total .... | 24,096 | 155,883,945 | 69,997,163 | 116,067 | 6,297 | 30,154,078 | 138,780,537 |

| Eastern States. | | | | | | | |
|---|---|---|---|---|---|---|---|
| Maine ....... | 3,974 | $14,699,152 | $13,553,144 | 21,853 | 6,167 | $7,485,588 | $24,661,057 |
| Massachusetts | 8,259 | 83,357,642 | 85,856,771 | 96,261 | 69,677 | 39,784,116 | 151,137,145 |
| N. Hampshire | 3,211 | 18,242,114 | 12,745,466 | 14,103 | 12,989 | 6,123,876 | 23,164,503 |
| New Jersey .. | 4,106 | 22,183,580 | 21,990,236 | 28,547 | 8,762 | 9,202,680 | 39,711,206 |
| New York ... | 23,553 | 99,904,403 | 134,655,674 | 147,737 | 51,712 | 49.131,000 | 237,597,249 |
| Pennsylvania. | 21,605 | 94,473,810 | 87,206,377 | 124,688 | 22,078 | 37,163,322 | 155,044,910 |
| R. Island .... | 853 | 12,923,176 | 13,183,909 | 12,837 | 8,044 | 5,008,656 | 22,093,258 |
| Vermont..... | 1,849 | 5,001,377 | 4,172,552 | 6,894 | 1,551 | 2,202,468 | 8,570 920 |
| Connecticut.. | 3,482 | 23,890,348 | 23,589,397 | 31,287 | 16,483 | 11,695,236 | 45,110,102 |
| Total .... | 71,842 | 382,366,732 | 397,347,569 | 487,398 | 197,363 | 170,908,574 | 715,846,142 |
| Grand Total... | 123,025 | 533,245,351 | 555,123,822 | 731,137 | 225,922 | 236,755,464 | 1,019,106,616 |

In the table of manufactures the largest item is flour and grist mills, reaching $136,056,736. This manufacture is common to all sections, and Virginia ranks the fourth State in that respect. If we draw off from the official report the proportion of leading manufactures in each section, the results are as follows:

| | EAST. | WEST. | SOUTH. | *Total.* |
|---|---|---|---|---|
| Boots and shoes........... | $45,259,305 | $2,179,086 | $6,529,017 | $53,967,408 |
| Hats and caps.............. | 13,043,495 | 449,556 | 826,813 | 14,319,864 |
| Clothiers................. | 33,837,691 | 4,037.900 | 10,436,118 | 48,311,709 |
| Cutlery and tools ......... | 3,382,520 | 251,370 | 179,351 | 3,813,520 |
| Distilleries ................ | 8,420,747 | 5,361,304 | 1,987,189 | 15,770,240 |
| Iron-forges............... | 6,429,160 | 831,692 | 1,741,843 | 9,002,705 |
| Iron foundries............ | 13,969.980 | 3,313,152 | 2,828,385 | 20,111,517 |
| Iron furnaces............. | 8,580,674 | 1,714,902 | 3,196,322 | 13,491,898 |
| Hardware. ................ | 6,725.720 | 164,010 | 78,040 | 232,050 |
| Nails..................... | 6,796,335 | 68,254 | 797,555 | 7,662,144 |
| Iron railing............... | 5,540,570 | 197,500 | 1.593.011 | 6,936,081 |
| Lumber................... | 31,897,614 | 14,243,265 | 12,379,085 | 58,520,966 |
| Cabinet ware ............. | 9,376,371 | 3,025,423 | 5.261,266 | 17,663,054 |
| Carpenters and builders .... | 11,080,491 | 931.882 | 4,874,446 | 16,886,819 |
| Tanners and curriers ....... | 27,136,467 | 3,808.657 | 6,757,209 | 37,702,333 |
| Woollens.................. | 35,950,609 | 2,318,102 | 1,579,846 | 39,848,557 |
| Cottons ................ ... | 52,062,953 | 438,900 | 9,367,331 | 61,867,884 |
| Total................. | $319,450,652 | $43,334,955 | $62,212,821 | $455,226,769 |
| Flour mills ................ | $67,529,922 | $25,415,048 | $43,111,766 | $136,056,736 |

If we deduct the flour product from the aggregate of manufactures, the remainder is $883,050,880; and the 17 heads of manufactures here enumerated, it appears, are rather more than one-half of that amount. Of the aggregates of these 17 leading articles the South manufactures 50 per cent. more than the West. In clothing of all kinds the South exceeds the West in the manufacture. But in the article of rum the West seems to have the advantage: whether that manufacture, like that of hay, is to be taken as an indication of superior thrift, or morality, or philanthropy, in the free-labor section over the slave-labor region, may be determined by the disposition of those who have the matter under consideration.

If now we compare the white population of each section with the number employed in manufactures, and give the product per head of the whole population, the results are as follows :

| | *White population.* | *Hands employed.* | *Product.* | *Per head.* |
|---|---|---|---|---|
| South................. | 6,222,418 | 151,944 | $164,579,937 | $26.50 |
| West ................. | 4,900,368 | 122,354 | 138,780,537 | 28.00 |
| North ................ | 8,626,852 | 684,761 | 725,846,142 | 83.00 |
| Total ............. | 19,749,638 | 959,069 | $1,019,106,616 | $51.60 |

If it is assumed that the quantity produced in this country is equal to its consumption of domestic manufactures, then the average consumption is, it appears, $51.60 per head, of the whites; but it is probable that the North and East consume more per head than the other sections, and that the South, by reason of the negroes, consumes more than the West. If we take Northern consumption at $60 per head, the Southern at $50, and the West at $40, the results will be as follows:

|  | Consumed. | Made. | Surplus. | Deficit. |
|---|---|---|---|---|
| North .............. | $517,601,120 | $715,846,142 | $198,145,022 | .......... |
| South .............. | 311,120,900 | 164,579,937 | .......... | 146.520,163 |
| West .............. | 196,014,720 | 138,780,537 | .......... | 57,234,183 |
| Total .......... | $1,024,736,740 | $1,019,206,616 | $198,145,022 | $203,754,346 |

Thus the balance of Southern purchases from the North, in manufactures, would be $146,520,163 per annum, and of Western $57,234,183. This balance is composed of dry-goods, shoes, hats, hardware, &c., as their chief items.

The Boston *Post* contains a long and able article, showing the extent of the trade between New England alone and the South, from which we make the following extract:

" The aggregate value of the merchandise sold to the South annually we estimate at some $60,000,000. The basis of the estimate is, first, the estimated amount of boots and shoes sold, which intelligent merchants place at from $20,000,000 to $30,000,000, including a limited amount that are manufactured with us and sold in New York. In the next place, we know from merchants in the trade, that the amount of dry-goods sold South yearly is many millions of dollars, and that the amount is second only to that of the sales of boots and shoes. In the third place, we learn from careful inquiry, and from the best sources, that the fish of various kinds sold realize $3,000,000, or in that neighborhood. Upwards of $1,000,000 is received for furniture sold in the South each year. The Southern States are a much better market than the Western for this article. It is true, since the establishment of branch houses in New York, Philadelphia, and other cities, many of the goods manufactured in New England have reached the South through those houses; but still the commerce of New England with the South, and this particular section of the country receives the main advantage of that commerce. And what shall we say of New England ship-building, that is so greatly sustained by Southern wants? What shall we say of that large ocean fleet that, by being the common carriers of the South, has brought so large an amount of money into the pockets of our merchants? We will not undertake to estimate the value of these interests, supported directly by the South. If many persons have not become very rich by them, a very large number have either found themselves well to do, or else have gained a living."

This estimate of the *Post* for New England alone, is about half the aggregate that the census indicates as the sales of Northern manufactures to the South.

The South manufactures nearly as much per head, of the white population, as does the West. Both these sections hold, however, a provincial position in relation to the East. As we have seen, heretofore, the first accumulations of capital in the country were at the East, from the earnings of navigation and the slave-trade. These were invested in manufactures, "protected" by the tariffs imposed by the federal government. The operation of these tariffs was to tax the consumers in the South and West, *pro rata*, upon what manufactures they purchased of the East, and, by so doing, to increase Eastern capital at the expense of those other sections. The articles mostly protected, and of which the cost is enhanced to the consumers, in proportion to the duties, are manufactured at the East to the extent of $320,000,000, of which $200,000,000 are sold South and West. This gives an annual drain of $50,000,000 from the consumers of those sections, as a bonus or protection to the capital employed in manufacturing at the North. The claim for this protection is based upon the necessity of protecting home manufactures against the overwhelming capital of England. The manufacturers of the South and West have to contend, however, not only against the overwhelming capital of New England, created in manufactures, but against the drain of capital from each locality, caused by the protection to Eastern goods. In spite of this disability, as we have seen in the tables, the manufactures of those sections increase, and at the South faster than at the West. There is another feature of this manufacturing industry which deserves attention. It is, that one-third of the hands employed at the East are females, and the product of their labor is made efficient by steam-machinery. If we take the relative numbers employed in each section in the cotton trade, the result is as follows:

|  | NORTH. | WEST. | SOUTH. | *Total.* |
|---|---|---|---|---|
| Male | 27,392 | 334 | 5,569 | 35,295 |
| Female | 53,184 | 513 | 8,960 | 62,661 |

The Northern labor is largely performed by females, and this element of labor is supplied by immigration in nearly its whole extent, a very large proportion of the females employed in the factories being Irish. At the South, female labor is taking the same direction with great success.

If we compare the whole number of persons employed in manufactures of all kinds at the South, with those so employed at the West, as seen in the above census table, we find at the South the number employed is 151,944, or one in 41 of the white population. At the West the number so employed is 122,364, or one in 40 of the population. These figures give no advantage to the free-labor section, as opposed to the slave-labor section. There is here no evidence that the existence of slavery is in any degree opposed to the development of white industry. It is only another evidence in corroboration of that afforded by the history of the Northern States. The theory has been advanced against the extension of slavery into the territories, that slavery degrades labor, and drives out free industry. In 1790 the New England and Middle States had 1,968,455 inhabitants, of which 40,372 were slaves. Did that slave-labor drive out white labor? or has not the latter extinguished the former, and cast adrift the then well-cared-for negroes, to starve in little bands on the outskirts of the towns and villages, their former happy homes, the wasting monument of the incapacity of a race, and of the selfishness of that philanthropy which found a pecuniary relief in conferring the blessings of liberty on their henceforth useless servants?

What we do find in these figures is, that the South, having become possessed of capital, is prosecuting manufactures at a rate which will soon make a "home market" for its raw materials, and place it foremost in the rank of exporters of goods. The figures show that it is fast supplanting Northern and imported goods with its own industry. It will not, like the North, however, have provincial markets to supply, but having all within its own border, will annually diminish its purchases from the North. It will have foreign markets for its surplus. The countries of South America and Asia will be open to it, and if it there encounters British and New England competition it will have the advantage of having, unprotected, developed its manufactures in face of the competition of Northern goods in the home market, and therefore become able to meet those goods in any market. If, in a few years, it does not become a seller of cotton goods to the North, on a large scale, as it already is on a small scale, since Georgia and Alabama cottons are favorites in New York, it will take none from them. The North will, however, still require food and materials, and the scale of dependence may vibrate.

We have here confined our remarks to the actual figures of the census of 1850. It is to be borne in mind, however, that industry of all kinds has made rapid strides in all parts of the Union since the date of that census. There are, however, unfortunately, no general official figures for the state of industry since. The States of Massachusetts and New York give State returns for the year 1855, and those returns, as compared with 1850, show prodigious progress.

| | 1850. | | | 1855. | | |
|---|---|---|---|---|---|---|
| | *Capital.* | *Hands.* | *Value.* | *Capital.* | *Hands.* | *Value.* |
| Mass....... | 83,357,642 | 165,948 | 151,137,145 | 120,693,258 | 245,908 | 295,820,682 |
| New York.. | 99,904,403 | 199,449 | 237,597,249 | 106,349,977 | 214,899 | 317,428,331 |
| Total.... | 183,262,045 | 365,397 | 388,734,394 | 227,043,235 | 460,807 | 613,249,014 |
| Increase. | .......... | ...... | .......... | 43,781,190 | 95,410 | 224,514,620 |

This rate of. increase has been immense. Those two States, according to the national census of 1850, produced more than half the whole amount of Northern manufactures. If they hold the same proportion now, the Northern manufactures will reach $1,230,000,000, and of these the sales to the South will reach $300,000,000. On the other hand, the Southern manufactures will have increased in as rapid a ratio—the demand for goods being in the double proportion of increasing numbers, and of greater wealth per head. We have seen that the agricultural wealth of the South swells annually in volume. A late number of the *New York Herald* contains, from a correspondent, the following figures in relation to mills near Columbus, Georgia:

"The Eagle mills, established since 1850, use 300,000 lbs. wool, and 736,000 lbs. of cotton. It has 136 looms, employs 70 girls, who earn 50 cents to $1 per day. It employs 225 hands, and pays 10 per cent. dividends. Other mills are as follows:

| | *Spindles.* | *Looms.* | *Hands.* | *Goods.* |
|---|---|---|---|---|
| Eagle.................... | .... | 136 | 225 | Cotton and woollen. |
| Howard.................. | 5,000 | ... | 200 | Cotton. |
| Grant.................... | .... | ... | 100 | " |
| Columbus................ | .... | ... | 200 | " |
| Corvetta................ | 2,700 | ... | 75 | " |
| Macon .................. | .... | ... | 180 | " |
| Planters ................ | 3,200 | ... | 75 | " |
| Milledgeville............. | 3,136 | ... | 120 | " |
| Meetwater .............. | 6,000 | 80 | 200 | " |
| Rovers.................. | .... | ... | 50 | " |
| Athens.................. | 2,500 | ... | 50 | " |
| Princeton ............... | 2,424 | ... | 70 | Cotton and woollen. |
| Mars Hill ............... | 350 | 12 | ... | Cotton. |
| Whites.................. | 1,740 | 20 | ... | " |
| Schleys ................. | .... | ... | ... | " |
| Rowell.................. | 10,000 | ... | 350 | " |
| Augusta ................ | 10,000 | 200 | 400 | " |

| | Spindles. | Looms. | Hands. | Goods. |
|---|---|---|---|---|
| Broad River | 5,000 | ... | 100 | Cotton. |
| Eaton | 1,836 | 36 | ... | " |
| Richmond | 1,500 | 40 | 70 | " |
| Troup | 1,600 | ... | 65 | " |
| Franklin | 1,320 | ... | ... | " |
| Waymans | 1,664 | 26 | ... | " |
| Flint River | 1,560 | 26 | ... | " |
| Thomaston | 1,260 | ... | 50 | " |
| Rock Mills | 600 | ... | 40 | " |
| Brothers | 1,000 | ... | 30 | " |
| Joy | .... | ... | 50 | " |

"The operatives in all these factories are white people, chiefly girls and boys from twelve to twenty years of age. On an average they are better paid, and worked easier than is usually the case in the North. Country girls from the pine forests, as green and awkward as it is possible to find them, soon become skilful operatives, and ere they have been in the mills a year they are able to earn from four to six dollars a week. They are only required to work ten hours a day. Particular attention is paid to the character of the operatives, and in some mills none are received but those having testimonials of good moral character and industrious habits. Churches and Sunday-schools are also attached to several of the manufactories, so that the religious training of the operatives may be properly attended to."

The movement of population is to be taken into the account, in connection with this subject of the manufactures and sectional industry. We have already stated that the New England female labor is largely foreign. We may now turn to the official statistics, and take therefrom the number of aliens who arrived in the country in 20 years, ending with 1850, and we find it is 2,466,200 souls. Of these, very few went South. The number, according to the census, living at the South, of foreign origin, was 316,670. Of these, a considerable number were annexed by the purchase of Louisiana and Florida. The number living at the North, of foreign origin, was 1,923,865. Of these, 601,928 dwelt at the West. The greater proportion of these emigrants at the North were mechanics of various descriptions, and very many of them brought their own capital into the country. The estimate of what each brought has not been less than $100, which would give $60,192,800 carried into the West, and $132,183,700 located North and East, or very nearly two hundred millions of the capital of the North and West was brought in by immigrants, who prosecuted with it those small trades, the products of which found such ready market from Southern buyers.  German hatters, cabinet-makers, tailors, &c., swarm in the Northern cities.  A "turn-out" of 3000 German tailors alone took place on one occasion in New York city.  Although these persons are located at the North, their employment comes almost altogether from the South.  Indeed, without the growing capacity of the South to absorb larger amounts of goods annually, the North would be utterly unable to keep employed the crowds of foreign artisans which arrive each week.  While the South gives them the employment, their arrival is a blessing to the whole country.  In the North, the female portion of the community have, as we have seen, also become producers.  This immigrant movement has added an element to Northern and Western progress which the South has not received, but it has nevertheless well maintained its relative position.

The sales of Northern manufactures to the South, as part of the offset to the large receipts of Southern produce, may be placed at $150,000,000, and from the West at possibly $30,000,000 ; making $180,000,000 worth of domestic merchandise purchased by the South, in addition to the imported goods.

The efforts which are being now made at the South to foster the production of goods there to the exclusion of Northern wares, are very similar to those which were made by the New England colonies, when dissatisfaction began to run high against the mother country.  In the year 1764, there had been imposed restrictions upon trade which gave great offence.  The colonies, therefore, determined to wear no more English cloth, but to manufacture for themselves, and home-spun became the fashion.  " Associations were entered into to retrench all superfluous expenses (and particularly funeral mournings), and to encourage every species of manufacture ; and they actually set about it with so much ardor, that they soon produced such specimens as caused them to think they could do without the foreign trade."—*McPherson.*

In the year 1767, General Phineas Lyman applied for a grant to settle the Ohio country as a military colony, and his memorial states : " The time will doubtless come when North America will no longer acknowledge a dependence on any part of Europe.  But that period seems to be so remote, as not to be at present an object of rational policy or human prevention; and it will be made still more remote by opening new scenes of agriculture, and widening the space which the colonists must first completely occupy."

Twelve years after the rude "specimens" of manufacture were produced; and nine years after General Lyman's remarkable letter, the separation, which all treated as chimerical, took place, and the facts are a lesson to the existing times. That North which, 96 years since, was derided by the English for adopting home-spun in self-defence, is now deriding the South for a similar determination. The North derides Southern separation, and, in the lead of purblind politicians, is pushing dissatisfaction to an extent as great as did the absurd ministers of George III., but for far more futile reasons. England sought revenue. The North, now in the enjoyment of every possible advantage, seeks, in the mere wantonness of prosperity, to enforce abstractions upon the South, that must prove as fatal to that section as to the whole Union. The South is not now in the destitute condition that the colonies were. They have, as we have seen, a large manufacturing industry, and they have already begun to apply to it that spur which was so effective with the colonies. Our ancestors smiled when a swaggering Colonel in Parliament assured ministers that "with a single regiment he could march through the colonies, from one end to the other, with fire and sword." In our day, a swaggering Congressman asserts that the "eighteen millions of people at the North will not permit separation." The fatuity of our day is expressed in the same language as was that of Lord North. Gov. Pettus has recommended to the Legislature of Mississippi the imposition of five or ten per cent. taxes on all wares offered for sale in that State, which are not made in it. The Governor of Virginia has made a similar proposition. In Louisiana the following language is held: "Better rely upon encouragement than repression. Offer five, or some other per cent., upon every thing made in the State, and manufactories would soon spring up which would gradually shove the manufactures of other communities out of the market. At the same time it would lead to no litigation, cause no bad blood, produce no sectional reaction elsewhere, and oppress no portion of the people of the State. It would have a tendency to create home manufactures, and thus make the State independent.

"Let the Legislature of Louisiana adopt the encouraging system, rather than the system of repression. The latter is exceedingly difficult to enforce, and generally fails of its objects at last."

All the States are active in this direction, and great results will follow. If there is no more serious consequences from their movements, a large increase of manufactures will supply the local demand, and a struggle take place between the Northern and the local manufacturers. In the long run the latter must triumph, even if the Northern States should adopt the French system, and give a drawback upon exports from the States.

It certainly is one of the most extraordinary spectacles of the age to see a great, intelligent, and manufacturing people voluntarily permitting a few political aspirants to attack their best customer, and seek to destroy his means of purchase, and merely for a chimera. The French Emperor has proclaimed that France alone "goes to war for an idea." But America presents the spectacle of a people who go to destruction for an "idea." That political party which threatens with fire and sword every Southern hearth, with violent death every Southern man, and with dishonor every Southern female, amid a saturnalia of blood, receives countenance from merchants whose trade depends upon the good-will of their threatened neighbors, and yet vainly hope that they will continue to buy Northern* wares, and make no effort to prepare for that hour which the tendency of that party, for the last 30 years, makes inevitable.

---

## CHAPTER V.

### IMPORTS AND EXPORTS.

In the preceding chapters we have observed the extraordinary progress which the Union as a whole has made, since the formation of the government, in material well-being. In 60 years its whole agricultural production has risen from an unimportant sum to $1,070,000,000, and its manufactures from nothing to $1,019,000,000. All sections have contributed more or less to this progress, which has met those popular wants that have increased in the double ratio of greater numbers and affluence. It follows from this immense increase in the products of industry, that a considerable surplus of many articles above the wants of the people remained for exchange with the products of foreign nations. We find accordingly year by year as the production went on, that external commerce extended itself. In 40 years last past the imports and exports from an aggregate of $39,500,000, rose to $681,000,000. The surplus of the country flowed off in exchange for such articles of foreign origin, as were wanted to supply necessaries or pamper increasing luxury.

The nature of international trade is for two countries to exchange such products as each by peculiarity of climate or natural facilities can produce to the best advantage. Where two countries having nearly the same soil and climate occupy themselves with the same pursuits, an extensive trade between them is not possible. Each produces for itself a sufficiency of what the industry of the other turns out. This was very early recognized in the case of the New England colonies and was the leading motive for prohibiting them from manufacturing. They were confined to catching fish, and selling it, with lumber, &c., to the West Indies, for tropical products, to send to England, in payment of the manufactures she furnished them.

The trade of the North American colonies with England up to the time it was interrupted by the growing difficulties with the mother country, may be seen in the figures for the year 1764:

|  | *Imported from England.* | *Exported to England.* |
|---|---|---|
| New England......................... | 459,765 | 88,157 |
| New York............................ | 515,416 | 53,697 |
| Pennsylvania........................ | 435,191 | 36,258 |
| Total........................... | £1,410,372 | £168,112 |
| Virginia and Maryland............... | 515,192 | 559,408 |
| Carolina............................ | 305,808 | 341,727 |
| Georgia ............................ | 18,388 | 31,325 |
| Total........................... | £839,388 | £932,460 |
| Grand total..................... | £2,249,760 | £1,100,572 |

It is here observed that the " balance" against the Northern colonies was very large, while there was a balance due the South. The Northern colonies at that time, as ever since, had nothing fitted to the English market, and yet they purchased largely of England, and paid well. They managed to do this by sending small, cheaply-built vessels to the West India islands, laden with the inferior sort of fish, caught by their fishers, beef, pork, butter, horses, poultry, corn, flour, cider, apples, cabbages, onions, &c., and these were sold mostly for coin, which was remitted to England. They also sold the best fish to the Catholic countries of Europe, and remitted to London the bills drawn against it. This was the simple business of New England. The trade of the Northern colonies with Europe and the West Indies stood thus:

|  | *Exported to* | *Imported from* |
|---|---|---|
| New England....................... | 407,314 | 340,339 |
| New York........................... | 118,524 | 113,046 |
| New Jersey ........................ | 2,531 | 1,990 |
| Pennsylvania....................... | 382,644 | 194,841 |
| Total........................... | $911,013 | $650,216 |

The exports of the South paid for all they imported, and trade being then far more direct than it has since become, the real state of their balances could easily be distinguished. The New England vessels returning from Europe made the African coast for slaves, which they sold in the Southern ports, and by so doing, absorbed the balance due those colonies from England.

When the American Union was formed, and the North embarked so eagerly in manufacturing, that circumstance of itself would soon have brought all trade between New and old England to an end, if the former could not have commanded produce to send thither. Accordingly, we find that the growth of the trade has been almost altogether in Southern produce, swollen from time to time with some Western grain, when famine abroad caused an extra demand for food, and latterly California gold has increased the exports. The growers of the Southern produce are they who have required the imports. As the *Colonies* had obtained Southern produce for slaves, so the *States* extracted it in exchange for manufactures. The aggregate imports and exports have been as follows, since the accounts began to be regularly kept:

### United States Imports and Exports.

|  | *Imports.* | *Domestic exports.* |
|---|---|---|
| 1821........................ | $23,180,862 | $16,339,109 |
| 1831........................ | 41,854,323 | 28,841,436 |
| 1841........................ | 45,730,007 | 44,184,357 |
| 1851........................ | 90,612,236 | 105,121,921 |
| 1857........................ | 360,890,141 | 348,043,635 |
| 1859........................ | 338,768,130 | 342,279,591 |

The general trade of the country is governed by the amount

of domestic productions to be sold.  Thus a certain amount of cotton, tobacco, rice, wheat, corn, &c., is required for the consumption of the people.  The quantity produced beyond what is required for those wants, or beyond what the people can pay for, is exported to meet the wants of other nations, and it goes, through the unerring skill of the merchants, to those countries that want it most.  Of cotton and tobacco there is not enough raised to meet the demand, and those countries get it which pay the best for it.  In some years this is the case with food.  In 1846, '7, and 1854, '5, there was not enough, and all countries bid against each other for it.  The United States sold largely, except in 1855, when there was no surplus here beyond the wants of the people, and none was sold.  In usual years a good deal of grain can be spared.  These raw products, nearly all furnished by the South, compose two-thirds of the domestic merchandise exported.  The proceeds of all return into the country mostly in the shape of manufactures.  The amount is increased by the earnings of American ships abroad, and also by the sums sent to this country for investment.  From this aggregate is to be taken the interest due abroad, and the expenses of American travellers there, or nearly as follows, for the last year.

| | | |
|---|---:|---:|
| Exports—domestic produce | | $278,392,080 |
| Surplus California gold product | | 42,000,000 |
| Freight earnings—estimate | | 30,000,000 |
| Total to credit | | $350,392,080 |
| Interest due abroad | $15,000,000 | |
| Expenses of travellers | 20,000,000 | |
| | | 35,000,000 |
| | | $315,392,080 |
| Actual net imports, 1859 | | 316,823,370 |

This gives the amount of goods that are received in exchange for produce sold.  It is obvious that unless the produce is given away, something must be taken in payment.  As we produce gold in sums larger than we require, that cannot be imported to advantage.  We have food and raw material in excess, and can therefore, if we trade at all, take only such foreign wares as those who buy of us can supply to the best advantage.  The food, the gold, and the cotton which we sell, Europe must have, and sales of these regulate the quantities of goods, pretty nearly, that come back.  The kinds of goods so received depend, in some degree, upon their ability to compete with the Northern manufactures, which have the preference.  If a Massachusetts factory can make a certain style of cotton goods as cheap as the

English, it has a duty of 20 per cent., and 10 per cent. charges, or 30 per cent. preference over the English, which insures it the market at a large profit. The account is sometimes disturbed by credit. As in the case of the recent railroad speculation, large sums are sent from England here for investment. If these in one year reach, say, $30,000,000, goods to that amount may be, and are, imported, in addition. It also happens, at such seasons, that sellers supply goods on credit to other than regular merchants. Those dealers sustain themselves by bank operations until explosion takes place. The trade then settles back to the real staple exports of the country; and these, as we have said, are of Southern origin.

The leading exports from the country, from time to time, have been as follows:

### United States Exports.

| Year. | Cotton. | Tobacco. | Flour and provisions. | Rice. | Manufactures. | Total. |
|---|---|---|---|---|---|---|
| 1790.... | 42,285 | 4,349,567 | 5,991,171 | 1,753,796 | .......... | 19,666,101 |
| 1803.... | 7,920,000 | 6,209,000 | 15,050,000 | 2,455,000 | 2,000,000 | 42,205,961 |
| 1807.... | 14,232,000 | 5,476,000 | 15,706,000 | 2,307,000 | 2,309,000 | 48,699,592 |
| 1816.... | 24,106,000 | 12,809,000 | 20,587,376 | 2,378,880 | 2,331,000 | 64,781,896 |
| 1821.... | 20,157,484 | 5,648,962 | 12,341,360 | 1,494,387 | 2,752,631 | 43,671,894 |
| 1831.... | 31,724,682 | 4,892,388 | 12,424,701 | 2,016,267 | 5,086,890 | 59,218,583 |
| 1836.... | 71,284,925 | 10,058,640 | 9,588,359 | 2,548,750 | 6,107,528 | 106,916,680 |
| 1842.... | 47,593,464 | 9,540,755 | 16,902,876 | 1,907,387 | 7,102,101 | 91,799,242 |
| 1847.... | 53,415,848 | 7,242,086 | 68,701,921 | 3,605,896 | 10,351,364 | 150,574,844 |
| 1851.... | 112,315,317 | 9,219,251 | 21,948,651 | 2,170,997 | 20,136,967 | 178,620,138 |
| 1859.... | 161,434,923 | 21,074,038 | 37,987,395 | 2,207,148 | 32,471,927 | 278,392,080 |

These figures are from the Treasury tables. In 1790 the same general state of trade existed as before the war. The temporary free trade with France had given some little impulse to business, but the Northern ships no longer enjoyed the same privileges in the English ports, and the slave-trade was injured by the want of coast goods, and by the great depression in the value of blacks in the South. With the French wars, however, the carrying trade became active, and a large market for provisions was opened up on the continent. The Middle States and New England then supplied considerable quantities, and in 1803 business was flourishing. In 1807 the trade was large. The embargo was to take place in the following year, and produce was hurried forward, and cotton, tobacco, and rice were one-half the whole. The embargo and the war had a serious effect upon Southern staples; but the events of those years conferred fortune on many a Northern merchant. New York has just buried one of her oldest merchants, whose princely fortune was begun by the large profits on cotton. The princely Girard owed his fortune to

the slave accumulation of St. Domingo; and there are few " old
families" North whose fortunes are not dated from slave connections. With the return of peace, in 1816, the exports were
largely developed; the produce accumulated during the war
went forward in great affluence. The New England States
had, however, then embarked in manufactures, and the population of the North, soon absorbed in those employments, consumed all their own provisions and breadstuffs, and there was
little to export beyond that sent from the South to the South
American States. With the great development of manufactures in England and Western Europe, the same circumstances
occurred, and an outside supply of provisions became yearly
more necessary. The West nearly reached a condition to supply this demand when the "free trade" policy was adopted by
England, in 1842. The famine of 1846 carried the export of
breadstuffs and provisions from the U. States to its highest
point; and it has since subsided because in some cases the surplus growth of the West did not suffice to feed the Eastern
States, even with the aid of the South, and leave any thing for
export.

The manufacturers of the north have not afforded much surplus for export. They were bred up under the protective system, avowedly because they could not compete with the
English manufacturer in this market, and it was not to be expected that they could, under such circumstances, do so in a
third market. The greatest increase that has taken place in
manufactures has been in cotton goods, and these have increased in the proportion in which, as we have seen in a former
chapter, the progress of manufactures at the South has occupied the home market. The South affords the material for that
manufacture. The exports of breadstuffs and provisions are
also due to the South, since but for the quantities of these
which are sent North to feed the Eastern States, little or no
Western produce could be spared for Europe, even at high
prices. In this respect the West is situated like the English
West Indies. There is prolific land enough to raise abundance
for export, but no labor. The introduction and use of labor-
saving machines alone enables the West to export at all. The
use of these requires more capital than the agriculturalists
generally possess; but with time, no doubt, they will increase.

The West enjoys within its bosom almost limitless supplies
of raw material for every description of manufacture except

cotton. Its metals, coal, lumber, building materials, raw materials, every thing exists in abundance; requiring only capital to develop them rapidly. In this it contrasts strongly with the barren hills of New England, which are as destitute of metals as of fertility. They afford no materials for the employment of her busy people, not even a sufficiency of wool. They have hitherto had their food and materials brought to them, and have sent back goods in return, manufactured under cover of those protective tariffs which all consumers have submitted to for their benefit and the convenience of the Federal Union. That state of things cannot last; the West will acquire capital and manufacture for itself. The South is making long strides in the same direction, and all the sooner that the North insists upon manufacturing morality as well as woollens, and fitting the South with new principles as well as new shoes.

If we analyze the export trade of the country in respect of the origin of the exports, we shall find that more than one-half the whole is exclusively of Southern origin ; that of those articles that are common to all sections, one-half goes directly from the South ; and that of the Northern manufactures that are exported, much of the raw material is also of Southern origin.

The following exports for the years 1857 and 1859 distinguish the origin :

*United States Exports for* 1857 *and* 1859.

| Of Southern origin. | **1857.** | **1859.** |
|---|---|---|
| Cotton........................... | $131,575,859 | $161,434,923 |
| Tobacco.......................... | 21,707,799 | 21,074,038 |
| Rice ............................ | 2,290,400 | 2,207,148 |
| Naval stores..................... | 2,494,530 | 3,695,474 |
| Sugar............................ | 190,012 | 196,735 |
| Molasses......................... | 108,003 | 75,699 |
| Hemp............................. | 33,687 | 9,227 |
| Total...................... | $157,402,290 | $188,693,496 |
| Other from South.................. | 24,398,967 | 8,108,632 |
| Cotton manufactures............... | 3,669,106 | 4,989,733 |
| Total from South.............. | $185,470,263 | $198,389,351 |
| From the North................ | 93,416,350 | 78,217,202 |
| Total merchandise........... | $278,886,613 | $278,392,080 |
| Specie............................ | 60,078,352 | 57,502,305 |

The cotton manufactures exported in 1857 amounted to $6,115,177. The raw material was valued at 60 per cent., or $3,669,106 as the interest of the South in that export. The " other exports" were composed of breadstuffs, &c. Thus the wheat and corn exportation in that year reached the following figures:

|  | Wheat. | Flour. | Corn. | Total. |
|---|---|---|---|---|
| From South............ | $4,145,787 | $7,888,167 | $1,225,098 | $13,259,052 |
| " North............ | 18,094,070 | 17,994,149 | 3,959,567 | 40,047,786 |
| Total................ | $22,240,857 | $25,882,316 | $5,184,665 | $53,306,838 |

The quantity of these articles (40,047,786) which went direct from the Northern States did not exceed the quantities which that section received from the South and from Canada. The fact was, therefore, that with the exception of manufactures, the South furnished nearly the whole, or substitutes for the whole exportations of the country.

On the other hand, if the larger portion of the importations were made at the North, for the reason that capital, shipping, and geographical advantages are there concentrated, the destination of those goods has been largely in the direction of the sources of the exports of the country. The goods swelling the current of manufacture, that sets South through New York and Philadelphia by means of coasting tonnage and railroads, helps to cancel the large debt which the North annually contracts. The annual report of the Secretary of the Treasury for the year 1856, page 101, gives the amount of imported goods consumed in the United States in 1850 at $163,186,510, or $7.02 per head of the whole population. The distribution of that amount was to the South, $43,000,000; West, 35,000,000; North, $85,180,000. In the past year these importations have risen to $317,882,059, or a consumption of $10.59 per head, which would give, in the same proportion, for Southern consumption, $106,000,000; for Western, $63,000,000; and for the North and East, $149,000,000. If, then, the sales of domestic manufactures to the South were, in 1850, $146,000,000, according to the data furnished by the census, and as we have seen on other data, the manufacture at the North has since increased 50 per cent., while the means of the South to pay have increased in even a greater ratio, the trade of 1859 would give Northern manufactures sold to the South $240,000,000; imported goods sold to the South $106,000,000; brokerage, interest, freight, commissions, insurance, &c, on Southern produce and funds 15 per cent., or $63,000,000. The number of whites at the South over 20 years of age is about 3,000,000. It is estimated that if 50,000 come North every year, their expenditure, at $1000 each, would amount to $50,000,000, disbursed for Northern board, goods, fares, &c. If we then recur to the Southern credits given in a preceding chapter, the account will stand thus :

| Sent North. | | Sent South. | |
|---|---|---|---|
| Bills and raw materials.... | $262,560,394 | Domestic goods........... | $240,000,000 |
| Other produce............ | 200,000,000 | Imported    "   ......... | 106,000,000 |
| | | Interest, brokerage, &c ... | 63,200,000 |
| | | Southern travellers....... | 53,360,394 |
| Total ............... | $462,560,394 | Total................ | $462,560,394 |

This is the vast trade which approximates the sum of the dealings between the North and the South. These transactions influence the earnings, more or less direct, of every Northern man. A portion of every artisan's work is paid for by Southern means. Every carman draws pay, more or less, from the trade of that section. The agents who sell manufactures, the merchants who sell imported goods, the ships that carry them, the builders of the ships, the lumbermen who furnish the material, and all those who supply means of support to them and their families. The brokers, the dealers in Southern produce, the exchange dealers, the bankers, the insurance companies, and all those who are actively employed in receiving and distributing Southern produce, with the long train of persons who furnish them with houses, clothing, supplies, education, religion, amusement, transportation, &c., are dependent upon this active interchange, by which at least one thousand millions of dollars come and go between the North and South in a year. The mind can with difficulty contemplate the havoc and misery that would be caused on both sides by the breaking up and sundering of such ties, if indeed it were possible. If we were to penetrate beyond a rupture, and imagine a peaceable separation, by which the North and South should be sundered without hostilities, we might contemplate the condition and prospects of each. From what has been detailed above, as revealed to us from the returns of the census, it is quite apparent that the North, as distinguished from the South and West, would be alone permanently injured. Its fortune depends upon manufacturing and shipping; but, as has been seen, it neither raises its own food nor its own raw material, nor does it furnish freights for its own shipping. The South, on the other hand, raises a surplus of food, and supplies the world with raw materials. Lumber, hides, cotton, wool, indigo—all that the manufacturer requires—is within its own circle. The requisite capital to put them in action is rapidly accumulating, and in the long run it would lose—after recovering from first disasters—nothing by separation. The North, on the other hand, will have food and raw materials to buy in order to employ its labor; but who will then buy its goods? It cannot supply England; she makes the same things cheaper. The West will soon be able to supply itself. The South, while having the world as an eager customer for its raw produce, will not want Northern goods; but she will supply with her surplus manufactures the Central and South American countries, as now with her flour. As the world progresses, manufacturing nations will deal less with each other, because they make the same things. Their customers must be tropical and agricultural communities. But if they quarrel with the manners and customs of those countries to the extent of attempting to force upon them a new system of morality, their piety will be its own reward, and the crown of commercial martyrdom may be mistaken for a zany's cap.

There is probably no wish on any side to separate. Each section is steadily growing in wealth and strength, and each develops its natural resources in the same ratio that its population and capital increase. There is this difference: both the South and West have vast natural resources to be developed, and the time for that development is only retarded by the present profits that the North derives from supplying each with those things that they will soon cease to want. The North has no future natural resources. In minerals, both the other sections surpass it. In metals, it is comparatively destitute; of raw materials, it has none. Its ability to feed itself is questionable. Its commerce is to the whole country what that of Holland once was to the world, viz., living on the trade of other people. Its manufactures occupy the same position, awaiting only the time when the other sections will do their own work. When that moment arrives, Massachusetts, which now occupies the proudest rank in the Union, will fall back upon her own resources, and still claim to be an agricultural state, since her summer crop is granite and her winter crop is ice. This period the North supinely permits a few unscrupulous politicians, clerical agitators, and reprobate parsons to hasten by the most wanton attacks upon the institutions of their best customers. They are forcing the Northern Slave States to assume to the South the same position that New England held to the South on the formation of the Union. They are holding out to them the bright prize of becoming the manufacturers, importers, and carriers for the South, as the North has been. They offer them this brilliant premium to cut their connection with the North, in order to enjoy those branches of industry in relation to the South which have conferred such wealth and prosperity upon New England and the Middle States. England became rich by the colonies—repelled them. Her mantle fell on New England; she has become rich, and in her turn repels the South in favor of the Northern Slave States. These latter see the prize falling to them, and may become eager to grasp it before the North shall have awakened to its danger.

------

## CHAPTER VI.

### TONNAGE AND RAILROADS.

THE early occupation of the Northern States being navigation, they have pursued the art of ship-building until they have become models of the world. In doing so they have acquired large capital, and are the owners of an immense tonnage.

The development of this industry of the North American colonies, and their trade, was probably the first real opposition on the ocean that the Dutch received. So much did it flourish in the 17th century that Sir Joshua Childs, writing in 1670, states that " our American plantations employ nearly two-thirds of our English shipping, and thereby give constant subsistence to, it may be, 200,000 persons here at home." In 1676 Sir William Petty states the shipping of the American trade at 40,000 tons. 100 years later, in 1769, the vessels built in the colonies were as follows:

*Ships built in the Colonies in* 1769.

| | Square-rigged. | Sloops and schooners. | Tonnage. |
|---|---|---|---|
| New Hampshire | 16 | 29 | 2,452 |
| Massachusetts | 40 | 97 | 8,013 |
| Rhode Island | 8 | 31 | 1,428 |
| Connecticut | 7 | 43 | 1,542 |
| New York | 5 | 14 | 955 |
| New Jersey | 1 | 3 | 83 |
| Pennsylvania | 14 | 8 | 1,469 |
| Maryland | 9 | 11 | 1,344 |
| Virginia | 6 | 21 | 1,269 |
| North Carolina | 3 | 9 | 607 |
| South Carolina | 4 | 8 | 789 |
| Georgia | .. | 2 | 50 |
| Total | 113 | 276 | 20,001 |

The number of tons built in the United States in 1820 was 47,780, not a large increase over the business of 1769. In the 40 years that succeeded 1820, the tonnage built rose to 583,450 tons in one year, step by step, with the increase of cotton. The employment of the colonial ships, during nearly 200 years, was fish and slaves,—the fish for the Catholic countries of Southern Europe, and the slaves for the South, and the West Indies. In all that time the construction reached up to 20,001, or 389 sail, of an average of 50 tons each. In 1820 the tonnage rose to 47,786, for 534 vessels, or 90 tons each; in 1855 there were built 2,034 vessels of 583,450 tons, or 290 tons average, showing the change in construction from the small cheap vessels built for the West India trade, to the large ships required for cotton transportation. The fisheries were the chief business of the Northern colonists, and they had not only the benefit of the large sale to the West Indies and to the Catholic countries of Europe, but the eating of fish in England had, by the law of Elizabeth, in 1563, been ordered on Wednesdays and Saturdays, for the encouragement of seamen, thus affording a large market, from which foreign fish were excluded. The same law became a custom down to our day, it being still almost universal in New England to eat fish on Saturday. Indeed, so strictly was this custom observed, that in the old slave days of Massachusetts, it being ordered that slaves should not be in the streets on Sunday, a black was arrested on the Common. He denied that it was Sunday, and proved his point by showing that " massa no hab salt fish yesterday." With all this encouragement the tonnage in 200 years made slow progress, until the union of the States and cotton growing began to open a broader field for navigation, and they have since not only carried the large produce of the South abroad, but have conveyed it coastwise. As this business has increased, the shipbuilding at the North has followed its expansion, and it has been fostered by the bounties of the federal government, paid to the fishermen of that section. Up to 1860 these bounties had reached nearly $12,966,998, paid out of the national treasury to encourage shipping at the North.

The fisheries being the great business of the North, when the Union was formed, a law of July 4, 1789, allowed a drawback on fish exported equal to the supposed quantity of salt used. This law in 1792 was changed to a bounty per ton on the vessels engaged in the fisheries, and has been continued down to the present time. The amount of tonnage and allowance paid to the fishing-vessels in the last 12 years was as follows:

*Federal Bounty to Fisheries.*

| Year. | Tonnage of vessels engaged in cod-fisheries. | Allowance paid to fishing vessels. |
|---|---|---|
| 1848 | 82,652 | $243,434 |
| 1849 | 73,882 | 287,604 |
| 1850 | 85,646 | 286,796 |
| 1851 | 87,476 | 328,267 |
| 1852 | 102,659 | 304,569 |
| 1853 | 99,990 | 323,199 |
| 1854 | 102,194 | 374,286 |
| 1855 | 102,928 | 346,196 |
| 1856 | 95,816 | 271,838 |
| 1857 | 104,573 | 464,178 |
| 1858 | 119,254 | 389,500 |
| 1859 | 129,637 | 426,962 |
| Twelve years | 1,186,717 | $4,046,929 |

Thus in twelve years the national treasury has paid out $4,046,929, as a direct bounty, to sustain one northern interest. The whole amount paid has been $12,944,998, and the following States have been the recipients of it:

*States that receive the Federal Bounty.*

| | |
|---|---|
| Maine | $4,175,050 |
| New Hampshire | 563,134 |
| Massachusetts | 7,926,273 |
| Connecticut | 182,853 |
| Rhode Island | 78,895 |
| New York | 18,319 |
| Virginia | 479 |
| Total | $12,944,998 |

Thus Massachusetts has received two-thirds of the whole amount, for the fostering of one of her interests. This bounty is paid out of the national treasury, into which it is collected from the Southern consumers of imported goods.

This has greatly aided the development of ship-building, not only in the branch of the fisheries, but in all others, and confirmed New England in its commercial predominance, and we shall see, as we progress, that ship-building has remained almost exclusively with the North, which owns about 80 per cent. of the present tonnage.

While they furnish the means of transportation, however, they, as we have seen in preceding chapters, with the exception of the fisheries, furnish very little employment for the shipping. There is probably no people in the world who do so much freighting, and derive so little of it from their own resources. They, in this respect, resemble Holland in the days of Van Tromp, when the inhabitants of the Flemish marshes were, by the carrying trade of the world, enabled to wear a broom at the mast-head. If the New Englanders have not swept the seas with their guns, they have done so by superior enterprise, and the enjoyment of the vast monopoly conferred upon them by the South. The carrying of the cotton crop has been the basis of the Northern freighting business, and the national tonnage has swollen in the following proportion, step by step with the cotton product:

*Tonnage owned and built annually in the United States, and the Cotton Crop.*

| Year. | Fisheries. | Steam. | Registered and enrolled. | Cotton crop. bales. | Vessels built. | Tonnage. |
|---|---|---|---|---|---|---|
| 1820........ | 158,430 | ..... | 1,119,736 | 225,000 | 534 | 47,784 |
| 1830........ | 137,245 | 64,471 | 990,260 | 976,845 | 637 | 58,074 |
| 1835........ | 234,457 | 122,815 | 1,580,481 | 1,254,328 | 507 | 46,238 |
| 1840........ | 233,112 | 198,184 | 1,709,318 | 2,177,885 | 872 | 118,309 |
| 1841........ | 229,282 | 174,342 | 1,691,092 | 1,634,945 | 762 | 118,893 |
| 1842........ | 218,047 | 228,349 | 1,612,950 | 1,638,574 | 1,021 | 129,083 |
| 1843........ | 219,192 | 236,867 | 1,668,271 | 2,378,875 | 482 | 63,617 |
| 1844........ | 262,961 | 272,178 | 1,707,160 | 2,030,409 | 766 | 103,537 |
| 1845........ | 282,142 | 325,988 | 1,769,387 | 2,394,503 | 1,038 | 146,018 |
| 1846........ | 296,398 | 347,892 | 1,885,284 | 2,100,537 | 1,420 | 188,203 |
| 1847........ | 295,486 | 404,841 | 2,095,236 | 1,778,651 | 1,598 | 243,732 |
| 1848........ | 318,822 | 427,890 | 2,261,804 | 2,347,634 | 1,851 | 318,075 |
| 1849........ | 297,010 | 462,393 | 2,527,772 | 2,728,596 | 1,547 | 256,577 |
| 1850........ | 309,773 | 525,946 | 2,609,544 | 2,096,706 | 1,360 | 272,218 |
| 1851........ | 319,658 | 583,607 | 2,753,182 | 2,355,257 | 1,367 | 298,203 |
| 1852........ | 368,982 | 643,240 | 3,070,431 | 3,015,029 | 1,444 | 351,493 |
| 1853........ | 342,942 | 604,617 | 3,388,637 | 3,262,882 | 1,710 | 425,572 |
| 1854........ | 319,136 | 676,607 | 3,747,212 | 2,930,027 | 1,774 | 535,616 |
| 1855........ | 311,399 | 770,285 | 4,069,162 | 2,847,339 | 2,034 | 583,450 |
| 1856........ | 315,162 | 673,077 | 3,841,047 | 3,527,845 | 1,703 | 469,393 |
| 1857........ | 328,740 | 705,784 | 3,862,812 | 2,939,519 | 1,434 | 378,804 |
| 1858........ | 339,082 | 729,390 | 3,933,453 | 3,113,962 | 1,225 | 242,286 |
| 1859........ | 347,646 | 768,762 | 3,977,970 | 3,851,481 | 870 | 156,602 |
| 1860, est..... | ....... | ....... | 4,000,000 | 4,300,000 | .... | ....... |

The sail vessels, under the head of "enrolled," as well as "registered," are, to a considerable extent, employed in the transportation of cotton. As a general rule, a registered ton of shipping will carry three bales of cotton. A good deal of the cotton is subject, however, to several distinct transportations. It is delivered at the Southern ports, by steam and other boats, hence sent to Northern ports, thence again shipped to England, or to manufacturing towns. This movement so governs the shipping trade that whenever the quantity of shipping has been stimulated beyond one ton to a bale of cotton produced, in the aggregate, there has been, invariably, reaction and depression. In 1820 the shipping was large, because there was in existence the remains of the trade during the French Wars, and the tonnage lost, condemned, and sold, had not then been fully marked off from the official registers. Since then, the account has been accurately kept. The quantity built was small, up to 1830, when the proportion of one ton to a bale of cotton existed. From 1835, when the same proportion was apparent, there was little variation in the quantity built per annum, and the proportion of shipping to cotton held good up to the large crop of 1843, which immediately gave an impulse to the business of ship-building, and tonnage increased annually up to 1846, when the amount had again reached the proportion of one ton to a bale. In that year, however, took place the Irish famine, causing a demand for shipping all over the world, for transportation of grain. This demand was aided by the Mexican war, for which the government required much transport service. The ship-building reached 318,075 tons in 1848, in which year those two elements had ceased to act, and there was a heavy depression in the trade, since the tonnage exceeded the proportion of one ton to a bale, in 1850 and 1851. In 1852 the proportion was recovered, but then took place the revolution in ship-building, caused by California. Clipper ships, became the rage, and the gold trade carried the tonnage far beyond the regular cotton proportion. The result was the same as before; a terrible depression overtook the shipping, and the building which had been carried to its greatest height, in 1855, when it reached 2,034 vessels, with a tonnage of 583,450, has year by year, declined. The quantity "lost, condemned, and sold" to foreigners has been more than equal to the production, and the sail tonnage is now 91,192 tons less than at its highest point, in 1855. The cotton crop has, however, increased, until it has resumed its proportion of one bale to the ton. There can be no clearer proof than these figures afford, of the utter dependence of the Northern shipping upon the great Southern staple.

If we turn to the official tables, distinguishing the three sections, we shall have the ownership of the tonnage as follows, comparing the years 1830 and 1858, both cotton crop and tonnage having quadrupled in that period.

| | 1830. | | | 1858. | | |
|---|---|---|---|---|---|---|
| | | *Enrolled.* | | | *Enrolled.* | |
| | *Registered.* | *Sail.* | *Steam.* | *Registered.* | *Sail.* | *Steam.* |
| South ....... | 109,182 | 82,849 | 33,605 | 391,518 | 297,394 | 229,180 |
| West......... | 54 | 2,090 | 219 | 50,236 | 219,416 | 104,009 |
| North....... | 380,826 | 471,682 | 20,010 | 1,781,369 | 1,381,893 | 318,174 |
| Total.... | 490,062 | 556,621 | 54,036 | 2,223,123 | 1,898,693 | 651,363 |

It is not only the owners of that shipping that derive the benefits of that crop, but the builders and their affiliated trades, lumbermen, riggers, &c., who reap the benefit of the business. If we turn to official sources, we find that the number and tonnage built in each section of the Union has been as follows:

*Number of Vessels built in each section of the Union, with the aggregate tonnage.*

| NORTH. | 1849. | 1855. | 1856. | 1857. | 1858. |
|---|---|---|---|---|---|
| Ships ............... | 185 | 360 | 286 | 228 | 114 |
| Brigs............... | 129 | 120 | 93 | 39 | 36 |
| Schooners ........... | 367 | 335 | 319 | 295 | 267 |
| Sloops and canal-boats. | 314 | 604 | 406 | 293 | 220 |
| Steamers ............ | 95 | 155 | 101 | 128 | 102 |
| Total.......... | 1,090 | 1,574 | 1,205 | 983 | 739 |
| Tons................ | 196,386 | 497,069 | 376,647 | 294,472 | 170,570 |
| SOUTH. | | | | | |
| Ships ............... | 12 | 18 | 16 | 20 | 2 |
| Brigs............... | 14 | 6 | 9 | 17 | 9 |
| Schooners ........... | 223 | 192 | 183 | 134 | 112 |
| Sloops and canal-boats. | 46 | 38 | 56 | 38 | 147 |
| Steamers ............ | 61 | 54 | 64 | 75 | 73 |
| Total.......... | 356 | 308 | 328 | 284 | 343 |
| Tons................ | 40,015 | 54,252 | 45,538 | 47,831 | 43,576 |
| WEST. | | | | | |
| Ships ............... | 1 | 3 | 4 | 3 | 4 |
| Brigs............... | 5 | .. | 1 | 2 | 1 |
| Schooners ........... | 33 | 76 | 92 | 69 | 52 |
| Sloops and canal-boats. | 10 | 27 | 17 | 27 | 33 |
| Steamers ............ | 52 | 44 | 56 | 62 | 51 |
| Total.......... | 101 | 150 | 190 | 153 | 141 |
| Tons................ | 20,176 | 32,129 | 47,208 | 36,501 | 29,140 |
| Total.......... | 256,577 | 583,850 | 469,393 | 378,804 | 242,286 |

The building of ships and brigs is confined almost entirely to New England, with the exception of those that are built in Maryland. The sloops and canal-boats of Southern construction are nearly all in the District of Columbia. The construction of shipping at the West has hitherto concerned river and lake navigation only, but of late some sea-going vessels have been there built. Flat-bottomed vessels have been built in Chicago for the Sea of Azoff; that trade is, however, comparatively unimportant. With every impulse given to ship-building, it is the North which has derived the benefit. In the town of Medford, in Massachusetts, from 1803 to 1846, inclusive, the whole number of vessels there built was 382, which, at a valuation of $45 per ton for hull, spars, and blocks (which items constituted the original terms of contract), amounted to $5,995,035—the aggregate tonnage being nearly 133,225 tons. The greatest number of ships constructed in one year was in 1845, when there were thirty, amounting in tonnage to 9,712 tons, and in value to $437,040. In the five years preceding April 1st, 1837, sixty vessels were built at Medford, upon which there were employed two hundred and thirty-nine workmen, and of which the measurement was twenty-four thousand one hundred and ninety-five tons, and the value one million one hundred and twelve thousand dollars. From April 1st, 1844, to April 1st, 1845, twenty-four ships were launched in Medford, upon which were employed two hundred and fifty men, and whose aggregate tonnage was nine thousand six hundred and sixty tons, and whose value was half a million of dollars

The value of the tonnage built in New England in 1855 was $20,000,000; in the South, $1,160,000; in the West, $980,000. With the reaction of the "clipper" excitement, the New England shipping industry fell to $6,800,000 in 1858, and the South suffered some reaction, but not in proportion. In 1855, the South built 11 per cent. of the tonnage built at the North; in 1858, 25 per cent. The demand in that section for steamers and schooners in the coasting trade was supplied at home. The cotton crop requires an ever-increasing supply, in spite of the railroads. At the West, the falling off in the European demand for breadstuffs at the time of great development in railroads, evidently injured the schooner-building. The fact is apparent, that the South is the only section which maintained its construction of enrolled tonnage, and it did so to supply the wants of its great staple. The supply of tonnage is now very large, but an unprecedented crop of cotton is coming to market, and more active freighting induced by it, will again give employment to Northern builders. The value of the 4,000,000 sail tonnage in the Union is $160,000,000, divided as in the following table, which also shows the proportion of freight furnished by each section.

| | Registered Tons. | Value of shipping. | Extent of freights furnished. |
|---|---|---|---|
| North................. | 1,781,368 | 73,145,879 | 2,000,000 |
| South................. | 391,518 | 17,618,111 | 24,500,000 |
| West................. | 50,236 | 2,260,620 | 1,500,000 |
| Total............ | 2,223,122 | $93,024,700 | $28,000,000 |

The South furnishes six-sevenths of the freight, but owns less than one-sixth of the tonnage. The North owns 80 per cent.

of the tonnage, and supplies 7 per cent. of the freights. The value of these freights is given much less than the actual amount. Thus, the cotton crop of the present year will reach 2,070,000,000 lbs., and the present rate of freight is one cent per pound, or 10 per cent of the value ; this gives nearly $21,000,000 freights for one transportation of the crop, and it requires several. The other articles of export bear a similar freight of the registered tonnage at the North. New York city holds one-half of the outward freights from New York. A large portion of that put down to the West is supplanted by Southern produce received coastwise, and it could not otherwise be spared from Northern consumption. These are the outward freights only. The return freights into the country are also, to a considerable extent, on Southern account. At the same rate per cent. on the value as that paid by cotton, the amount derived on the importations is $35,000,000 per annum, of which pro rata $12,000,000 is paid by Southern consumers. We have, then, $36,000,000 paid by the South to the shipping per annum, or a sum double the value of all the tonnage she owns, and this without taking into account in any degree the coasting freights. This large sum is distributed among the merchants, owners, seamen, ship-builders, stevedores, carmen, and all their business connections, as the value of the Southern connection. That section consents to the profits thus enjoyed by the North, while she has it in her power to withdraw them by a resort to her own forests and ship-yards. The North thus monopolizes the freights, for the reason that she has hitherto been able to furnish the cheapest ships. The South has no doubt, however, profited by the cheap freights. Had the two sections not been united by the bond of free trade, a very little legislation would have caused ship-building to grow faster at the South than it has hitherto. The evils of disunion would be not unconnected with some benefit for the Maryland and Delaware ship-builders in this respect. The coasting tonnage is supported in nearly the same manner as the registered tonnage, and it is the North that draws the benefit.

The official Treasury returns give the tonnage built in 1850 at 272,218. The census returns give the distribution of the labor as follows for that year :

*Ship-building in the United States, per Census.*

|  | No. | Capital. | Cost of materials. | Hands. | Cost of labor. | Value of product. |
|---|---|---|---|---|---|---|
| Connecticut.......... | 42 | $289,400 | $205,600 | 707 | $325,944 | $522,410 |
| Maine .............. | 172 | 887,886 | ,981,750 | 2,054 | 938,752 | 2,146,380 |
| Massachusetts........ | 140 | 655,900 | 1,282,690 | 1,835 | 1,028,904 | 2,711,885 |
| New Hampshire...... | 5 | 29,800 | 574,855 | 349 | 137,160 | 739,360 |
| Vermont............ | 1 | 150,000 | 60,000 | 100 | 36,720 | 120,000 |
| Rhode Island........ | 6 | 41,400 | 43,082 | 115 | 51,180 | 117,750 |
| New York .......... | 125 | 1,513,000 | 2,625,162 | 3,478 | 1,745,160 | 6,150,185 |
| New Jersey.......... | 27 | 91,310 | 65.497 | 155 | 65,796 | 171,900 |
| Pennsylvania........ | 192 | 478,253 | 574,963 | 1,507 | 585,636 | 1,424,909 |
| NORTH.......... | 710 | 4,136,949 | 6,413,599 | 10,300 | 4,915,252 | 14,304,779 |
| Illinois .............. | 1 | 100 | 250 | 4 | 1,920 | 2,500 |
| Indiana............. | 18 | 81,950 | 57,597 | 157 | 55,152 | 153,263 |
| Michigan ........... | 1 | 200 | 80 | 3 | 900 | 1,210 |
| Ohio............... | 17 | 155,200 | 74,018 | 292 | 106,308 | 209,560 |
| WEST.......... | 37 | 236,350 | 131,945 | 456 | 164,280 | 366,533 |
| Delaware .......... | 7 | 70,400 | 42,485 | 135 | 54.516 | 124,050 |
| Dist. of Columbia .... | 2 | 7,700 | 12,000 | 33 | 7,800 | 25,000 |
| Florida ............. | 4 | 10,200 | ...... | 40 | 16,476 | 17,700 |
| Georgia ............ | 2 | 5,500 | 1,697 | 11 | 4,776 | 8,000 |
| Kentucky........... | 7 | 25,500 | 81,400 | 122 | 63,360 | 182,900 |
| Louisiana........... | 7 | 167,500 | 107,361 | 129 | 100,620 | 251,701 |
| Maryland .......... | 68 | 210,820 | 344,583 | 929 | 413,160 | 1,061,250 |
| Missouri............ | 4 | 126,150 | 42,625 | 68 | 61,344 | 183,750 |
| North Carolina....... | 8 | 77,950 | 43,900 | 144 | 37,140 | 98,000 |
| Tennessee .......... | 1 | 500 | 2,800 | 9 | 4,320 | 5,400 |
| Texas.............. | 3 | 3,000 | 2,720 | 8 | 4,320 | 14,600 |
| Virginia ............ | 32 | 102,700 | 59,286 | 239 | 75,192 | 152,020 |
| SOUTH.......... | 145 | 808,660 | 740,857 | 1,867 | 843,044 | 1,924,371 |
| Total .............. | 892 | 5,182,309 | 7,286,401 | 12,623 | 5,922,576 | 16,595,683 |

The ship-building interest of the South far exceeds that at the West, according to this return, which corresponds pretty nearly with the return of tons built in the above table from the annual navigation returns of the Treasurer's department. There are at the North, it appears, 10,300 hands employed directly in ship-building; and as a curious incident of the growing availability of female labor, Vermont returns four females engaged in ship-building, and Virginia reports two so employed. The 10,300 hands of the North receive nearly 5 millions per annum wages, or an average of $500 each. The material costs $6,413,699, and is purchased of the 27,000 persons who, at the North, are engaged in getting out $31,897,000 worth of lumber per annum. That is, the ship-builders take one-fifth of their product in order to build ships to carry cotton. The South has become ambitious of carrying its own produce, and, as seen in the returns, it has 145 establishments for ship construction. These turned out 43,000 tons, at a value of $2,000,000; and the lumber resources of Florida and Georgia are at hand to give the business an immense development, under the action of the growing capital of the South.

The growth of steam tonnage on the Western and Southern rivers has been large; but this, as well as the sail tonnage, has been much affected by the influence of railroads, which has directed much produce from the water-carriage, changing the direction, in many cases, from down stream to across the country, thus influencing the Northern roads in favor of the Southern exports. The sugar, cotton, and tobacco of the South finds its way, to a considerable extent, across the country into the Western States; and these roads have been built in the western section, to a very large extent, with borrowed money. They have consequently been expensively built—far more so than those which have been built at the South. The aggregate length and cost of railroads has been, at two periods, as follows:

| | 1853. | | 1860. | | |
|---|---|---|---|---|---|
| | *Length.* | *Cost.* | *Length.* | *Cost.* | *Per mile.* |
| North............. | 7,222 | $287,691,587 | 9,665 | $481,874,434 | $50,000 |
| West............. | 5,535 | 110,389,337 | 9,191 | 365,109,701 | 40,080 |
| South............. | 4,663 | 91,522,204 | 9,053 | 221,857,503 | 24,100 |
| Total.......... | 17,420 | $489,603,120 | 27,909 | $1,068,841,638 | |

These returns, for 1854, are from the census returns, and those for 1860 are from the *Boston Railway Times*, compiled by an eminent engineer. We have then the fact that the South has as many miles of railroad as either of the other sections, and that they cost per mile less than half the cost of the Northern roads, and two-thirds the expense of the Western roads, a fact which shows the economy with which the Southern roads were built. We now take from *Stow's Railway Annual* the railroads delinquent on the interest of the bonds:

| | | | *Amount.* |
|---|---|---|---|
| South...................... | 3 companies. | | $2,025,000 |
| North...................... | 9 " | | 39,000,000 |
| West...................... | 21 " | | 68,120,000 |
| Total .............. | 33 companies. | | $109,215,000 |

The business of the South has, it appears, paid the cost of 9,053 miles of railroad, where the North has been unable to do so, and the West has shown still less ability to sustain that length of road. The capital supplied to the latter section for construction of the roads came from England and the East, and was expended in a lavish manner, stimulating business and speculation, which has fallen through, leaving a disastrous condition of affairs in all that region. The railroads themselves show, in the declining revenues, the fact that they owed their former prosperity less to the effects of free labor than to the factitious activity caused by a passing speculation. The crops of that region are not, like those of the South, in constant and active demand, pressing always by the shortest road to market. They depend for realization upon short crops abroad. In ordinary seasons the price will not pay for transportation by rail, while the South becomes an active competitor with the West for the supply of the Northern and Eastern States by water.

In illustration of the great progress which the South has made in the means of transportation afforded by railroads, we take the following from the most accurate sources:

RAILROADS OF THE UNITED STATES.—*Southern.*

| | Length | Cost | | Length | Cost |
|---|---|---|---|---|---|
| Annapolis and Elkridge...... | 20 | $462,000 | King's Mountain ............ | 22 | 196,230 |
| Baltimore and Ohio ......... | 387 | 24,802,645 | Laurens ................... | 32 | 213,476 |
| Baltimore and Phila. Central.. | 30 | 1,650,000 | Northeastern................. | 102 | 1,907,277 |
| Chambersburg and Hagerstown ...................... | .. | 395,000 | South Carolina.............. | 242 | 7,583,038 |
| Cumberland Coal and Iron, Eckhardt ................. | 11 | 500,000 | Spartanburg and Union...... | 25 | 1,000,000 |
| Cumberland and Pennsylvania | 22 | 800,000 | Total South Carolina .... | 778 | $18,431,560 |
| George's Creek Coal and Iron. | 21 | 600,000 | | | |
| Northern Central............ | 142 | 7,238,541 | Atlanta and La Grange ...... | 86 | $1,171,706 |
| Philadelphia, Wilmington, and Baltimore.................. | 102 | 8,568,369 | Augusta and Savannah ...... | 53 | 1,030,100 |
| Western Maryland ...... | 14 | 300,000 | Barnesville and Thomaston .. | 16 | 200,000 |
| Sundry coal railroads ........ | 40 | 800,000 | Brunswick and Florida ...... | 31 | 538,649 |
| | | | Central of Georgia .......... | 191 | 3,750,000 |
| Total Maryland. ........ | 789 | $46,116,555 | Etowah..................... | 9 | 112,500 |
| | | | Georgia.................... | 232 | 4,174,492 |
| Alexand., London, and Hampshire .... ....... | 193 | $509,689 | Macon and Western ........ | 102 | 1,500,000 |
| Clover Hill. coal............ | .. | 299,999 | Main Trunk (Atlantic and Gulf)...................... | 4 | 68,767 |
| Manassas Gap............. | .. | 2,843,403 | Milledgeville and Gordon.... | 17 | 212,500 |
| Norfolk and Petersburg...... | .. | 1,453,723 | Milledgeville and Eatonton .. | 22 | 275,000 |
| Northwestern Virginia ...... | .. | 5,928,754 | Muscogee................... | 50 | 931,213 |
| Orange and Alexandria ...... | 121 | 3,010,399 | Rome and Kingston ........ | 20 | 250,000 |
| Fredericksburg and Gordonsville...................... | 45 | 231,573 | Savannah, Albany, and Gulf.. | 68 | 1,151,750 |
| Petersburg and Lynchburg .. | 132 | 3,786,837 | Southwestern ............... | 137 | 3,034,839 |
| Petersburg and Roanoke .... | 80 | 1,204,115 | Western and Atlantic........ | 138 | 5,901,497 |
| Richmond and Danville...... | 142 | 8,487,584 | Total Georgia........... | 1176 | $24,297,712 |
| Richmond, Fredericksb'g, and Potomac..... .......... | 75 | 1,817,179 | | | |
| Richmond and Petersburg.... | 25 | 1,205,411 | Florida .................... | 104 | $2,500,000 |
| Richmond and York River .. | 38 | 893,272 | Florida and Alabama ....... | 25 | 450,000 |
| Seaboard and Roanoke ...... | 80 | 1,462,800 | Florida, Atlantic, and Gulf Central .................. | 15 | 500,000 |
| Virginia Central ............ | 195 | 7,517,768 | Pensacola and Georgia...... | 29 | 800,000 |
| Virginia and Tennessee ..... | 214 | 6,765,155 | Tallahassee ................. | 21 | 425,000 |
| Winchester and Potomac .... | 32 | 575,485 | Total Florida.......... | 198 | $4,675,000 |
| Washington and Alexandria.. | 6 | 150,000 | | | |
| Sundry coal railroads ....... | 30 | 300,000 | Alabama and Florida ....... | 48 | $1,000,000 |
| | | | Alabama and Mississippi Rivers ...................... | 22 | 600,000 |
| Total Virginia .......... | 1410 | $42,670,674 | Alabama and Tennessee Rivers ...................... | 99 | 2,390,717 |
| | | | Marion .................... | 14 | 280,000 |
| Atlantic and North Carolina.. | 95 | $1,800,000 | Mobile and Girard .......... | 37 | 1,500,000 |
| North Carolina.............. | 223 | 4,235,000 | Mobile and Ohio ............ | 324 | 12,500,000 |
| Raleigh and Gaston......... | 97 | 1,240,271 | Montgomery and West Point. | 117 | 2,522,979 |
| Roanoke Valley............. | 22 | 450,073 | Northeast and Southwest Alabama .................... | 28 | 112,194 |
| Western, coal .............. | 43 | 18,637 | Tennessee and Ala. Central... | 26 | 65,194 |
| Wilmington and Manchester. | 161 | 2,379,168 | Total Alabama .......... | 785 | $19,962,038 |
| Wilmington and Weldon .... | 162 | 2,776,404 | | | |
| Total North Carolina.... | 803 | $12,899,423 | Delaware .................. | 71 | $1,146,810 |
| | | | Newcastle and Frenchtown .. | 16 | 741,355 |
| Blue Ridge................. | 13 | $1,720,023 | Newcastle and Wilmington .. | 4 | 93,900 |
| Charleston and Savannah ... | 29 | 1,000,000 | Total Delaware ......... | 91 | $1,980,665 |
| Charlotte and South Carolina. | 109 | 1,719,045 | | | |
| Cheraw and Darlington...... | 40 | 600,000 | | | |
| Greenville and Columbia .... | 164 | 2,487,461 | | | |

| | Length. | Cost. | | Length. | Cost. |
|---|---|---|---|---|---|
| Grand Gulf and Port Gibson. | 8 | $200,000 | East Tennessee and Georgia.. | 110 | 2,981,643 |
| Mississippi Central.......... | 122 | 3,583,298 | East Tennessee and Virginia. | 130 | 3,208,133 |
| Raymond.................... | 7 | 95,000 | Memphis and Charleston..... | 287 | 6,024,642 |
| Southern Mississippi........ | 83 | 3,500,000 | Memphis and Ohio.......... | 81 | 2,500,000 |
| West Feliciana.............. | 26 | 620,000 | Memphis, Clarksv'le, & Louisville...................... | 73 | 195,864 |
| Total Mississippi........ | 246 | $7,998,298 | Mississippi and Central Tennessee..................... | 55 | 1,294,275 |
| | | | Mississippi and Tennessee... | 60 | 1,338,289 |
| Baton Rouge, Grosse Tete, and Opelousas............. | 17 | $225,000 | McMinnville and Manchester | .. | ........ |
| Clinton and Port Hudson.... | 22 | 750,666 | Nashville and Chattanooga... | 34 | 558,959 |
| Mexican Gulf .............. | 27 | 662,911 | Shelbyville branch.......... | 159 | 4,468,907 |
| Milnesburg and Lake Pon-chartrain............. ... | 6 | 212,398 | Nashville and Northwestern.. | 172 | 600,000 |
| New Orleans and Carrollton. | 13 | 497,220 | Tennessee and Alabama...... | 43 | 1,000,000 |
| New Orleans, Jackson, and Great Northern........... | 206 | 7,142,563 | Winchester and Alabama.... | 15 | 300.000 |
| New Orleans, Opelousas, and Great Western........... | 80 | 3,877,525 | Total Tennessee ........ | 1137 | $26,337,427 |
| Vicksburg, Shreveport, and Texas..................... | 21 | 929,418 | Breckenridge, coal.......... | 8 | $312,000 |
| Total Louisiana......... | 393 | $14,297,801 | Covington and Lexington.... | 80 | 4,135,971 |
| | | | Lexington and Big Sandy.... | 17 | 694,024 |
| Cairo and Fulton............. | 11 | $210.000 | Lexington and Danville..... | 13 | 824,483 |
| Hannibal and St. Joseph..... | 162 | 8,533,228 | Lexington and Frankfort..... | 29 | 658,256 |
| North Missouri.............. | 107 | 5,473,914 | Louisville and Frankfort.. ... | 65 | 1,379,345 |
| Pacific...................... | 163 | 10,643,596 | Louisville and Nashville, and Lebanon branch........... | 137 | 8,834,980 |
| Southwestern branch........ | 19 | 967.962 | Maysville and Lexington.... | 18 | 575,000 |
| St. Louis and Iron Mountain. | 84 | 5,042,660 | Paducah and Mobile........ | 26 | 800,000 |
| Total Missouri........., | 547 | $30,871,360 | Portland and Louisville..... | 5 | 100,000 |
| | | | Total Kentucky........... | 399 | $13,314,059 |
| Central Southern............ | 48 | $300,000 | Texas...................... | 205 | $5,000,000 |
| Cleveland and Chattanooga... | 30 | 867,210 | Arkansas.................... | 38 | 1,093,161 |
| Edgefield and Kentucky..... | 30 | 750,000 | Total South............. | 8171 | $221,857,503 |

*Northern and Western.*

| States, etc. | Length. | Cost. | States, etc. | Length. | Cost. |
|---|---|---|---|---|---|
| Maine.................. | 486.2 | $19,315,567 | Ohio.............. | 2978 | $124,821,055 |
| New Hampshire........ | 653.0 | 10,087.422 | Michigan ............ | 777 | 36,362,812 |
| Vermont .............. | 557.6 | 21,235,184 | Indiana.............. | 1989 | 31,055,603 |
| Massachusetts.......... | 1327.8 | 63,691,110 | Illinois .............. | 2774 | 94,338,008 |
| Rhode Island.......... | 101.1 | 2,750,450 | Wisconsin............ | 837 | 500,000 |
| Connecticut............ | 601.8 | 25,098,678 | Iowa ................ | 343 | 11,260,169 |
| New York............. | 2726.2 | 135,314,197 | Minnesota............ | 105 | 500,000 |
| New Jersey........... | 553.6 | 24,886,531 | | | |
| Pennsylvania.......... | 2678.1 | 140,570,271 | N. Interior States..... | 10,706 | $298,837,647 |
| | 8685 | $451,949,410 | Total............ | 27,562 | $972,644,560 |

If the South has not built as much tonnage as it required for its business, allowing the North to carry its produce, it has not been behind in the building of railroads. It has built them, however, with its own capital. The effect of this large construction at the South was to absorb the capital which, earned by cotton, had of late accumulated, and prevent it from going more into manufacturing. It will be observed that the South built more miles of railroads in the six years to 1860 than did the West, but they did not exhaust their means in so doing. The West is prostrate under the effort, while the South was never more solid. It has now before it the roads to assist in an active development of other interests under the influence of the cotton proceeds.

# CHAPTER VII.

### BANKING.

BANKING, in its legitimate commercial character, is confined to the utilizing of funds, which, without its intervention, would for a certain time remain idle in the hands of merchants and dealers. Thus, if we suppose a certain number of persons being possessed of means, buy a quantity of goods to sell again, they will immediately be in the receipt of money from the sales of a portion of their goods. What each thus receives he would keep by him until it became necessary again to purchase. In this manner, the aggregate amount lying idle in the hands of all, would be very large. The contrivance of a common depository, called a bank, for all those funds, was obviously a great invention. The ability to loan the money thus collected to each dealer, at the time of making his purchases, in proportion to his wants, greatly facilitated business, and virtually increased the capital necessary to its conduct. As long as the business could be confined to the simple transactions of those actually engaged in trade, it was eminently safe and useful. The money loaned to each merchant began immediately to be replaced by his deposits, and there was no danger that a demand would ever spring up except for the regular known purpose of business. The notes on which the loans were made were all represented by goods. The moment, however, that these funds, that are supplied by trade, begin to be diverted to purposes of speculation, stock loans, &c., transactions which represent only an imaginary future value, the foundation of disaster is laid. In agricultural regions the course of banking is different. The agriculturists, who create the real wealth of the country, are not in the daily receipt of money. Their produce is ready but once in the year, whereas they buy supplies the year round, of stores, and when the crop is ready it is turned into the stores or factories, or sold to dealers. The produce itself, after supplying the local wants, leaves a surplus, which seeks a distant market, and becomes the medium by which alone all the goods imported into the country or section can be paid for. The storekeeper of every town has purchased goods, generally on credit, and has sold them to those who raise the produce ; when the latter is ready it must go forward to cancel the debt. To effect this exchange money is required. Usually the dealer in produce—possibly flour—will make a draft on New York at 60 to 90 days. For this the local bank gives him bank-notes: with these the grain is purchased, floured, sent to New York, sold, and the proceeds lodged in a New York bank to meet the draft coming on for payment. In the mean time, the farmer who received the notes for grain paid them to the store in settlement of his bill for supplies. The storekeeper having his payments maturing for the goods, buys of the local bank the draft on New York at 60 to 90 days, forwards it to his creditor in discharge of his account. In all this operation the produce finds a market, and the goods consumed by the growers have been paid for, and all the paper created to effect the exchange has been cancelled. This operation is, at times, disturbed by speculation, as in 1856, '57. Some of the Western merchants, when they received money, spent it for wild lands, and asked the New York creditor to wait. Formerly the New York merchants would take notes for goods, payable at the local banks, because they thought the country dealer would pay promptly to keep his credit good at home. It was found, however, that when the note fell due the payer would meet it by an accommodation note discount, which, although it made the payment good for the New York merchant, still left due from the country bank to the city bank a balance, which was not always paid. The rule was then notes payable in the city—the result of this is to force all financial currents towards the general centre. All the paper, foreign and domestic, growing out of the crops, to the value of at least \$1,000,000,000 per annum, draws directly or indirectly upon New York, and, as a consequence, funds tend in the same direction to meet the paper. The cotton crop alone is the basis of at least \$500,000,000, foreign and domestic bills, operated upon in New York. A very large portion of the cotton is shipped from the South, but it is sold in New York, *in transitu*, and the bills are negotiated in New York, for the reason that the larger proportion of goods are there imported, and under the present exchange system the demand is there for bills. In 1859 the whole importation of goods into the country was \$338,768,130 ; of this \$229,181,349 was at the port of New York. That is to say, of the \$350,000,000 worth of foreign bills drawn against produce shipped, a demand for

$229,000,000 existed from the New York importers. The market for bills grows out of that fact.

The whole banking system of the country is based primarily on this bill movement against produce. As the railways all tend towards New York, so do all financial transactions follow the same direction.

The concentration of capital at New York promotes its own development, or "makes the meat it feeds on." The manufacturers of Europe, and of the East, and the agriculturists of the West and the South, all send their capital to New York on credit, and, singularly enough, to obtain credit. All Europe contributes to her apparent capital, and swells the deposits in her banks. The process is a very simple one. The European manufacturer ships to a New York factor dry-goods, consisting of silks, laces, &c. He is apprised that long credits must be given to insure a sale of these goods, say 8 to 12 months from day of sale. The factor disposes of these goods to the jobber, taking his paper in settlement. This paper is generally at once placed on the market, and sold at market rates for money. Thus the factor is at once supplied with money, belonging, in fact, to his European correspondent, which he can use in any way he thinks proper, only taking care to be able to transmit money to Europe at the time that the notes taken for the goods fall due. The wholesale jobber repeats the same operation in his sale in like manner to the wholesale and retail merchant. Their paper is at once turned into cash, giving to the jobber great appearance of strength at his bank, and also a large cash capital, to be invested in stocks, or shaving paper, or any other manner fancy or judgment may dictate. The wholesale merchant sells in like manner to country merchants, whose paper is also thrown on the market, where it is salable. Thus, the same article, sold successively on time, furnishes the appearance of real capital to several different merchants. The same operation is repeated in the sale of the various other articles imported from Europe to this country. In like manner the manufacturers of New England furnish capital to New York. They consign their manufactures to a New York agent, and have a time draft on him discounted at their home banks. If the agent succeeds in selling the goods promptly, he has the use of the money till the maturity of the draft. Again, the money to buy this paper is not by any means contributed alone by New York capitalists. Some of the banks of South Carolina are charged with buying up the paper of Southern men through their agents in New York. Large amounts of capital are known to be sent on from Virginia, and other parts of the South, for the same purpose.

With the Southern banks a preference is given to a four-months' draft upon New York to a four-months' note on personal security. The manufacturers of tobacco are compelled, in order to raise money to carry on their business in Virginia, to have a Northern correspondent, upon whom they draw these bills, and to whom their tobacco must be consigned. As the bills are drawn on the consignment of tobacco, that must go forward, no matter what is the state of the market in New York, and no matter how much depressed the article may be by reason of want of demand or a glut in the market.

When the tobacco arrives in New York, the agent there sells the tobacco as soon as he thinks proper, generally for an eight-months' note. He immediately takes the note, places it in the hands of a broker, who sells it at the current rates for similar paper. The proceeds, less the commission and a shave, are returned to the agent, who uses it in paying other acceptances falling due, it may be to other parties, or he applies the money to purposes of private speculation, thus being supplied with capital by the Virginia banks. The value of the manufactured tobacco is estimated at $15,000,000.

A planter in the South cannot borrow money from the bank upon a pledge of his land and negroes, or on good personal security, or even upon a promise to turn over to the bank the proceeds of his crop when sold. He can, however, borrow by drawing on his factor, who sells his cotton. These drafts, from the nature of the case, fall due during the early part of the crop year. In like manner, the shipper of cotton to England cannot obtain money except by drawing a sterling bill, which is a bill payable sixty days after sight. Formerly, an advance to a planter really meant what it purports to be. Now, an advance consists in the acceptance of a draft; and if the planter's cotton is not in time to protect it, long and loud are the complaints against the dishonesty of planters in withholding their crops to meet their just debts. It is easy to see how this mode of banking affects the price of cotton, and depresses it beyond its true value. No one expects to obtain any thing like full value from a sale by a pawnbroker of a watch pledged for a debt, even in prosperous times. Of course, when times are bad, the sacrifice is much greater. But the Southern people have made the movement of the sale of cotton dependent, in a great degree, upon the condition of affairs in New York. If there is no demand for sterling bills in New York, caused either by their want of ability or willingness to pay their debts to Europe, then our Southern banks cannot buy sterling bills, and the shipper cannot buy cotton. Even when cotton is bought and shipped, either to New York or Europe, it becomes completely in the power of the buyers to control the price of cotton. The banks, refusing to give the acceptor of the bills any accommodation, necessitates the sale of the article pledged on arrival to meet the bill at maturity. However honest he may be, and anxious to promote the interest of the consignor, necessity having no law, he is compelled to sell at prices dictated by the buyer.

The capital of all sections, in all shapes, is thus poured into New York, through the hands of the bankers, and becomes the means of floating a large amount of securities, of all descriptions. The Southern produce which comes here pays a large profit to agents of all kinds, through whose hands it passes, and the goods which come here are, to a large amount, sold to the South on credit, on which Southern money lying in New York is advanced, to be used in such purposes of speculation as frequently bring on a panic, and depress the price of both bills and cotton. The summer is the season when the largest supply of Southern funds becomes apparent, and it is then the banks are most anxious to make it draw interest. They lend it upon stocks, and cause an inflation by speculators, who bid high for money. In the fall, when those funds are again wanted for their legitimate purposes, they cannot be recalled from speculation so readily, and the notes of the mercantile people are thrown out rather than that the paying loans to the speculators should be disturbed. The pretence is that specie is going abroad, and that it is the importers who send it. Their paper is consequently thrown out, preventing them from buying bills. By the same operation the price of cotton is depressed. Thus at the same time the value of bills drawn against cotton is depressed at the same moment that the price of the article itself falls.

The financial system of advances is one, no doubt, by which the shippers of produce on advances are yearly victimized. The complaints were formerly loud and long against the " slaughtering" of American tobacco and cotton in the foreign cities to

which they were consigned on advances. The merchandis
generally sold at the most unfavorable moment and adver
cumstances, and not unfrequently bought in at the low
thus produced by the acceptor, to hold for his own advar
This is one of the evils of a want of capital in producing
tries. They are the victims of the lenders; and it is one
means by which the large capital of England has been in
ed at the expense of her colonies, and of the tropical cou
with which she deals. She buys for cash and sells on
credits, and a large margin exists between the two prices.
operation of capital is not different in America from wha
elsewhere; and it is against this operation that the Sou
required to contend.

In the vast circle of the States the 1500 corporate banks,
a capital of $401,000,000; and the 800 private banks, w
capital of $150,000,000, all base their operations upon
York exchange, and the combined 2300 banking concern
erating on the circle, make New York the focus of their
To this point comes all paper, sooner or later, for negoti
and as a consequence, all surplus funds come here for em
ment. The banks and bankers of New York encourage
tendency, as a matter of course, and their united strength
follows:

|  | *No.* | *Capital.* |
|---|---|---|
| New York corporate banks.......................... | 55 | $69,333,( |
| "        private      "  .......................... | 80 | 60,000,( |
| Total......................................... | 135 | $129,333,( |

The Secretary of the Treasury, in his report for 1856,
141, gave the capital of the private banks in New York C
$41,500,000. By addition of firms the amount has since
to the figure stated. The course of business usually req
the use of money to purchase the crops in the autumn, an
that purpose the distant banks discount or buy bills on
York at 60 to 90 days, by which time the produce will
been realized, and the amount applied to the liquidation o
bill. It follows that before much produce has been sold
demand for money is large. On the other hand, when the
of the produce has been sold, the realization is greater tha
demand, and money becomes plenty. In this operatior
Southern products—cotton, rice, and tobacco—play the
part; and the proceeds of these crops accumulate in New Y
as the season advances, in the shape of " balances due ba

The quarterly returns of the New York banks will show the course of this movement.

### New York Banks.

| | Loans. | Specie. | Deposits. | Due Banks |
|---|---|---|---|---|
| 1857, July........ | $103,954,777 | $14,370,434 | $104,350.420 | $27,319,817 |
| "    December... | 162,807,376 | 29,313,421 | 83,043,357 | 21,268,562 |
| 1858, March....... | 170,436,240 | 31,071,074 | 93,738,878 | 28,710,077 |
| "    June........ | 187,468,510 | 33,597,211 | 100,762,909 | 34,290,766 |
| "    September .. | 194,734,996 | 29,905,291 | 103,481,741 | 33,610,448 |
| "    December... | 200,577,108 | 28,335,984 | 110,461,798 | 35,134,049 |
| 1859, June........ | 185,027,449 | 22,107,782 | 99,597,772 | 30,175,329 |
| "    September .. | 182,420,134 | 22,026,137 | 103,106,666 | 23,992,116 |
| "    December... | 191,596,617 | 20,921,141 | 102,109,393 | 28,807,249 |

The cotton crop begins to come forward in September, and causes a demand for money until about 60 days have elapsed. When the first purchases begin to be realized, the sales of sterling bills on Southern bank account cause the balances in the New York City banks to rise, as seen, December, 1857, in the table of corporate banks, when they were $21,268,562, and continue to rise to $34,290,766 in June, 1858. In that month the crop is nearly all realized, and the bills sold. The idle balances are then large. The New York City banks, in order to increase these balances, allow an interest of 4 per cent. on them; and they use them, not in legitimate banking, but in "loans on call," on stocks, and other securities, in competition with the private bankers, who at that season begin to supply the market with exchange at high rates, the supply against cotton having run out. The proceeds of these bills they also lend, and the competing lenders foster speculation, to be nipped when the renewed demand for money to move the crops takes place. The accumulation of funds in New York, and the facility with which they are loaned, favors the negotiation of paper, and state, city, and county bonds reach that point for sale, and are made payable there for the same object. It is obvious that the amount of "balances" in New York to the credit of the South depends upon two circumstances relatively : first, the amount of crops to be sold; second, the quantity of goods purchased. In 1858 the sales of crops were large. The cotton crop alone realized $160,000,000, and at the same time the goods purchased were less than usual, it resulted that the balances, after having reached an unusual sum in June, went South in specie. In the past year the imports of goods have been much larger, but the sales of produce still greater. The cotton crop has realized $200,000,000, and the shipments of coin to the South were active. The specie held by all the banks of the Union, and by the Southern banks, has been as follows:

|  | 1857. | 1858. | 1859. | 1860. |
|---|---|---|---|---|
| North.............. | $22,853,924 | $26,065,503 | $42,038,635 | $40,618,624 |
| South.............. | 35,495,914 | 48,347,329 | 62,497,783 | 48,359,072 |
| Total.......... | $58,349,838 | $74,412,832 | $104,537,818 | $88,977,696 |

The South never held so large a proportion of the aggregate specie before, and in this respect it is exercising the power which proceeds from its large crop production.

The continued large exports from the South, which will be larger this year than ever before, exercise a controlling power upon Northern funds; and only a small decline in the purchase of goods, or the amount of expenditure at the North, would produce a great derangement of the present system. The city of New Orleans is the great centre of exports, and New York of imports. If we compare the imports of the one and the exports of the other, we have results as follows:

| Year. | New York imports. | Population. | N. Orleans exports. | Receipts from the interior. | Population. |
|---|---|---|---|---|---|
| 1804.......... | 10,739,250 | 60,489 | 1,392,093 | .......... | 8,056 |
| 1810.......... | 14,198,204 | 96,373 | 1,753,974 | .......... | 17,242 |
| 1820.......... | 23,629,246 | 123,706 | 7,242,415 | .......... | 27,176 |
| 1830.......... | 35,624,070 | 202,589 | 13,042,740 | .......... | 46,310 |
| 1840.......... | 60,440,750 | 312,710 | 30,077,534 | 43,716,045 | 102,193 |
| 1850.......... | 111,123,524 | 515,547 | 38,105,350 | 96,897,873 | 116,375 |
| 1859.......... | 245,165,516 | 900,000 | 100,734,952 | 172,952,664 | 175,000 |

These foreign exports from the port of New Orleans swell with great rapidity, and they furnish the sterling bills against 40 per cent. of the imports into New York, while the other Southern ports give as large a quota. Against those bills, as we have seen, run the large supply of inland bills. It is now obvious that if the South is disposed to carry out its determination of reviving the old colonial non-intercourse as a means of redress, that an immense financial balance would be thrown against the North. It is true that the sterling bills then would have but a limited market in New York, but what would follow? Precisely what followed when the panic produced the result, that is exhibited in the following table:

|  | Rates of Sterling Bills in New Orleans. | | Bills on New York. | Imports of specie at N. Orleans. | Amount in Banks of N. Orleans. |
|---|---|---|---|---|---|
|  | Lowest. | Highest. | Discount. |  |  |
| 1855.............. | 107 | 110½ | 1   a 2¾ | 3,746,037 | 8,570,568 |
| 1856.............. | 106¾ | 109¾ | 1¼  a 2½ | 4,913,540 | 8,191,625 |
| 1857.............. | 107 | 110 | 1¼  a 2⅝ | 6,500,015 | 16,811,162 |
| 1858.............. | 91½ | 109 | 1½  a 6 | 13,268,013 | 10,370,701 |
| 1859.............. | 107¾ | 110 | 1⅛  a 2¼ | 15,627,016 | 16,218,027 |

The decline in the imports of 1858, following the panic, had an immense effect upon sterling bills, which fell to 20 per cent. below the actual par, and bills on New York to six per cent. discount, and became *unsalable* at any price. The current of specie went southward, broad and deep. That was produced by "non-intercourse" through "panic," and diminished intercourse from any other cause develops the same power of the Southern crops over Northern finances. The table also displays the growing power of the Southern banks ; from an amount of $1,845,808 in 1848, of specie held by the banks, the amount has risen to a sum larger than it was the custom of the New York banks to hold before the panic ; and the New Orleans banks have shown great prosperity while carrying so large an amount of specie.

The exchange system of the country favors this process of centralization in New York. The whole external trade of the country is based upon buying bills for remittance abroad, while there hardly exists a market, in the countries with which we deal, for bills on America. The produce of the country is shipped and drawn against supplying, in round numbers, 350 millions of exchange. Nearly the whole of this amount is sold to banks and bankers, who hold it as a sort of monopoly, awaiting the demand of merchants who, having imported $330,000,000 worth of goods, must pay for them. There is also $20,000,000 to be remitted for interest on debts, public and corporate, and probably $30,000,000 more as the expenses of Americans travelling abroad. Now the only mode for making these remittances is to buy bills, and the remitters must pay the price asked. In all the cities of Europe there is a variety of counter-exchanges, by which the merchant may arbitrate his remittances as he pleases. If in Paris he wants to remit to London, he may buy a bill on London, or may order his creditors in London to draw on him ; or he may buy a bill on any other city, to remit or order a draft on any other city, to be sold. Twenty combinations may be calculated, and the cheapest acted upon. The American merchant has but one choice. He may give the banker his price for a bill, or remit the coin himself. The effect of this monopoly of the exchange market by the bankers, aids the concentration of money in New York, and in a similar manner the internal exchanges are more or less controlled. The rate is always at a premium in New York, and that frequently when New York is in debt, the real rate of exchange being disguised in depreciation of local currency. The Southern banks, having large deposits in New York drawing interest, do not sell exchange against those funds, but in some cases buy commercial exchange for depreciated notes, and then supply the market only as it will bear a premium. If their funds did not draw interest at the North, and their own paper was payable on demand, actually as well as nominally, the exchange rate would be as often below as above par. At bottom, the same system exists as with the external exchange, viz., always to draw, and never to be drawn upon. As we have seen in a former chapter, the South sends north per annum $522,000,000 in value, which becomes the basis of at least 1000 millions of exchange, which the banks monopolize ; and the proceeds are the basis of large moneyed operations at the North.

It is not a matter of surprise, under all these circumstances, that notwithstanding the large production of wealth at the South, capital accumulates there so slowly. All the profitable branches of freighting, brokering, selling, banking, insurance, &c., that grow out of the Southern products, are enjoyed in New York ; and crowds of Southerners come north in the summer to enjoy and spend their share of the profits. The profits that importers, manufacturers, bankers, factors, jobbers, warehousemen, carmen, and every branch of industry connected with merchandising, realize from the mass of goods that pass through the Northern cities, are paid by Southern consumers. There can then be no matter of wonder that the North accumulates, or that the South does so slowly. When, however, people at the North reproach the South with these advantages, derived from them as some of the " blessings of free labor," the depth of ignorance and the sublimity of impudence seem to have combined. Nevertheless capital does accumulate at the South. As we have seen, her net-work of railroads has been built well, and more economically than in any other section, and with less foreign aid. The bonds and stocks are not only better paid, but held at home ; and there is no more efficient means of building up local capital than by the operation of 9000 miles of railroad, with its employees, and $200,000,000 of certificates of cost, all paid from their traffic. The growth of manufactures is another efficient aid to accumulation. If the South has a smaller leak than in the West in the matter of interest and dividends, it has a larger one in the shape of "absenteeism," since a considerable portion of the annual profits are spent North and in Europe. The sums so expended would, in ten years, give her more manufacturing capital than exists at the North, and multiply itself thereafter with great rapidity. That time is approaching, and the faster by reason of the ill blood so wantonly stirred up by unprincipled party-leaders and their abolition coadjutors.

---

## CHAPTER VIII.

### POPULATION.

In estimating the relative growth of the three sections, population and its movement have a very important influence upon the result. The South has depended only on its own natural increase of whites and blacks; while the North and West have had immense accessions of men and capital from abroad to stimulate their industry.

The census returns of the total white population, indicate the fact that, including the blacks, the South has multiplied in number faster than the North, notwithstanding that the latter has had the whole benefit of immigration, with all the wealth it has brought with it.

During the speculative years that ended, in 1840, with the repudiation of many of the States, the South received much money, from the North and from Europe, for the establishment of banks, which failed, and the money was lost. The numbers of Southern population were not increased by the movement. The large immigration from Europe, on the other hand, not only increased the numbers of the Northern and Western population, but largely increased the wealth of those sections, by means of the capital brought in by the immigrants. Of these latter, great numbers were mechanics and artisans, who, remaining in the Northern cities, added greatly to the manufacturing productions.

The following table comprises the aggregate census returns from the formation of the government, with the area of each State :

### United States Census.

| North. | Area in sq.miles. | 1790. | 1800. | 1810. | 1820. | 1830. | 1840. | 1850. |
|---|---|---|---|---|---|---|---|---|
| Maine ......... | 31,755 | 96.540 | 151,719 | 228,705 | 298,335 | 399,455 | 501,793 | 583,169 |
| New Hampshire | 9,280 | 141,899 | 183,762 | 214,360 | 244,161 | 269,328 | 284,574 | 317,976 |
| Vermont ...... | 10,212 | 85,416 | 154,465 | 217,713 | 235,764 | 280,652 | 291,948 | 314,120 |
| Massachusetts.. | 7,800 | 378,717 | 423,245 | 472 040 | 523,287 | 610,408 | 737,699 | 994,514 |
| Rhode Island .. | 1,306 | 69,110 | 69,122 | 77,031 | 83,059 | 97,199 | 108,830 | 147,545 |
| Connecticut.... | 4,674 | 238,141 | 251,002 | 262,042 | 275,202 | 297,675 | 309,978 | 370,792 |
| New York ..... | 47,000 | 340.120 | 586,756 | 959,049 | 1,372,812 | 1,918,608 | 2,428,921 | 3,097.394 |
| New Jersey.... | 8,320 | 184,139 | 211,949 | 245,555 | 277,575 | 320,823 | 373,306 | 489,555 |
| Pennsylvania.. | 46,000 | 434,373 | 602,365 | 810,091 | 1,049,458 | 1,348,233 | 1,724,033 | 2,311,786 |
| **Total North..** | **160,747** | **1,968,455** | **2,634,385** | **3,486,496** | **4,339,653** | **5,532,383** | **6,761,082** | **8,626,851** |
| *South.* | | | | | | | | |
| Delaware ..... | 2,120 | 59.096 | 64,273 | 72,674 | 72,749 | 76,748 | 78,085 | 91,532 |
| Maryland ..... | 11,124 | 319,728 | 341,548 | 380.546 | 407,350 | 447,040 | 470,019 | 583,034 |
| Dist. of Columb. | 60 | ...... | 14,093 | 24.023 | 33,039 | 39,834 | 43,712 | 51,687 |
| Virginia ...... | 61,352 | 748,308 | 380,200 | 974,622 | 1,065,379 | 1,211,405 | 1,239,797 | 1,421,661 |
| North Carolina. | 50,704 | 393,751 | 478,103 | 555,500 | 638,829 | 737,987 | 753,419 | 869.039 |
| South Carolina. | 29,385 | 249,073 | 345,591 | 415,115 | 502,741 | 581,185 | 594,398 | 668,507 |
| Georgia....... | 58,000 | 82,548 | 162,101 | 252,433 | 340,987 | 516,823 | 691,392 | 906,185 |
| Florida........ | 59,268 | ...... | ...... | ...... | ...... | 34,730 | 54,477 | 87,445 |
| Alabama...... | 50,722 | ...... | ...... | 144,317 | ...... | 309,527 | 590,756 | 771.623 |
| Mississippi ... | 47,156 | ...... | 8,850 | 40,352 | 75,448 | 136,621 | 375,651 | 606,526 |
| Louisiana..... | 41,255 | ...... | ...... | 76,556 | 153,407 | 215,739 | 352,411 | 517,762 |
| Texas ......... | 237,504 | ...... | ...... | ...... | ...... | ...... | ...... | 212,592 |
| Arkansas ..... | 52,198 | ...... | ...... | ...... | 14,273 | 30,388 | 97,574 | 209,897 |
| Tennessee .... | 45,600 | 35.791 | 105,602 | 261,727 | 422,813 | 681,904 | 829,210 | 1,002,717 |
| Missouri....... | 67,380 | ...... | ...... | 20,845 | 66,586 | 140,455 | 383,702 | 682,044 |
| Kentucky .... | 37,680 | 73,077 | 220,955 | 406,511 | 564,317 | 687,917 | 779,828 | 982,405 |
| **Total South..** | **871,458** | **1,961,372** | **2,621,800** | **3,480,994** | **4,522,224** | **5,863,619** | **8,340,531** | **9,664,050** |
| *West.* | | | | | | | | |
| Ohio .......... | 39,964 | ...... | 45,365 | 230,760 | 581,434 | 937,903 | 1,519,467 | 1,980,329 |
| Indiana ....... | 33,800 | ...... | 4,875 | 24,520 | 147,178 | 343,031 | 685,866 | 988,416 |
| Illinois ....... | 55,405 | ...... | ...... | 12,282 | 55,211 | 157,445 | 476,183 | 851,470 |
| Michigan ..... | 56,243 | ...... | ...... | 4,762 | 8,896 | 31,639 | 212,267 | 397,654 |
| Wisconsin..... | 53,024 | ...... | ...... | ...... | ...... | ...... | 30.945 | 305,391 |
| Iowa .......... | 50,914 | ...... | ...... | ...... | ...... | ...... | 43,112 | 192,214 |
| California..... | 155,980 | ...... | ...... | ...... | ...... | ...... | ...... | 92,597 |
| Minnesota .... | 166,025 | ...... | ...... | ...... | ...... | ...... | ...... | 6,077 |
| New Mexico ... | 207,007 | ...... | ...... | ...... | ...... | ...... | ...... | 61,547 |
| Oregon ........ | 185,630 | ...... | ...... | ...... | ...... | ...... | ...... | 13,294 |
| Utah .......... | 269,170 | ...... | ...... | ...... | ...... | ...... | ...... | 11,380 |
| Kansas ........ | 114,798 | ...... | ...... | ...... | ...... | ...... | ...... | ...... |
| Nebraska..... | 335,882 | ...... | ...... | ...... | ...... | ...... | ...... | ...... |
| Washington... | 123,022 | ...... | ...... | ...... | ...... | ...... | ...... | ...... |
| **Total West..** | **1,417,991** | | | **50,210** | **272,324** | **792,719** | **1,470,018** | **2,967,840** | **4,900,369** |
| **Grand Total..** | **2,470,196** | **3,929,827** | **5,305,925** | **7,239,814** | **9,654,596** | **12,866,020** | **17,069,453** | **23,191,876** |

The progress of the white population in the three sections, with the immigration decennialy, ran as follows :

### White Population and Immigration.

| | SOUTH. | NORTH. | WEST. | Immigration in 10 years. |
|---|---|---|---|---|
| 1790........... | 1,271,692 | 1,902,475 | ........ | ........ |
| 1800........... | 1,702,980 | 2,551,585 | 49.740 | ........ |
| 1810........... | 2,208,785 | 3,383,259 | 268,870 | ........ |
| 1820........... | 2,842,340 | 4,225,692 | 783,679 | 150,000 |
| 1830........... | 3,660,758 | 5,407,170 | 1,454.127 | 128,502 |
| 1840........... | 4,632,640 | 6,616,761 | 2,738,317 | 538,381 |
| 1850........... | 6,221,868 | 8,476,709 | 4,854,517 | 1,427,337 |
| 1860 (est.) ..... | 8,097,000 | 11,190,000 | 7,867,000 | 2,518,054 |

The estimate of the population for 1860 is based on the known progress of the population in the previous returns, and the known number of immigrants. The number of persons who arrived in the country up to the census of 1850, was given officially at 2,244,220, and the census reported 2,210,839 as residing in the country, a number which very nearly agrees; but a large number of those who had arrived were, of course, dead, and many had left the country. There were, also, numbers in the annexed territories who were born abroad, but who were not reported as arrivals. The latter were mostly at the South, and the census shows that of 2,210,839 persons living in the U. States, and born abroad, there were 316,670 only at the South.

The census of 1850 gave the nativities of the population of the three sections ; these we condense as follows :

*United States White Population—1850.*

|  | Living South. | Living North. | Living West. | Total. |
|---|---|---|---|---|
| Born South....... | 5,510,687 | 69,501 | 660,142 | 6,240,330 |
| " North....... | 337,765 | 6,941,510 | 1,090,814 | 8,370,089 |
| " West........ | 57,296 | 19,696 | 3,060,177 | 3,137,169 |
| " Abroad...... | 316,670 | 1,292,241 | 601.928 | 2,210,839 |
| Total......... | 6,222,418 | 8,342,938 | 5,413,059 | 19,958,427 |

These numbers include only the white population, and it is matter of much regret that the same detail was not preserved in respect of the black population, since the origin of the free blacks, particularly those living in the West, is matter of much interest. The—in round numbers—two millions of foreigners living at the North and West, at the date of the census, according to the estimates of the Emigrant Commissioners, brought into the country $200,000,000 in capital, which was applied by them in prosecuting that productive industry which, in its results, so largely swells the sum total of Northern prosperity. This is an element in which the South has not participated. It is sometimes alleged that the reason the South does not get its share of the immigration is, that slavery is objected to by the new-comers ; that is, however, a superficial reason, since they can know little of the institution, or of blacks, until they arrive here. The true reason is, probably, that they follow the parallels of latitude to which they have become accustomed, as do the emigrants from the Northern States. A considerable number of alien laborers have, of late years, been employed

South in the winter, in drainage and such employments as careful masters think too unhealthy for valuable blacks; these, however, return North when the work is done. All that large class of immigrants that are employed in domestic service at the North, certainly would find the same position filled by blacks at the South; but it is due to their presence at the North almost entirely that Northern housekeepers can find servants at all. The Irish and Germans perform almost all the domestic service of the Northern cities, and the former form almost the whole factory force.

The dearth of servants causes always a rise in the rate of wages at the North, when immigration from any cause diminishes, as has been the case in the last few years. This is likely to diminish still more, as the migration from Europe has taken a turn which promises to dry up that source of a supply of labor. The hold which is had upon the Irish, is the economy of those already in service. These save and remit a large portion of their earnings to their friends, in order to aid in paying the passages of relatives, who continue to seek service in the Atlantic cities as the first means of livelihood. The amount of money sent to their parents, brothers, and sisters, and other relatives, by the Irish servant-girls in this country, may well astonish the public. Rev. Dr. Cahill, who is now lecturing in this country with so much *éclat* and success, took the pains to ascertain the amount sent to Ireland in a single year. He obtained returns from the different offices in this city which transmit money to that country, and found that, in the year 1859, the aggregate sum amounted to $1,350,000— one million three hundred and fifty thousand dollars. But for this source domestic servants would scarcely be had at all, since very few of those born here will take service; they eke out a scanty living in the various employments which are dependent upon Southern purchasers to pay at all, and consider service as quite degrading. It is probably the case that this kind of work is considered far more degrading than even at the South, where it is mostly done by blacks. It is said that slavery injures free labor by degrading work; domestic service certainly is held to be so degrading at the North that no natives will do it.

The West has one-ninth of its population born abroad, and they have arrived with funds with which they have bought land, settled it, and added to the supply of surplus produce exported. The mass of persons born at the North, who have

moved West, carried thither a large amount of capital, applied
to agriculture, manufactures, mines, &c.   The accession of
persons born South, it appears, was larger than that from
European countries.   The figures show that the South has
mainly depended upon its own resources for increase of population, since it has lost more to the North than it has gained
thence and from abroad.

The figures show that the South contains 711,731 not born
on its soil; while there are North and West 729,643 persons
born South.   Its acquisitions have, therefore, nearly equalled
its losses by migration.   The North, on the other hand, has
lost largely of its native population, and comparing it with the
South, the results are as follows :

|  | NORTH. | SOUTH. |
|---|---|---|
| Born.......................... | 8,370,089 | 6,240,330 |
| Living........................ | 6,941,510 | 5,510,687 |
| Emigrated, 17 per cent..... | 1,428,579 | 729,643, or 12 per cent. |

An incendiary publication, after showing that the census
gives as above a migration of 729,640 persons from the South,
remarks :

" This last table, compiled from the 116th page of the Com-
pendium of the Seventh Census, shows, in a most lucid and
startling manner, how negroes, slavery, and slaveholders, are
driving the native non-slaveholding whites away from their
homes, and keeping at a distance other decent people.   From
the South the tide of emigration still flows in a westerly and
northwesterly direction, and so it will continue to do until
slavery is abolished."

If this very clear reasoning is true of the South, whence less
than 12 per cent. of the population has migrated, what inference is to be drawn from the fact that 17 per cent. of those
born at the great, opulent, free North have emigrated ?   What
has " driven them away from their homes ? "   Is it slavery, or
the want of it ?   If this fact of migration proves any thing, it
is that the poor whites are better off at the South than at the
North, since they show less disposition to avail themselves of
the promise of the West—a promise which, as yet, is very far
from being fulfilled.   The attractions of the fertile lands of the
West have, no doubt, proved very powerful for great numbers
in both the Atlantic sections, but much more so to those who
dwell in the sterile regions of the North, than to those of the

sunny South. The numbers who have left the Northern section have been replaced, it appears, by the immigrants; for these there has been less attraction at the West; the results are as follows:

Born abroad............................................ 2,210,839
Living North............................... 1,292,241
    " South................................. 316,670
    " West.................................. 601,928
                           ————— 2,210,839

The north has received 136,138 less from abroad than she has lost of her native population. The latter were agriculturists, and the former were domestic servants, factory hands, and artisans, who remain in the cities, and find employment in furnishing goods to meet the demand from the South. That they live at the North, is the case; but they are not the less supported by Southern patronage. All those concerned in the trades, would not the less promptly feel the effects of a non-intercourse, because the proceeds of their labor find a market through third hands. The state of the shoe trade is indicative of what must result from a continuance of a restricted Southern trade. A Boston paper describes this interest as follows:

" Commission houses, agencies, manufacturing firms, have increased, and there are to-day over two hundred wholesale and jobbing boot, shoe, and leather dealers, and over one hundred hide and leather dealers in Boston, transacting a business amounting to the enormous aggregate of about *sixty millions of dollars annually.* The manufactures of one single city, within seven miles of Boston, are in value between four and five millions of dollars annually, more than the entire produce of the State twenty-five or thirty years ago; and that city, with others like it, is pouring its wealth of home manufactures into Boston for a market. *Eighty thousand people in the Commonwealth of Massachusetts are occupied in the manufacture of boots, shoes, and leather,* of every conceivable and desirable variety, style, and material; and from their workshops and their factories there is an incessant transit to the metropolis of hundreds of thousands of boxes and cases of boots and shoes."

The exports of shoes from Boston were as follows, during the year 1859 :

*Cases of Shoes Exported from Boston,* 1859.

|  | First quarter. | Second quarter. | Third quarter. | Fourth quarter. | Total year. |
|---|---|---|---|---|---|
| To Baltimore.............. | 14,238 | 9,585 | 24,767 | 13,924 | 62,461 |
| " Charleston............ | 4,233 | 1.484 | 9,379 | 1,581 | 17,177 |
| " Louisville............. | 7,870 | 2,373 | 8,872 | 2,004 | 21,119 |
| " Lexington............. | 768 | 259 | 958 | 160 | 2,158 |
| " Memphis.............. | 1,515 | 552 | 1,011 | 220 | 3,338 |
| " Mobile............... | 807 | 279 | 618 | 1,261 | 2,940 |
| " Nashville ............. | 4,302 | 921 | 7,267 | 1,291 | 18,781 |
| " Natchez.............. | 2 | 9 | 41 | 45 | 97 |
| " Paducah ............. | 184 | 96 | 689 | 177 | 1,146 |
| " Petersburgh........... | 23 | 72 | 331 | 101 | 529 |
| " Pine Bluff, Ark........ | 358 | 77 | 199 | 41 | 683 |
| " Richmond ............ | 681 | .... | 219 | 522 | 1,452 |
| " San Antonio.......... | 157 | 186 | 434 | 23 | 750 |
| " Savannah, Geo........ | 610 | 458 | 1,323 | 135 | 2,526 |
| " St. Louis.............. | 24,246 | 4,347 | 28,956 | 8,215 | 55,774 |
| " Vicksburg, Miss....... | 75 | 82 | 227 | 37 | 371 |
| " New Orleans.......... | 9,490 | 6,290 | 12,470 | 9,436 | 37,686 |
| Total............. | 69,559 | 27,070 | 97,756 | 39,182 | 233,567 |
| " Other Southern towns. |  |  |  |  | 17,791 |
| Total direct South. |  |  |  |  | 251,358 |
| " Philadelphia .......... | 17,242 | 9,688 | 23,635 | 4,604 | 56,119 |
| " New York............ | 29,238 | 45,469 | 55,208 | 22,237 | 182,207 |
| " All others............. |  |  |  |  | 228,307 |
| Total cases....... | 215,836 | 136,612 | 260,329 | 105,714 | 717,991 |

The decline in the quantities shipped in the fourth quarter is very marked. The total value sent South directly in the year is about $12,000,000; but a large portion of those cases that were sent to New York and Philadelphia were to supply the Southern market; at least half the whole quantity was taken South, and the returns of the last quarter of the year shows a decline of 154,615 cases; and the depression in the shoe trade, leading to the great strike, results from the diminished business. The same general state of affairs shows itself, more or less, in all the trades; because it is the slave earnings that all depend upon for business. It is not to be understood by this, that there is no other demand except that which originates South; but that demand is of so large a proportion that a diminution of it makes lower prices, and strikes inevitable. When there is less work, the alternative is to discharge part of the hands, or to work all short time; when prices fall for the goods, lower cost of production becomes inevitable, and this is reached by less wages, which the workers resist. They make common cause, and production ceases at their cost, until the lowered supply overtakes the demand, and prices are restored. Under the present circumstances, the remedy would be migration, or the carrying of the workshops nearer to the consumer. This, no doubt, will be the case when the prejudices in relation to Southern climate shall have been overcome. The census gives us the following view of the healthiness of climates:

*Deaths in the Free and in the Slave States*—1850.

| Free States. | No. of deaths. | Ratio to the No. living. | Slave States. | No. of deaths. | Ratio to the No. living. |
|---|---|---|---|---|---|
| Connecticut........ | 5,781 | 64.13 | Alabama ......... | 9,084 | 84.94 |
| Maine ............. | 7,545 | 77.29 | Arkansas......... | 2,987 | 70.18 |
| Massachusetts ...... | 19,414 | 51.23 | Delaware........ | 1,209 | 75.71 |
| New Hampshire.... | 4,268 | 74.49 | Florida.......... | 933 | 93.67 |
| New Jersey........ | 6,467 | 75.70 | Georgia.......... | 9,920 | 91.93 |
| New York......... | 44,339 | 69.85 | Kentucky ........ | 15,206 | 64.60 |
| Pennsylvania ....... | 28,318 | 81.63 | Louisiana ......... | 11,948 | 42.85 |
| Rhode Island....... | 2,241 | 65.83 | Maryland........ | 9,594 | 60.77 |
| Vermont .......... | 3,132 | 100.13 | Mississippi ....... | 8,711 | 69.93 |
| | | | Missouri........ | 12,211 | 55.81 |
| North.......... | 121,505 | 71.04 | North Carolina.... | 10,207 | 85.12 |
| | | | South Carolina.... | 7,997 | 83.59 |
| Illinois ............. | 11,619 | 73.28 | Tennessee ........ | 11,759 | 85.34 |
| Indiana............ | 12,728 | 77.65 | Texas ............ | 3,046 | 69.79 |
| Iowa.............. | 2,044 | 94.03 | Virginia.......... | 19,053 | 74.61 |
| Michigan........... | 4,520 | 88.19 | | | |
| Ohio............... | 28,949 | 68.41 | South........ | 133,865 | 71.82 |
| Wisconsin.......... | 2,884 | 105.82 | | | |
| West.......... | 62,744 | 78.10 | | | |

This does not give the true state of affairs, since those who go to the West are robust emigrants, while they leave the sickly at home; by which means the mortality of the East would show much larger than the West. The South, also, would show a much larger mortality, for the reason that such numbers who leave the North for their health, generally die where they expect to find it. Massachusetts has less attraction on the score of health than any State, except Louisiana, which the tables represent as the most unhealthy State. There is, therefore, nothing on the score of health which should deter the migration of hands to the Southern markets, as capital progesses there to encourage it. The attractions of the North to those who go there to buy goods, are largely depended upon as a means of preventing any very serious interruption of the bonds of trade. There are, no doubt, many reasons why a good understanding should continue to exist, since mutual advantages result; but so thought the politicians of the mother country in respect of the colonies. They depended upon those advantages to hold the countries together while they pushed a distasteful course, until the disadvantages outweighed the advantages, awakening counter-interests, and separation became inevitable.

If we now take from the census the employments of the free people in each section, we have results as follows:

*Employments of Free People.*

|  | North. | West. | South. | Total. |
|---|---|---|---|---|
| Manufacturing.................. | 684,761 | 122,364 | 151,944 | 957,059 |
| Commerce, trades, and mining... | 230,282 | 226,581 | 180,334 | 639,206 |
| Agriculture.................... | 823,220 | 728,127 | 769,236 | 2.400,583 |
| Labor......................... | 547,458 | 198,582 | 247.680 | 993.620 |
| Navigation.................... | 79.675 | 10,093 | 26,573 | 116,341 |
| Domestic service.............. | 13,861 | 4,205 | 4,177 | 22,243 |
| Army......................... | 1,788 | 1,548 | 2,047 | 5,370 |
| Professions................... | 38,496 | 22,262 | 38,807 | 94,515 |
| Government service............ | 11,861 | 3,668 | 9,437 | 24,966 |
| Other pursuits................ | 37,522 | 16,073 | 36.939 | 95,814 |
| "      occupations .............. | 14,058 | 2,322 | 5,779 | 22,159 |
| Total employed............ | 2,482,890 | 1,335,733 | 1,653,255 | 5,371,876 |
| Population.................... | 8,342,938 | 5,413,059 | 6,222,418 | 19,958,424 |

The proportion employed in these industries is, it appears, larger at the South, in proportion to the white population, than it is at the West, and the ratio falls but a little behind that of the North. This, it will be remembered, refers to the free population only, and while the population is as busily occupied as at the North, and more so than at the West, there is, over and above, the great slave population which carries on agricultural labor on a scale superior to that of any other section. If the number of workers is as large at the South in proportion to the population as in the other sections, the capital so employed is less, for the reason that the commercial system of the country has given advantages to that at the North. If we compare the number of families and dwellings in each section, the results are as follows:

|  | North. | West. | South. |
|---|---|---|---|
| Families...................... | 1,582,951 | 876,748 | 1,128,534 |
| Dwellings .................... | 1,390,005 | 856,607 | 1,116,725 |

At the South, where dwellings are the least required, the number per family is the greatest. In the large cities of the North, the numbers that crowd into one house are frightful. In respect to the number of dwellings, the South is at least quite as well provided as the other sections.

In respect to the morality of the people, the census furnishes some figures. It is to be borne in mind that these cannot be very accurate, however, since much depends upon the manner in which the law is administered. There may be more promptness in arrests, more facility of conviction, in one place than another, and various causes may interpose to prevent the actual number punished from being a true test of the prevalence of crime. Nevertheless we have given, in the chapter upon black population, the numbers in jail, showing that the South has no cause of shame on that score.

---

## CHAPTER IX.

### THE BLACK RACE AT THE NORTH.

THE principle has been well recognized, that it is the duty, not only of communities, but of individuals, to contribute each its share towards the general well-being. The source of all wealth being originally land and labor, no set of people have a right to seize and withhold from the service of humanity at large any portion of the earth's surface. This is the question that underlies land reform, and it is also that which underlies servitude, as no race of men have a right either to monopolize the gifts of Providence, or the right to live without labor. The exigencies of society require that all should, in a greater or less degree, be producers, and in the early stages of society slavery was universal, and ordered by the divine command, for the reason that the masses of men had not learned to appreciate industry. This coercion of labor prevailed very generally down to very recent dates. It is only in modern times that human intelligence, even of the white race, has induced men to labor for the rewards it confers. The desire to possess property was found to be a sufficient stimulus for the majority of the white race to labor in a free state; accordingly, servitude ceased to be necessary. Indeed, it became detrimental to the general interests, for the reason that the free worker produced more than the servile laborer. This was not universally the case, however, but pauperism and crime were resorted to by those who had a distaste for labor. The law of servitude held good for these exceptions, and the workhouses and prisons of most civilized countries are illustrative of its application. The history of the poor-laws of England is fraught with instruction upon this head. In the reign of Henry VIII., when servitude was dying out, the laws against paupers were very severe; not only were "sturdy beggars" subjected to severe punishment, but those who relieved or harbored them were also visited severely by the law. With the progress of civilization, some

amelioration of these laws took place; but, alas for human nature, it was found that pauperism increased as relief was extended. Numbers of persons were content with idleness and
the sustenance afforded by law, and wrung from the earnings
of the industrious. It was also shown in the Parliamentary
reports that thrift and a disposition to save were checked by
the knowledge that, in the event of distress, the parish must
support the pauper. Nevertheless, as a general thing, the
white race will work eagerly for the reward of labor. In this
fact exists the broad distinction between the white and the
black race. The latter, it is sufficiently proved by the world's
experience, will not work at all if he can help it. Idleness is
his chief good, and pauperism and theft are for the race not an
unwelcome means of attaining their object. The *vis inertia* of
the black blood is so great, that even a large mixture of white
blood will overcome it only so far as to induce the individual
to perform menial offices, clinging to the skirts of white society.
It never suffices to impart energy or enterprise to the black
descendant.

The fact of the inertness of the black is singularly corrobo-
rated by a correspondent of the *New York Herald* of February
6th, who sought to apologize for the condition of the refugee
blacks in Canada.

" It is not generally known to the world, that full one-half
of the arrivals from the South are children of white fathers.
Startling as this declaration may be, it is nevertheless true.
And some of them are men known and distinguished in our
national councils. Is it not a slander upon these illustrious
sires, to say they have begotten a race that cannot take care of
themselves?

" I have known whole families to arrive in Canada from the
South with scarcely a particle of African blood visible in their
faces. The philosophy of the case is, therefore, clearly on the
side of the runaways."

Those only who have a good deal of white blood have sufficient energy to migrate; the true black, never. Enough of
the black nature remains in the runaway, however, to unfit
him for any useful purpose. This fact is within the knowledge
of every citizen of the United States. In all the Northern
States, there are hanging on the outskirts of towns and villages
pauper blacks, the miserable remnant of former well-fed slaves.
These are always a nuisance, and so well known is it that, even

Ohio—which was settled on the territory given by Virginia, and devoted to freedom forever by Nathan Dane's resolution in Convention—among ·its first laws, enacted one excluding blacks from the State on any pretence. The white person who brought in a free negro must give security in $500 for the behavior of that black, and that he should not come upon the town. Illinois, and other States, enacted the same law, and very justly. The free black, without referring to the fact that he is here through no fault of his own, will not contribute his share to the exigencies of society, and it is too much to impose his support upon the labor of industrious whites. He claims to be free, but lives only to prey upon society. Why should he be exempt from the rules that apply to similar white persons? Although the grown white man will work for support and property, youth are, as a general thing, disinclined to do so, because they have still a sense of dependence. The law, consequently, provides for their coercion—every white male may be bound by his parents or guardians, or overseers of the poor, to a trade, and compelled to work for his master until 21, his earnings belonging to his parents. If he escapes from service, he may be arrested and sent back. The police reports of the city contain many such arrests. The provision of the United States Constitution which provides for the surrendering of persons escaped from service, applies as well to these as to blacks, and is always executed without any clamor from " underground railroad" agents, or demand for trial by a jury of runaway apprentices or confederate idlers. Again, for mature white persons who are afflicted with poverty, the law makes provision for their support, and also to compel them to labor where they are capable of it. Perhaps the most barbarous laws in this respect exist in some parts of New England—especially Connecticut. The rule is to *sell* the paupers annually at so much per head, usually from $15 to $20. The "lot" is put up at auction, and the man who bids the lowest sum to keep these poor persons a year takes the lot. He then provides as cheaply as he can for them, intending of course to make money by the operation, and they are required to work for him. Thus, in the fishing section, they must clean fish and feed on the offal; if they die in the course of this treatment, so much the better for the contracror, whose interest under the system is directly that they may perish before his year is out, and there are none to make inquiries.

In reply to inquiries respecting the pauper laws of Connecticut, we received the following from high authority:

"It is the custom in many towns in Connecticut to set up the paupers at auction every year, and knock them off to the lowest bidder; that is, to the man who will take them for the year at the lowest price. This was the case, to my knowledge, in several counties. I have always understood it to be a general thing in Connecticut. When we were in H. they were sold, to the number of sixty, for the year, to our next-door neighbor, for $15 a head; and he got all the work out of them that he could, though most of them were infirm, and not able to do much. They hoed his corn, and sawed his wood, and weeded his garden; and being an extensive fisherman, they assisted in dressing his fish, and "did chores" generally. They are made to work all that they are able. In H. the contractor, as I said, was a fisherman, and during the fishing season a principal article of food for the paupers was the heads and tails of shad, which were cut off when dressed for salting. They were all lodged in a little one-story house, with an attic not to exceed 25 by 30 feet; were all stored in together, male and female, with, as appeared to me, very little regard to decency. In case of the death of any of them, the contractor got a specified sum for their burial, and also, I think, secured the whole amount contracted for for the year; indeed, I believe the probable death of some of them was a contingency calculated on in making the bid, so that the contractor had a direct interest in starving them to death, or in neglecting them when sick."

This may be philanthropy, but the manner in which it works is certainly food for philosophy. The person who officially superintended the sale of the above-mentioned sixty white paupers was some time after appealed to on behalf of a runaway slave. His "phelinks" were so wonderfully stirred by the color of the applicant that he gave him $10, took him home, clothed and fed him, at an expense equal to what he had sold a white pauper fellow-townwoman for under the hammer. This virtue, however, proved its own reward, since the "runaway slave" turned out to be a knavish wood-sawyer from a distant town, who was making a raise on the "fugitive dodge."

That part of the white race which prefers crime to labor is provided for in the prisons, and their coerced labor turned to account. With the black race idleness is the rule. There is no need of quoting authorities on this head, since the public prints are full of them, corroborating every man's experience. Fifty years since the idea was indulged that the black, like the white, was possessed of ambition that would induce him to work when free. Benevolent and large-hearted men eagerly adopted the idea that the black race was different from the white only in color of their skin, and he was eagerly adopted as a "brother." This being once settled, the rules of white conduct were applied to him. Dr. Channing, on the West India emancipation question, thus states it:

"The planters in general would suffer little, if at all, from emancipation. This change would make them richer rather than poorer. One would think, indeed, from the common language on the subject, that the negroes were to be annihilated by being set free; that the whole labor of the South was to be destroyed by a single blow. But the colored man, when freed, will not vanish from the soil. He will stand there with the same muscles as before, only strung anew by liberty; with the same limbs to toil, and with stronger motives to toil than before. He will work from hope, not fear; will work for himself, not for others; and unless all the principles of human nature are reversed under a black skin, he will work better than before. We believe that agriculture will revive; worn-out soils will be renewed, and the whole country assume a brighter aspect under *free labor*."

This has proved to be an illusion. The first who properly recognized this fact was Toussaint L'Ouverture, in St. Domingo. The French republic had hastily emancipated the blacks, and frightful carnage succeeded. Toussaint, himself a slave, had risen to control and respect by his capacity to swallow draughts of blood and gunpowder at negro rites; but, notwithstanding all the attempts to glorify him, the only evidence of intellect he displayed was in recognizing the necessity of labor, while convinced of the unwillingness of the blacks to work; and he promptly re-enslaved the whole of them. The English committed a similar folly to the French, in their W. I. Islands, by freeing the blacks in the expectation that they would work. They now confess the bitterness of their disappointment, and admit the error they committed in abandoning a territory so necessary to the service of mankind as Jamaica and the other islands to a horde of black savages, who will neither make the land available nor permit others to do so. The necessity of dispossessing or re-enslaving has become urgent.

The *London Times* of January 6, 1860, in a long article upon "The State of the Islands, by Mr. Trollope," remarks as follows:

" Negroes, coolies, and planters—what is the position of each, and what are the rights of each? In England it is too much the custom to regard only the first of these. Floods of pathetic eloquence and long years of parliamentary struggling have taught us to imagine that the world was made for Sambo, and that the sole use of sugar is to sweeten Sambo's existence. The negro is, no doubt, a very amusing and a very amiable fellow, and we ought to wish him well; but he is also a lazy animal, without any foresight, and therefore requiring to be led and compelled. We must not judge him by ourselves. That he is capable. of improvement everybody admits, but in the mean time he is decidedly inferior—he is but very little raised above a mere animal. The negroes know this themselves. They have no idea of country and no pride of race. They despise themselves. They know nothing of Africa, except that it is a term of reproach, and the name which offends them most is that of a nigger. So little confidence have they in any being who has an admixture of their blood that no negro will serve a mulatto when he can serve a European or a white creole. In his passion he calls the mulatto a nigger, and protests that he is not, never will be, like buckra man. These colored people, too, despise themselves, and in every possible way try to deny their African parentage. They talk contemptuously of the pure blacks, whom they describe as dirty niggers, and nasty niggers, and mere niggers.

" He is a very funny sort of animal, and there is something interesting in a being so dependent as he is on the sympathy of others; but it is evident that he is scarcely fitted to take care of himself. He has no care for to-morrow, and it is enough if he can strut for a little hour in his finery. His virtues and his vices are alike those of momentary impulse. Although he is desperately fond of life, yet if he can lie in the sun for an hour without pain he will not drag himself to the hospital to be cured of a mortal disease. Although he loves his children, he will in his rage ill-use them fearfully. Although he delights to hear them praised, he will sell his daughter's virtue for a dollar. A little makes him happy, and he is so entirely a creature of the present that nothing can make him permanently wretched. Mr. Trollope compares him to a dog in his attachments. The dog is faithful to us, and so is the negro. In return for our protection the dogs give us all their hearts, but it is not given in gratitude; and they abstain with all their power from injury, but they do not abstain from judgment. The master may use either his dog or his negro ever so cruelly—yet neither has any anger against him when the pain

8

is over.  If a stranger should save either from such ill usage,
there would be no thankfulness after the moment.  Affection
and fidelity are things of custom with him.  As for the negro's
religion, our author has little faith in it.  The negroes, he says,
much prefer to belong to a Baptist congregation or to a so-
called Wesleyan body, because there an excitement is allowed
to them which is denied in the Church of England.  They sing,
they halloo, they scream, they have their revivals, they talk of
their ' dear broders,' and ' dear sisters,' and 'in their extatic
howlings get some fun for their money.'

   " A servile race, peculiarly fitted by nature for the hardest
physical work in a burning climate, the negro has no desire
for property strong enough to induce him to labor with sustained power.  He lives from hand to mouth.  In order that
he may have his dinner, and some small finery, he will work
a little, but after that he is content to lie in the sun.  This, in
Jamaica, he can very easily do, for emancipation and free-trade
have combined to throw enormous tracts of land out of cultivation, and on these the negro squats, getting all that he wants
with very little trouble, and sinking in the most resolute
fashion back to the savage state.  Lying under his cotton-tree,.
he refuses to work after ten o'clock in the morning.  ' No,
tankee, massa, me tired now ; me no want more money.'  Or,
by way of variety, he may say : ' No ; workee no more ; money
no 'nuff ; workee no pay.'  And so the planter must see his
canes foul with weeds because he cannot prevail on Sambo to
earn a second shilling by going into the cane-fields.  He calls
him a lazy nigger, and threatens him with starvation.  The
answer is—' No, massa ; no starve now ; God sent plenty yam.'
These yams, be it observed, on which Sambo relies, and on
the strength of which he declines to work, are grown on the
planter's own ground, and probably planted at his expense, and
Mr. Trollope suggests an inquiry into the feelings of an English
farmer if our laborers were to refuse work on the plea that
there is plenty of potatoes and bacon to be had—the potatoes
and bacon being the produce of the farmer's own fields.  There
lies the shiny, oily, odorous negro under his mango-tree, eating
the luscious fruit in the sun.  ' He sends his black urchin up
for a breadfruit, and, behold,' says Mr. Trollope, ' the family
table is spread.  He pierces a cocoanut, and, lo ! there is his
beverage.  He lies on the ground, surrounded by oranges, ba-
nanas, and pineapples.  Why should he work?'  Let Sambo
himself reply.  ' No, massa, me weak in me belly ; me no
workee to-day ; me no like workee just 'em little moment.'

   " The evil which thus cruelly embarrasses the planters is
chiefly felt in Jamaica, and in some of the smaller islands,
Grenada, Dominica, and St. Lucia, where the negro has the
chance of squatting.  The negro imagined that his emancipa-

tion was to be an emancipation not merely from slavery, but from work, and British philanthropy proposes to protect him in his laziness from the competition of the coolies.

" As far as Jamaica is concerned, what is there to tempt the Englishman ? It is a fact that half the sugar estates, and more than half the coffee plantations have gone back into a state of bush, and a great portion of those who are now growing canes in Jamaica are persons who have lately bought the estates 'for the value of the copper in the sugar-boilers and of the metal in the rum-stills.' The Anti-slavery Society will scarcely believe in the poverty and ruin of the planter, because they hear wonderful accounts of his hospitality. 'We send word to the people at home that we are very poor,' say the planters. 'They don't believe us, and send out somebody to see. For this somebody we kill the fatted calf and bring out a bottle or two of our best. He goes home and reports that these Jamaica planters are princes who swim in claret and champagne.' The planter accordingly makes the complaint, 'This is rather hard, seeing that our common fare is salt fish and rum and water.' Mr. Trollope advised the planters to produce their ordinary fare on such occasions, but the reply was, 'Yes, and then we should get it on the other cheek. We should be abused for our stinginess. No Jamaica man could stand that.' "

The idea of working for pay never entered into black nature. Mungo Park, in his day, said : " Hired servants, by which I mean persons of free condition, voluntarily working for pay, *are unknown in Africa,*"—and no subsequent traveller, down to Dr. Livingstone, has reversed that judgment.

In " Lewis's West Indies," written 17 years before emancipation, it is remarked :

" As to the free blacks they are almost uniformly lazy and improvident; most of them half-starved, and only anxious to live from hand to mouth. Some lounge about the highways with pedler-boxes stocked with various worthless baubles; others keep miserable stalls, provided with rancid butter, damaged salt-pork, and other such articles; and these they are always willing to exchange for stolen rum and sugar, which they secretly tempt the negroes to pilfer from their proprietors; but few of them ever endeavor to earn their livelihood creditably. Even those who profess to be tailors, carpenters, or coopers, are, for the most part, careless, drunken, and dissipated, and never take pains sufficient to attain any dexterity in their trade. *As to a free negro hiring himself out for plantation labor, no instance of such a thing was ever known in Ja-*

*maica;* and probably no price, however great, would be considered by them as a sufficient temptation."

Captain Hamilton, on his examination as a witness before a select committee of Parliament, stated that Jamaica had become "*a desert*," and being asked if he thought the term "*desert*" was quite applicable to the state of things there, replied: "I should say, peculiarly applicable, *without any exaggeration.*"

In a memorial, addressed by the council and assembly of Jamaica, to her majesty, the Queen, dated February 19, 1852, after alluding to the distressed condition of the island, and the probable complete abandonment of sugar culture throughout the British Antilles, unless a remedy were provided, the moral deterioration of the island is thus noticed:

" In conclusion, we would humbly entreat the consideration of your majesty, to the moral effects which must be produced on the lower classes of the population of this island by the general abandonment of property and withdrawal of capital, now unhappily in progress. Convinced that in granting freedom to the British slave, it never was intended to allow him to sink into a state of barbarism and uncivilization, we still feel it our humble duty to assure your majesty, that the *downward progress of the agricultural resources of the colony has been already accompanied by a retrogression in moral conduct on the part of the lower classes,* and we are assured that this retrogression must and will, for obvious reasons, keep pace with the destruction of property, and the consequent expulsion from the colony of all whom necessity may not compel to residence, events that must speedily occur, unless your majesty shall be pleased graciously to receive our petition, and we obtain from the Imperial Parliament efficient aid, ere ruin and desolation shall have taken the place of prosperity and cultivation, and religion and morality shall have been superseded by barbarism and superstition."

There were liberated 633,000 blacks in the West Indies—a number equal to what these United States contained at the formation of the Union. Yet the products of the West Indies have nearly ceased, except what arises from coolie labor.

During the nine years between 1847 and 1856, 47,739 laborers were introduced into the West India islands and British Guiana.* These are just 47,739 protests against the abomina-

---

* Par. Rep., 1857, cited by Mr. Cave.—*Times, Dec.* 28, 1857.

ble laziness of the negro. The world has been scraped and
raked to bring laborers to the West Indies, to eat the bread and
hoard the wealth offered to the black man; laborers from
China, coolies from India, Portuguese from Modina, Africans
from Sierra Leone and from captured slave-ships, have all
been brought distances of from 5,000 to 15,000 miles to shame
this degraded race!—and still we are told there is no inducement for them to work, and that sufficient pay is not offered to
them. Is it a reasonable statement to make, to say that the
planters can fit out ships and send them to the antipodes for
laborers, under a contract to return them to their homes within
a given period, and pay them wages during all that period, and
yet that they would not rather pay the same money to a laborer
on the spot, and one, moreover, both stronger and better acquainted with his duties than the other? The truth is, the
blacks will *not* work without coercion, and this is the cause of
West India distress and negro retrogression. In endeavoring
to hide the truth from our eyes, we are continually hunting up
causes, when the real cause is patent before us; the sugar-du-
ties bill of 1846 is especially saddled with the burden of West
Indian miseries; but we do not know how this charge can be
better answered, or a higher authority cited in proof of the
idleness of the blacks, than by quoting the remarks of Earl
Grey, made in the House of Lords on the 10th of June, 1852.
He stated, "that it was established, by statistical facts, that
before the measure of 1846 came into operation, all those evils
which were now complained of were in actual existence; that
the negroes were becoming *idle, and falling back in civilization,* and the like, and to what principal cause had that been
attributed? It was attributed by every man who had looked
into the state of the colonies to this simple reason, that the
negroes had been relieved from the coercion to which they
were formerly subjected, and that they were living in a country where there was an almost unlimited extent of fertile land
open to them, where the climate did not render fuel or clothing
absolutely necessary to life; that *wages were so enormously
high* as to enable them to live, as well as they desired to live,
upon the production of one or two days' labor in the fortnight,
and that they had consequently no earthly motive to give a
greater amount of labor in return for their subsistence. The
demoralization of the negroes, and their disinclination to work,
arising from this cause, commenced long before the Act of

1846. . . . Sir H. Light and Governor Barkly had both shown, in their very able dispatches, that the true cause of the mischief was the want of any adequate stimulus to labor on the part of the negroes, from the manner in which the abolition of slavery had been effected."*

It is undeniable, then, that the majority of the free negroes of the West Indies are living in idleness; the proofs of this are abundant and varied; they are visible in the census reports, in the dispatches of governors, in the list of exports, and in the observations of travellers.†

The same experience has been earned by the French. They emancipated their blacks when under the influence of the same delusion. The same ruin attends their colonies. A work of M. Vacherot, recently published in Paris, holds the following propositions in relation to the free black population of French Guiana:

" The idlers should be punished by fine. The small proprietor ought to be forced to produce in the same ratio in which he would do when working on a large estate, at a salary. The owner who will neither cultivate nor produce is a vagabond to be punished. It is not enough that he remains at home, that he begs from no one, he should be compelled to make the land he owns produce its share. The landed vagabond is a greater nuisance than the wandering vagabond."

These ideas are a very curious "capsizing" of the socialist doctrines of 1848, '49. It was then asserted that the people had a "right to labor;" that it was the duty of the government to employ them. The constitution of 1848 declared it the duty of government to provide for citizens " by procuring employment for them." This was based upon the desire of the white to work. The black, however, will not work, and the authorities of Guiana claim the right to make him. How those "idle vagabonds" are to be fined is, however not so clear.

In the United States there are 4,000,000 of these blacks, who,

---

* Par. Deb., Hansard, 3 S. V. 122, p. 384.

† Nearly a fourth part of the whole adult population of Trinidad are returned by the last census as living in idleness. (See Lord Harris's dispatch, May 18, 1852.) If we compare this with Great Britain there are two hundred and fifty persons among the poor population of Trinidad to eight among the wealthy of Great Britain who are idlers—the difference is, the one race *likes*, and the other *hates* work ; and a people who will not work *must* be slaves—or, as St. Paul says, in substance, whoever will not work, let him not eat.

as slaves, are eminently useful to themselves and to humanity at large. To emancipate them is to convert 4,000,000 productive workers into as many idle paupers. Who is to support those paupers in their idleness, which with them is synonymous with freedom? In the West Indies they eat the spontaneous fruits of the earth. In the United States there are none for them to eat. That the blacks are now kept to work as Northern white apprentices and paupers are kept to work, for their own and society's benefit, is true. In that respect the institution operates as a great workhouse, where the naturally idle are compelled to contribute their share to the services of mankind.

The highest rewards, political and social, have been, in the island of Jamaica, vainly held out to the black to induce him to work. John Bigelow, Esq., in his letters to the *Evening Post*, afterwards embodied in a book on the condition of Jamaica, with the best intentions in the world to favor the black, showed conclusively that labor is the last thing he will undertake. The land is, if not the most prolific, at least as much so as any in the world. It may be bought from $5 to $10 per acre, and the possession of five acres confers the right of voting, and eligibility to public offices. The planters offer freely $1.50 per day for labor; 16 days' labor will buy such a piece of land, and the market of Kingston offers a great demand for vegetables at all times. These facts, stated by Mr. Bigelow, place independence within the reach of every black. Yet what are the results? There has been no increase of black voters in the last 20 years. The land runs wild. Kingston gets its vegetables from the United States, even from New York, and 50,000 coolies have been imported to raise sugar on the plantations—the sensual black, meanwhile, basking in the sun, and feeding on yams and pumpkins. That is black nature. The omnipotent Deity, who placed those blacks under white control, will not hold those guiltless who have, from hope of greater gain, shirked from the responsibility of masters, and allowed the blacks to sink back to their savage condition.

Freedom for the blacks in the United States is quite a different affair, since they cannot there exist without labor. Nevertheless, the process of emancipation goes on at a rate of which the public are not fully apprised. The following table of number of free and bond blacks in all the States of the Union, is composed of the returns of the federal census:

## BLACK POPULATION OF THE UNITED STATES.

| Names of States | 1790 Free Blacks | 1790 Slaves | 1800 Free Blacks | 1800 Slaves | 1810 Free Blacks | 1810 Slaves | 1820 Free Blacks | 1820 Slaves | 1830 Free Blacks | 1830 Slaves | 1840 Free Blacks | 1840 Slaves | 1850 Free Blacks | 1850 Slaves |
|---|---|---|---|---|---|---|---|---|---|---|---|---|---|---|
| Maine | 538 | ..... | 818 | ..... | 969 | ..... | 929 | ..... | 1,190 | ..... | 1,355 | ..... | 1,356 | ..... |
| New Hampshire | 630 | 158 | 856 | 8 | 970 | ..... | 786 | ..... | 604 | 3 | 537 | ..... | 528 | ..... |
| Vermont | 255 | 17 | 557 | ..... | 750 | ..... | 903 | ..... | 881 | ..... | 730 | ..... | 711 | ..... |
| Massachusetts | 5,463 | ..... | 6,452 | ..... | 6,737 | ..... | 6,740 | ..... | 7,048 | ..... | 8,669 | ..... | 9,064 | ..... |
| Rhode Island | 3,469 | 952 | 3,304 | 381 | 3,609 | 108 | 3,554 | 48 | 3,561 | 17 | 3,238 | 5 | 3,670 | ..... |
| Connecticut | 2,801 | 2,759 | 5,330 | 951 | 6,453 | 310 | 7,844 | 97 | 8,047 | 25 | 8,105 | 17 | 7,693 | ..... |
| New York | 4,654 | 21,324 | 10,374 | 20,343 | 25,333 | 15,017 | 29,980 | 10,088 | 44,870 | 75 | 50,027 | 4 | 49,069 | ..... |
| New Jersey | 2,762 | 11,423 | 4,442 | 12,422 | 7,843 | 10,851 | 12,609 | 7,557 | 18,303 | 2,254 | 21,044 | 674 | 23,810 | 236 |
| Pennsylvania | 6,537 | 3,737 | 14,561 | 1,706 | 22,492 | 795 | 32,153 | 211 | 37,930 | 403 | 47,854 | 64 | 53,626 | ..... |
| **Total** | 26,831 | 40,370 | 46,654 | 35,946 | 75,156 | 27,081 | 95,960 | 18,001 | 122,434 | 2,779 | 143,558 | 765 | 149,906 | 236 |
| Delaware | 3,899 | 8,887 | 8,268 | 6,153 | 13,136 | 4,177 | 12,958 | 4,509 | 15,855 | 3,292 | 16,919 | 2,605 | 18,073 | 2,290 |
| Maryland | 8,043 | 103,036 | 19,587 | 105,635 | 33,927 | 111,502 | 39,730 | 107,398 | 52,938 | 102,994 | 62,078 | 89,737 | 74,723 | 90,368 |
| District of Columbia | ..... | ..... | 783 | 3,244 | 2,549 | 5,395 | 4,048 | 6,377 | 6,152 | 6,119 | 8,361 | 4,694 | 10,059 | 3,687 |
| Virginia | 12,766 | 293,427 | 20,124 | 345,796 | 30,570 | 392,518 | 37,139 | 425,153 | 47,348 | 469,757 | 49,842 | 448,987 | 54,333 | 472,528 |
| North Carolina | 4,975 | 100,572 | 7,043 | 133,296 | 10,266 | 168,824 | 14,612 | 205,017 | 19,543 | 245,601 | 22,732 | 245,817 | 27,463 | 288,548 |
| South Carolina | 1,801 | 107,094 | 3,185 | 146,151 | 4,554 | 196,365 | 6,826 | 258,475 | 7,921 | 315,401 | 8,276 | 327,038 | 8,960 | 384,984 |
| Georgia | 398 | 29,264 | 1,019 | 59,404 | 1,801 | 105,218 | 1,763 | 149,656 | 2,486 | 217,531 | 2,753 | 280,944 | 2,931 | 381,682 |
| Florida | ..... | ..... | ..... | ..... | ..... | ..... | ..... | ..... | 844 | 15,501 | 817 | 25,717 | 932 | 39,310 |
| Alabama | ..... | ..... | ..... | ..... | ..... | ..... | 633 | 47,439 | 1,572 | 117,549 | 2,039 | 253,532 | 2,265 | 342,844 |
| Mississippi | ..... | ..... | ..... | ..... | ..... | ..... | 458 | 32,814 | 519 | 65,659 | 1,369 | 195,211 | 930 | 309,878 |
| Louisiana | ..... | ..... | ..... | ..... | 7,585 | 34,660 | 10,960 | 69,064 | 16,710 | 109,588 | 25,502 | 168,452 | 17,462 | 244,809 |
| Texas | ..... | ..... | ..... | ..... | ..... | ..... | ..... | ..... | ..... | ..... | ..... | ..... | 397 | 58,161 |
| Arkansas | ..... | ..... | ..... | ..... | ..... | ..... | 77 | 1,617 | 141 | 4,576 | 465 | 19,935 | 608 | 47,100 |
| Tennessee | 361 | 3,417 | 309 | 13,584 | 1,317 | 44,535 | 2,779 | 80,107 | 4,555 | 141,603 | 5,524 | 183,059 | 6,422 | 239,459 |
| Kentucky | 114 | 11,830 | 741 | 40,343 | 1,713 | 80,561 | 2,741 | 126,732 | 4,917 | 165,213 | 7,317 | 182,258 | 10,011 | 210,981 |
| Missouri | ..... | ..... | ..... | ..... | 607 | 3,011 | 376 | 10,222 | 569 | 25,091 | 1,574 | 58,240 | 2,618 | 87,422 |
| **Total** | 32,635 | 657,527 | 61,241 | 857,095 | 108,265 | 1,163,854 | 135,304 | 1,524,580 | 182,070 | 2,005,475 | 215,568 | 2,486,226 | 238,737 | 3,204,051 |
| Illinois | ..... | ..... | 163 | ..... | 613 | 168 | 506 | 917 | 1,637 | 747 | 3,598 | 331 | 5,436 | ..... |
| Indiana | ..... | ..... | 337 | ..... | 393 | 237 | 1,230 | 190 | 3,629 | 3 | 7,165 | 3 | 11,262 | ..... |
| Ohio | ..... | ..... | ..... | ..... | 1,899 | ..... | 4,862 | ..... | 9,568 | 6 | 17,342 | 3 | 25,279 | ..... |
| Michigan | ..... | ..... | ..... | ..... | 120 | 24 | 305 | ..... | 261 | 32 | 707 | ..... | 2,583 | ..... |
| Wisconsin | ..... | ..... | ..... | ..... | ..... | ..... | ..... | ..... | ..... | ..... | 185 | ..... | 635 | ..... |
| Iowa | ..... | ..... | ..... | ..... | ..... | ..... | ..... | ..... | ..... | ..... | 172 | 16 | 333 | ..... |
| California | ..... | ..... | ..... | ..... | ..... | ..... | ..... | ..... | ..... | ..... | ..... | ..... | 962 | ..... |
| Minnesota | ..... | ..... | ..... | ..... | ..... | ..... | ..... | ..... | ..... | ..... | ..... | ..... | 39 | ..... |
| Oregon | ..... | ..... | ..... | ..... | ..... | ..... | ..... | ..... | ..... | ..... | ..... | ..... | 207 | ..... |
| Utah | ..... | ..... | ..... | ..... | ..... | ..... | ..... | ..... | ..... | ..... | ..... | ..... | 24 | 26 |
| New Mexico | ..... | ..... | ..... | ..... | ..... | ..... | ..... | ..... | ..... | ..... | ..... | ..... | 22 | ..... |
| **Total** | ..... | ..... | 500 | ..... | 3,025 | 429 | 6,933 | 1,107 | 15,103 | 788 | 354 | ..... | 46,852 | 26 |
| **Grand total** | 59,466 | 697,897 | 108,395 | 893,041 | 186,446 | 1,191,364 | 238,197 | 1,543,688 | 319,599 | 2,009,043 | 386,348 | 2,487,355 | 434,495 | 3,204,313 |

This table comprises many singular facts not generally borne in mind. The legal abolition of slavery at the North, it appears, did not extinguish the slaves. It also appears that the free blacks gain rapidly on the slave population, even at the South. Nor could all the black laws of the Northwest territory keep blacks out of Ohio and Illinois. The old, worthless, and thieving blacks will penetrate across the borders, to prey upon the white settlers.

The remarkable fact in the above table is the increase of free blacks at the South, where they choose to remain, notwithstanding all the blandishments of the North. The increase of that class in Maryland, Delaware, and Virginia, is worthy of observation. In Delaware the black population may be said to be all free. In Maryland they were 8 per cent. of the slaves in 1790, and have since gained at each census, until they are 80 per cent. in 1850. They do not migrate, and this fact is characteristic of the race. Being without energy they dislike any exertion, even the requisite daily employment, far more so migration to better their condition. If we compare the aggregate progress of the blacks in the three sections, the result is as follows:

*Blacks in the United States.*

|  | NORTH. | WEST. | SOUTH | |
|---|---|---|---|---|
|  |  |  | *Free.* | *Slave.* |
| 1790 | 66,080 | .... | 32,635 | 657,047 |
| 1800 | 82,800 | 500 | 61,241 | 857,095 |
| 1810 | 103,237 | 3,454 | 108,265 | 1,163,854 |
| 1820 | 113,961 | 8,040 | 135,304 | 1,524,580 |
| 1830 | 125,213 | 15,891 | 182,078 | 2,005,475 |
| 1840 | 144,321 | 29,523 | 215,568 | 2,486,226 |
| 1850 | 150,142 | 46,852 | 238,737 | 3,204,051 |

The Northern black population progresses at a very slow pace, notwithstanding the aid it acquires by migration. The free blacks at the South, on the other hand, increase rapidly, notwithstanding some loss by migration. Nevertheless, the aggregate increase at the North is far less than the natural increase of the whites. If the black race have been petted anywhere on the face of the earth, it has been in Massachusetts, Rhode Island, and Connecticut. Yet the fact shows that in 1820 there were in those States 18,559 blacks. 30 years after, in 1850, there were 20,427, an increase of less than 10 per cent. in 30 years. In Massachusetts alone there were, in 1800, 6,452 blacks; in 1850 these had increased to 9,060—of these only 5,699 were born in the State, 3,361 having come from other

States, and thus the native blacks in 50 years declined 752 in actual numbers.

It is no doubt the fact that the Northern climate is too rigorous for the black nature, and that they do not increase for that among other reasons, but the great fact is, that no matter how high negro worship may run at the North, and how much soever the people of Massachusetts are disposed to educate, patronize, equalize, and evangelize the black race, they still inexorably require industry from him as one of the virtues. That, however, in the view of the black, counteracts all else that can be done for him. To live in Massachusetts not only is industry required, but a good deal of it, added to foresight and prudence, three qualities entirely foreign to the black nature. After all they have done for the black race, the New England philanthropy can get only a very scant supply of house-servants out of it. The fact of the small increase of blacks in a region where so many advantages are held out to him, contrasts strongly with his rapid increase in sections where his white friends allege he suffers great hardships.

The census of 1840 gave some very interesting facts in relation to the afflictions of the white and black race in respect of being deaf and dumb, blind and insane. The following are the figures taken from the census, arranged in parallels of latitude, as nearly as may be :

Blacks.—Deaf and Dumb, Blind, and Insane.

| | No. | Deaf & Dumb. | Blind. | Insane. | Ratio of Insane. |
|---|---|---|---|---|---|
| Louisiana................. | 193,554 | 17 | 36 | 45 | 4,310 |
| Florida................... | 26,534 | 2 | 10 | 12 | 2,211 |
| Mississippi............... | 196,580 | 28 | 69 | 82 | 2,397 |
| Alabama.................. | 255,371 | 53 | 96 | 125 | 2,011 |
| Georgia.................. | 283,697 | 64 | 151 | 134 | 2,117 |
| South Carolina........... | 335,314 | 78 | 156 | 137 | 2,447 |
| Latitude, 30 to 34.... | 1,291,250 | 242 | 518 | 535 | 2,413 |
| Virginia ................. | 495,105 | 150 | 466 | 384 | 1,219 |
| North Carolina........... | 268,549 | 74 | 167 | 221 | 1,245 |
| Tennessee ............... | 188,583 | 67 | 99 | 152 | 1,240 |
| Kentucky................. | 189,575 | 77 | 141 | 180 | 1,051 |
| Missouri................. | 59,814 | 27 | 42 | 68 | 879 |
| Maryland................. | 151,815 | 66 | 191 | 141 | 2 005 |
| Delaware ................ | 19,524 | 8 | 18 | 28 | 700 |
| Latitude, 34 to 38 .... | 1,372,695 | 469 | 1,124 | 1,174 | 1,170 |
| Rhode Island............. | 3,238 | 3 | 1 | 13 | 249 |
| Connecticut.............. | 8,105 | 8 | 13 | 44 | 184 |
| New Jersey............... | 21,718 | 15 | 26 | 73 | 297 |
| Pennsylvania............. | 47,918 | 51 | 96 | 187 | 256 |
| Ohio..................... | 17,345 | 33 | 33 | 165 | 105 |
| Indiana.................. | 7,168 | 15 | 19 | 75 | 955 |
| Illinois ................. | 3,929 | 24 | 10 | 79 | 497 |
| Iowa..................... | 188 | 4 | 3 | 4 | 47 |
| Latitude, 38 to 42 .... | 109,609 | 153 | 201 | 540 | 203 |

| | No. | Deaf & Dumb. | Blind. | Insane. | Ratio of Insane. |
|---|---|---|---|---|---|
| Maine .................. | 1,355 | 13 | 10 | 94 | 14.4 |
| Massachusetts........... | 8,666 | 17 | 12 | 200 | 43.3 |
| New Hampshire......... | 737 | 9 | 3 | 19 | 28.2 |
| Vermont................. | 730 | 2 | 2 | 13 | 56.1 |
| New York .............. | 50,031 | 68 | 91 | 194 | 21.2 |
| Michigan ............... | 707 | 2 | 4 | 26 | 27.2 |
| Wisconsin .............. | 196 | .. | .. | 13 | 65.2 |
| Latitude, 42 to 46 .... | 62,421 | 101 | 132 | 549 | 115. |

This table presents extraordinary results; the number of insane diminishes in the exact ratio in which we proceed South, with the exception of some of the Western States, where the blacks have mostly arrived in the State, and the infirm class do not accompany the others. Taking the parallels of latitude, the ratio of deaf, dumb, and blind to the whole number is as follows:

| | Latitude, 30 to 34. | Latitude, 34 to 38. | Latitude, 38 to 42. | Latitude, 42 to 46. |
|---|---|---|---|---|
| Deaf, Dumb, and Blind...... | 1 to 1,200 | 1 to 870 | 1 to 300 | 1 to 255 |
| Insane...................... | 1 " 2,413 | 1 " 1,170 | 1 " 203 | 1 " 115 |

These facts were disclosed by the census of 1840, and were brought to the notice of the public in an article in the "Democratic Review," in 1845, by the present writer. Attempts were immediately made to impeach the census return five years after it was taken, in order to invalidate its testimony. It was stated that in some towns of Massachusetts, there were more insane blacks reported than the whole black population consisted of. The fact that the insane blacks had, meantime, been removed to asylums, it was not, however, thought worth while to mention. Nevertheless, the effort prevented a correct return for the seventh census. That some errors did occur in taking the census is, no doubt, true; but its truthfulness in the aggregate is manifest from the fact it discloses. No, not only do the insane, but the other afflicted classes also increase in exact proportion to the climate. If important errors occurred, they could not have been made in such regular gradation. The fact, however, of the greater infirmity of the black race in Northern climes thus made manifest, is only corroborative of the small increase of the class, and of the testimony of the public hospitals. It is to be regretted that the Massachusetts State returns, generally so useful and so accurate, should have ceased to distinguish between the black and white races. If the returns did so distinguish, important scientific research would be aided, without in any degree degrading the blacks. Omitting to distinguish them on paper does not efface the indelible distinction which the Almighty has imprinted on them. The endeavor to smother up inquiry in relation to ethnological facts, savors a good deal of fear lest theories are not founded on solid foundations. If the truth makes against the black and mixed races, why cling to error? If it makes in their favor, by all means let it be developed. One reason of the greater infirmity of the blacks at the North is, that they are a hybrid race, and have always the well-known tendency of such races to die out, and revert to the original stock. It is evident from the facts collated, that the black race, even made entirely free, will never come north if they can help it.

If we, however, take the numbers confined in the jails of each section at the date of the census of 1850, we have the following extraordinary results:

| | Black population. | No. in jail. | One in | White population. | No. in jail. | One in |
|---|---|---|---|---|---|---|
| North......... | 150,142 | 478 | 310 | 8,342,938 | 2,710 | 3,000 |
| West ......... | 46,852 | 87 | 542 | 5,413,039 | 760 | 7,000 |
| South......... | 3,442,788 | 323 | 10,000 | 6,222,418 | 1,288 | 5,000 |
| Total ..... | 3,639,782 | 888 | | 19,978,395 | 4,758 | |

The North again presents the most extraordinary results for the morals of that race, in a region where they are by far the most petted of the community.

The white criminals confined at the North were as one to 3,000 of the whole. It is true that a large portion of these were foreign born, showing that if the North has advantages from immigration, it has also disadvantages. At the West the proportion is less than in the other sections for the white race; when we come to the blacks, however, we find that at the North one out of every 310 is in jail; at the West, one out of 542 is in jail; and the South, one in 10,000 of all; but confined to the free blacks, it is one in 800.

The black race is more vicious at the North, as a necessity of its position; it will not work; it cannot compete with the white man, and crime is its ready support! If they had sufficient energy to migrate at all, they would tend southward, where nature will aid them in the indulgence of sensual idleness. It is probable that the Almighty has in store singular and severe manifestations of His wrath against those self-righteous persons, who, in their own blinded folly, seek to thwart His manifest intentions to exalt both and all races through the medium of black servitude to white intelligence. By so doing, they strive to carry both back to the barbarism of the Middle Ages. It is, no doubt, the case that the condition of servitude admits of many modifications for the better. The most important improvement needed is to exact more industry from the blacks. Those employed in cities and as house-servants are notoriously indolent. Persons who visit the South are at once impressed with this fact. It is probably owing, in some degree, to the enervating effects of climate which takes from the energy required to direct black labor. There are vices and hardships in the system, it is true ; but there is no state of humanity exempt from these afflictions. The separation of families, and the sundering of domestic ties through the vicissitudes of life, are far less frequent among the black than among the white races. The Irish nation endures more misery from this source in a single year than afflicts the blacks in a quarter of a century. The records of the courts show that freedom is no bar against rape, seduction, and kindred villanies. If the blacks suffer least in this respect, they have also far less sensibility in relation to it when it occurs.

That the free black race is a nuisance in whatever section it settles, is sufficiently manifest, not only from the natural repulsion of the community, but from the action of State Legislatures. Ohio early adopted laws to exclude them from her soil, but repealed them to suit political parties during the "free-soil" campaign of 1850. The Northern States of Indiana, Illinois, Oregon, and Minnesota, have by law excluded them from their territories. The Legislature of Missouri has passed a law to the same effect. The State of Louisiana has also by law forbidden any free blacks to come into the State, and Arkansas has by law compelled the free blacks to leave the State or be enslaved. This disposition is extending even with the small number of negroes that are now free, and any accumulation of their numbers would, as in the West Indies, immediately evolve a war of races that would only end in the extermination of one. The antipathy is now strongly marked between them, and it requires only an increase in numbers to develop those characteristics of the blacks, which would make peace with them impossible.

# CHAPTER X.

## ACCUMULATION.

WE have followed briefly the progress which each national section has made in the production of wealth, and have shown that the greatest results, by all odds, have attended the Southern system. When we turn, however, to accumulation and possession, a different state of affairs presents itself. Neither the West nor the South hold much of what they produce. Wealth once extracted from the soil by labor, evinces a strong affinity for the North and East, and there piles up in a magnitude which dazzles the observer. As the opulent always become purse-proud, so does the affluent North regard with a degree of haughtiness the very useful sections which pour riches into her lap. Exercising the prerogative of wealth she assumes the right to dictate manners and morality to those who are less thrifty in worldly matters. It is the nature of capital to accumulate, and the more so when the laws are so framed as to favor that accumulation. From the earliest period of the government the federal revenues have been derived from duties on goods imported. The duties have not been levied with a single view to revenue, but have been so adjusted as to afford the largest protection to Northern manufactures. In other words, to tax the consumers of goods West and South for the support of Eastern manufactures. The amount of customs so collected in the past 70 years reaches 1100 millions of dollars, a large portion of which was disbursed at the North. This sum has been paid mostly by the South and West into the federal treasury, on goods imported. The sum of these may be 20 per cent. of the quantity home manufactured, and the value of which has been increased in the ratio of the duty. If, however, it is assumed that the home-made goods have been enhanced in value only to the extent of the customs revenue, then the Eastern manufacturers have obtained 1100 millions of dollars as tribute from the South and West. That large sum has been taken from agricultural industry and added to manufacturing industry. The fisheries of the Eastern States drew $5,000,000 as bounties paid to those engaged in them, out of the federal treasury, to the date of the abolition of those bounties. The North enjoyed a monopoly of the carrying trade, foreign vessels being excluded. These, and other circumstances drew the surplus capital from the agriculturist into the coffers of the manufacturer. The accumulation of capital thus brought about, became invested in stocks, banks, insurance companies, all of which drew large profits on credits granted to the other sections. The North has $600,000,000 so invested, of which $356,318,000 are in banks alone, which draws $60,000,000 per annum from the earnings of the other sections. The frequent pilgrimages from all sections to the Eastern cities for the purchase of goods, and in pursuit of pleasure, form a large item of cost charged upon goods, that is paid by the consumer. The profits of other business may be approximated as follows:

| | |
|---|---:|
| Bounties to fisheries, per annum........................ | $1,500,000 |
| Customs, per annum, disbursed at the North............ | 40,000,000 |
| Profits of Manufacturers.............................. | 30,000,000 |
| "      Importers.................................... | 16,000,000 |
| "      Shipping, imports and exports................ | 40,000,000 |
| "   on Travellers.................................. | 60,000,000 |
| "   of Teachers, and others, at the South, sent North. | 5,000,000 |
| "      Agents, brokers, commissions, &c............ | 10,000,000 |
| '      Capital drawn from the South................ | 30,000,000 |
| Total from these sources........................ | $231,500,000 |

This is an approximation of the annual load which Southern industry is required to carry, and the means of paying it depends upon black labor. The heavy drain of capital thus created prevents an accumulation at the South, and promotes it as effectively at the North, where every such accumulation only accelerates the drain. If we take the aggregate of these items for 10 years only, the result is the enormous sum of $2,315,000,000, and allowing 20 per cent. of the sum only as the aggregate of the 50 previous years, the amount 'is 2770 millions of dollars earned at the South, and added to Northern accumulation. The fishing bounties alone, as we have seen, reach $12,944,000, mostly paid to Maine and Massachusetts. It is not, therefore, a matter of surprise if we find the North very rich, and the South showing much slower accumulation. No matter how great may be the production of wealth at the South it pours off into Northern coffers as rapidly as it is created, and, singularly enough, the recipients of that wealth are continually upbraiding the South with its creation. As we have seen, in the quotation from the *London Times*, contained in a former chapter, English common-sense detects the absurdity, not to say indecency, of such conduct, and is disposed, at least, to be civil until they can do better.

If we take the census figures for the amount of wealth in the Union, distinguishing real from personal, we have the following results. To the figures as returned by the census-makers, the commissioner, Mr. De Bow, added a " true" value.

|  | Real. | Personal. | Total. | True. |
|---|---|---|---|---|
| North.......... | $1,835,063,613 | $546,768,966 | $2,381,782,579 | $2,095,833,338 |
| West.......... | 619,154,287 | 195,054,073 | 815,208,360 | 1,022,948,262 |
| South.......... | 1,445,008,447 | 1,381,727,523 | 2,826,735,970 | 3,947,781,366 |
| Total...... | $3,899,226,347 | $2,125,440,562 | $6,024,666,909 | $7,066,562,966 |

The Southern figures for personal property include the slave property, and in illustration of the manner in which incendiary partisan statistics have been propagated, we may refer to " Helper's Crisis." The above official figures give, it will be seen $1,445,008,447 as the real property at the South, and $1,381,727,523 as the personal, including slaves. " Helper's Crisis," p. 47, adds these two sums together, as follows :

| | |
|---|---|
| Valuation at the South............................. | $2,936,090,737 |
| Deduct value of slaves.............................. | 1,600,000,000 |
| True net value of the Slave States............. | $1,336,090,737 |

It will be observed that in pretending to give the census figures he deducts, for the value of "slaves" alone, a sum 218 millions greater than the census gave for all the personal property, including slaves, and the operation is disguised by bringing the real and personal valuations together.

The means of determining the increase of wealth are not very definite. If there had been a valuation at the date of each national census the task of comparison would have been light. But this has not been the case.

On the 14th July, 1798, Congress by law imposed a tax of $2,000,000 upon dwelling-houses, farm-lands, and slaves between the ages of 12 and 50. In consequence of this tax, a valuation took place of lands and houses separately. In 1815 a new valuation of houses, lands, and slaves took place together.

The valuation of lands took place again by the census of 1850, and the comparison of the number of acres and valuation at both periods, is as follows :

| | 1798. | | 1850. | |
|---|---|---|---|---|
| | *No. of acres.* | *Valuation.* | *No. of acres.* | *Valuation.* |
| New Hampshire....... | 3,749 061 | $19,028,108 | 3,392,414 | $55,245,997 |
| Maine ............... | } 7,831,628 | 59,445,642 | { 4,555,393 | 54,864,748 |
| Massachusetts........ | | | { 3,356,012 | 109,076,347 |
| Rhode Island......... | 565,844 | 8,082,355 | 563,938 | 17.070,802 |
| Connecticut.......... | 2,649,149 | 40,163,955 | 2,383,879 | 72,726,422 |
| Vermont............. | 4,918,722 | 15,165,484 | 4,125,822 | 63,367,237 |
| New York........... | 16,414,510 | 74,885,075 | 19,119,088 | 554,546,642 |
| New Jersey.......... | 2,788,282 | 27,287,981 | 2,752,946 | 120,237,511 |
| Pennsylvania ........ | 11,959,835 | 72,824,852 | 14,923,347 | 407,876,099 |
| Delaware............ | 1,074,105 | 4,053,248 | 956,144 | 18,880,031 |
| Maryland............ | 5,444,272 | 21,634,004 | 4,634,350 | 87,178,515 |
| Virginia ............. | 40,458,644 | 59,976,860 | 26,152,311 | 216,401,444 |
| North Carolina....... | 20,956,467 | 27,909,479 | 20,996,987 | 67,891,766 |
| South Carolina....... | 9,772,587 | 12,456,720 | 16,217,790 | 82,431,684 |
| Georgia.............. | 13,534,159 | 10,263,506 | 22,821,379 | 95,753,445 |
| Kentucky ........... | 17,674,634 | 20,268,325 | 22,340,748 | 154,330,262 |
| Tennessee ........... | 3,951,357 | 5,847,662 | 18,984,022 | 97,851,212 |
| Total........... | 163,746,686 | $479,293,263 | 188,286,480 | $2,275,730,124 |

Dividing the Northern from the Southern States, the aggregates of each compare as follows .

| | SOUTH. | | NORTH. | |
|---|---|---|---|---|
| | *Acres.* | *Value.* | *Acres.* | *Value.* |
| 1798....... | 112,869,655 | $162,409,811 | 50,877,031 | $316,883,452 |
| 1850....... | 133,113,641 | 820,718,319 | 55,172,839 | 1,455,011,805 |
| Increase.............. | | $658,308,508 | | $1,138,128,353 |

The land at the North has increased $20 per acre, and the land at the South has increased $4 per acre. The concentration of manufactures and commerce has given 1100 millions of dollars to the value of land in the Northern States, in 50 years. At the South, where the eight States named embrace about one-half the Slave States, the growing value of the product only has been relied on to raise the value of the land. If we take the remaining Southern States, that have grown up since the valuation of 1798, but which are reported in the census of 1850, the result is as follows :

| | *Acres.* | *Value.* |
|---|---|---|
| Old States, as above ............. | 113,112,641 | $820,718,319 |
| New " per census........... | 47,371,907 | 234,703,237 |
| Total South, 1850............. | 180,485,548 | $1,055,421,556 |

The South has thus added to the extent of its territory, and raised the value of the whole to 1055 millions. Those 47,371,907 acres that have been added since 1798, were bought of the Federal government for about $60,000,000, which has thus been contributed to the Federal expenses by slave-labor. We now come to the value of the slaves. These, by the law of 1798,

9

were taxed 50 cents each.   In 1815 the tax was again levied upon slaves, and they were included, as the Secretary expressed it, because they increased the ability of the State to pay.   The valuation of the blacks was then at $250 each, as follows :

|  | No. | Each. | Value. |
|---|---|---|---|
| 1798 | 893,041 | $200 | $178,608,200 |
| 1815 | 1,163,854 | 250 | 291,973,500 |
| 1850 | 3,204,313 | 550 | 1,603,758,656 |
| Increase from 1798 | 2,311,272 |  | $1,425,150,456 |
| Increase in land | | | 893,011,745 |
| Total increase in value of land and slaves | | | 2,318,162,201 |

We have seen, in a former chapter, that the product of these lands and slaves, sent out of the country, is $265,000,000, or 11 per cent. of the value.   That is, the value here given is equal to nine years' purchase; but the other products of the slaves and lands support the workers and their masters.   Thus this increased value of the land and hands is represented by the actual exchangeable productions, although the proceeds of those productions pour off into Northern coffers.   At the North, 55 million acres have increased $1,138,128,253, on account of their proximity to those manufacturing and commercial establishments that are employed by Southern expenditures and purchases of goods.   That value is the reflection of Southern industry.   The manufacturing capital that has accumulated at the North is to be added to the value of city property.   If we now take the value of Western lands from the census of 1850, we have the sum of 67,420,583 acres, valued at $760,299,733.   We may now include in the valuation the houses and improvements of the three sections, as follows :

*Real Estate Valuation.*

|  | 1798. | 1814-15. | 1850. |
|---|---|---|---|
| North | $422,271.673 | $1,036,319,513 | $1,835,063,613 |
| South | 197,705,574 | 533,990,496 | 1,445,008,447 |
| West | | 61,347,215 | 619,154,287 |
| Total | $619,977,247 | $1,631,657,224 | $3,899,226,347 |

Such has been the progress of valuation in each section. At the North, the same extent of land has received a value of 1400 millions additional.   At the South and West, the area has extended as it has increased in value.

If we turn to the census we find the valuation of farms and farm implements in each section to have been as follows :

*Acres of Land Improved.—Value of Farms and Farm Implements.*

| | Area. | Acres improved. | Value of farms. | Value of farm impl'ts. |
|---|---|---|---|---|
| Maine | 20,330,240 | 2,039,596 | $54,861,748 | $2,284,557 |
| New Hampshire | 5,939,200 | 2,251,488 | 55,245,997 | 2,314,125 |
| Vermont | 6,535,580 | 2,601,409 | 63,367,227 | 2,739,282 |
| Massachusetts | 4,992,000 | 2,133,436 | 109,076,347 | 3,209,584 |
| Rhode Island | 825,840 | 356,487 | 17,070,802 | 497,201 |
| Connecticut | 2,991,360 | 1,768,178 | 72,726,422 | 1,892,541 |
| New York | 30,080,000 | 12,408,964 | 554,546,642 | 22,084,926 |
| New Jersey | 5,324,800 | 1,767,991 | 120,237,511 | 4,425,503 |
| Pennsylvania | 29,440,000 | 8,628,619 | 407,876,099 | 14,722,541 |
| Total North | 106,459,020 | 33,956,158 | $1,455,008,795 | $54,170,160 |
| Ohio | 26,576,960 | 9,851,493 | 358,758,603 | 12,750,585 |
| Indiana | 21,637,760 | 5,046,543 | 136,385,173 | 6,704,444 |
| Illinois | 35,359,200 | 5,039,545 | 96,133,290 | 6,405,561 |
| Michigan | 35,995,520 | 1,929,110 | 51,872,446 | 2,891,371 |
| Wisconsin | 34,511,860 | 1,045,499 | 28,528,563 | 1,641,568 |
| Iowa | 32,584,960 | 824,682 | 16,657,567 | 1,172,869 |
| California | 99,827,200 | 32,454 | 3,874,041 | 103,483 |
| Territories | 631,021,740 | 320,416 | 4,976,839 | 361,652 |
| Total West | 917,515,260 | 24,089,742 | $697,186,522 | $32,031,533 |
| Delaware | 1,356,800 | 580,862 | 18,880,031 | 510,279 |
| Maryland | 7,119,360 | 2,797,905 | 87,178,545 | 2,463,443 |
| District of Columbia | ........ | 16,267 | 1,730,460 | 40,220 |
| Virginia | 39,165,280 | 10,360,135 | 216,401,543 | 7,021,772 |
| North Carolina | 32,450,560 | 5,453,975 | 67,891,766 | 3,931,532 |
| South Carolina | 18,805,400 | 4,072,651 | 82,431,684 | 4,136,354 |
| Georgia | 37,120,000 | 6,378,479 | 95,753,445 | 5,894,150 |
| Florida | 37,931,500 | 349,049 | 6,323,109 | 658,795 |
| Alabama | 32,027,490 | 4,435,614 | 64,323,224 | 5,125.663 |
| Mississippi | 30,179,840 | 3,444,358 | 54,738,634 | 5,762,927 |
| Louisiana | 26,403,200 | 1,590.025 | 75,814,398 | 11,576,938 |
| Texas | 152,002,500 | 643,976 | 16,550,008 | 2,151,704 |
| Arkansas | 33,406,720 | 781,530 | 15,265,245 | 1,601,296 |
| Tennessee | 29,184.000 | 5,175,173 | 97,851,212 | 5,360,210 |
| Kentucky | 24,115,200 | 5,968,270 | 155,021,262 | 5,169,037 |
| Missouri | 43,123,200 | 2,938,425 | 63,225,543 | 3,981,525 |
| Total South | 544,926,720 | 54,986,714 | $1,119,380,109 | $75,385.945 |
| Total | 1,568,901,000 | 113,032,614 | $3,271,575,426 | $151,587,638 |

These figures are from the census, and they show us that farm lands at the South are not much behind the West, but they give an inordinate value to the farms of the North. Seemingly the lands are valued higher in proportion to their sterility. The average value of the farm lands of the North is $42 per acre, at the West $29, and at the South $20 for improved lands. The value of farm implements is as great at the South, nearly, as in both the other sections. In Louisiana they nearly reach the value of those in Ohio. Comparing the agricultural West with the agricultural South, we have results as follows:

| | Improved area. | Value farm lands. | Value Implements. |
|---|---|---|---|
| West | 24,089,742 | $697,186,522 | $32,031,533 |
| South | 54,986,714 | 1,119,380,109 | 75,385,945 |
| In favor of the South | 30,897,972 | $422,193,587 | $43,354,412 |

The West, as we have seen, has received 600,000 foreign immigrants, and a great number of Eastern immigrants, together with hundreds of millions of dollars poured over her lands, while the South has depended only on itself, and yet it has 100 per cent. more land under the plough, 130 per cent. more value in farm implements, and 60 per cent. more value to its lands. This is free and slave labor in the same business. These are the means of production. It is the Northeast which retains the accumulation. With a far less area the value of lands is much greater, but this includes the numerous cities and manufacturing localities, which are made valuable by Southern traffic. The city of New York has a value of $551,928,122, or equal to the whole State of Pennsylvania, exceeding that of any Western State except Ohio, and of the Southern States except Virginia. The trade and valuation of New Orleans, and New York and Boston compare as follows:

|  | Imports and exports. | Real estate. | Personal estate. | Total. | Population. |
|---|---|---|---|---|---|
| Boston........ | $65,774,797 | $153,505,300 | $101,208,800 | $254,174,100 | 162,748 |
| New York..... | 382,861,703 | 378,954,930 | 172,961,192 | 551,923,122 | 629,904 |
| New Orleans.. | 117,413,044 | 76,485,970 | 28,370,942 | 104,856,912 | 124,385 |

The business of New Orleans embraces the large river receipts of produce, which go to swell its exports, and its external business is larger than that of Boston; yet its personal property is very small, and the value of its real estate nothing in proportion to its business. The real estate of New York is enhanced in value by the crowd of buyers from the South, to catch whose business high rents are paid for desirable sites, and the holders of the old Knickerbocker farms have grown immensely wealthy by the confluence in Broadway of the Yankee dealers and Southern buyers. The Western cities present no such rise in value. Cincinnati, with a population of 155,000, has its real estate valued at $55,595,825, or less than New Orleans.

The tendency at the North is to increase the wealth and population of the cities that enjoy the Southern trade, while the agricultural population diminishes by migration West. This has produced a declining value of farm lands. The census gave for New York the value of farm lands at $554,546,642, while the real estate in New York city alone is $378,954,930, or nearly three-fourths. The real estate in Boston exceeds the value of farm lands in Massachusetts by 44 millions. The sterile nature of the soil, as compared with that of the West, while its valuation is so much greater, prompts migration. Farm lands in Massachusetts are valued at $50 per acre, and much better are had at the West for $10. New York lands are valued at $45 per acre, and produce far less than Western lands at $5 per acre.

The valuations of land are, however, little to be depended upon, a fact which the revulsion in the Northwest brings home to the experience of vast numbers of individuals at the present moment. At the North everywhere, farm lands are greatly overvalued. It is true that nothing is more difficult than to affix values to landed property, and the value of such property varies rapidly. Thus, a farm of—say 100 acres—under fair management, may give the owner his living in exchange for his labor, and $600 per annum clear money. This would be the interest on $10,000, and he might, under such circumstances, estimate his land as worth $100 per acre. This, however, is not the case ; very few farms will, at the North, give any thing beyond a meagre support of a family in return for hard labor and care. Nevertheless, the universal valuation is $100 per acre for farms. Every owner feels that if he could sell at that price, and place the money at seven per cent. interest, he should be rich without working at all, compared with his farm life. Hence it is that throughout the length and breadth of the North and West, every farm is for sale. In England and Europe land is tenaciously held ; in this country no kind of property is more readily parted with. This fact grows out of the over valuation. In years of large exports of food, farm profits, as a matter of course, rise, and the holder is enabled to meet his mortgages readily ; for nearly all the farms are mortgaged. In a time of low prices, like the past year, the mortgages are paid with difficulty, and when the land comes to market $40 or $50 per acre is found to be nearer the realizable value. The holders of mortgages are they who reap the true value of the farm lands. The grasp which the money-lenders and speculators have upon the free labor of the North is universal and tenacious, and "financial talent" is always on the lookout to mortgage other peoples' labor for their own benefit. This was singularly the case with the Holland Land Company in the State of New York. That company held a large tract where the Western terminus of the Erie Railroad now is. The land was settled by numbers of industrious settlers, who had taken the lands of the company to improve

them, and to pay as they could.  When they paid up, they
were to have deeds.  These settlements were in a state of progress, when, in an evil hour, financial talent, in the shape of
William H. Seward, Esq., and his coadjutors, turned their attention to the "free labor" of that region, and concluded to
make it available by "bonds."  They agreed to buy out the
Holland Land Co. ; but in order to do it, they must enchain
the free laborers.  They persuaded these simple-minded men,
who were paying up the principal on their lands as best they
could, to take deeds, and give mortgages with "bonds," bear-
ing interest inexorably twice a year.  These mortgages the
financiers pledged with the American Life and Trust Co., for
loans with which to buy out the Land Co.  The free laborers
soon found that they were in the hands of the spoiler, and
when they could no longer wring from the earth the inevitable
semi-annual interest, they were cleared, as the negro-loving
Duchess of Sutherland cleared her estates of pauper residents,
they being driven forth to new homes in the West.  Their
departure left the lands in the hands of those who knew how
to profit largely by the construction of the Erie Railroad
over them.  Thus it is that free labor is made useful to those
who understand the "higher law" of finance.  The mortgage
holders generally are they who reap the profit of free farming
labor.  E. D. Mansfield, Esq., the able Commissioner of Statistics for the State of Ohio, gives the mortgages upon the lands
of that State at $50,000,000.

If we take from the State returns of last year the valuation
of such States as have been officially given, we get returns as
follows :

*State Returns of Taxable Acres, Valuation, Slave Value, Other Personal,
and Total Valuation, 1858.*

| | Acres taxed. | Value of land. | Slave value. | Other personal. | Total valuation. |
|---|---|---|---|---|---|
| Virginia..... | 37,000,000 | $374,989,888 | $313,148,275 | $355,827,765 | $1,043,965,928 |
| Georgia..... | 33,759,233 | 181,677,194 | 271,620,405 | 156,292,277 | 609,589,876 |
| Florida ..... | 2,265,503 | 13,910,981 | 27,250,551 | 8,299,932 | 49,461,466 |
| Texas ....... | 47,937,537 | 86,539,306 | 71,912,496 | 33,935,575 | 192,387,377 |
| Arkansas ... | 7,989,676 | 42,385,704 | 34,794,704 | 10,869,007 | 88,049,415 |
| Tennessee... | 25,362,726 | 166,417,907 | 82,319,723 | 11,581,981 | 260,319,611 |
| Kentucky... | 21,568.383 | 270,960,818 | 95,588,479 | 53,809,903 | 420,359,180 |
| Missouri.... | 26,525,338 | 235,892,792 | 45,090,028 | 39,072,373 | 320,055,193 |
| Total ... | 202,399,296 | $1,372,774,597 | $941,724,661 | $669,688,811 | $2,984,188,046 |

These are the figures for eight Southern States.  The value
of the lands given in the above table from the census in these
same States was $629,000,000, an increase of $743,000,000 ! in

eight years following the rise in the value of the cotton crop. It will be observed that the other seven Southern States, of which we have no official State returns, gave a value of $490,000,000 in the above census table. If these have increased in the same ratio as those for which we have returns, and there is no reason to doubt it, then the whole increased value in the Southern States is $1,333,000,000 !! There was no speculation in these States; but they were, to some extent, acted upon adversely by the land speculation of the North-west, which attracted capital thither even from the South. If we turn now to the State returns of seven Free States, the results are as follows:

| | Acres. | Value. | Personal value. | Total. |
|---|---|---|---|---|
| California ...... | 5,037,557 | 56,060,351 | 48,919,728 | 131,306,269 |
| Indiana ......... | 21,918,659 | 176,894,881 | 141,310,023 | 318,204,964 |
| Illinois ......... | 42,100,000 | 395,663,459 | 111,813,908 | 407,477,367 |
| Iowa ............ | 10,445,003 | 98,101,200 | 41,943,333 | 140,044,533 |
| Ohio ............ | 19,800,000 | 590,285,947 | 250,314,084 | 840,800,031 |
| Michigan ........ | 7,917,322 | 88,101,204 | 32,261,670 | 120,362,474 |
| Wisconsin ...... | 17,411,319 | 155,012,330 | 13,607,893 | 152,537,700 |
| Total ........ | 124,629,860 | $1,560,119,372 | $610,370,199 | $2,111,233,345 |

The valuation of these same States in the table, page 131, was $692,209,000, showing an increase of $867,910,000 as the result of the vast migration from abroad and the East, with the expenditure of many hundred millions in addition to the railroad expenditure. The territories may have increased so as to bring up the value to $1,000,000,000.

This increase is flattering, but what are the results? The West is bankrupt in face of that valuation; capital flows back from it as fast as it can be realized. The money sent there is sunk; the railroads do not earn expenses; and the lands, with their high valuation, do not give back an interest upon mort-gages. The South, on the other hand, has attained that valua-tion on a basis of the actual rise in value and sale of the produce of the land. The annual produce not only amply pays the in-terest, but it gives a higher value to the price of slaves, which have risen to $1500 to $2000 for a good field-hand. There is no " back set" in the values thus attained, while those of the West are a wreck. In these figures for the Southern States we have also the fact, that there is personal property in those States, over and above the value of slaves, more than equal to the amount of personal in the Western States. The fact is a com-plete refutation of that assertion which has been freely circu-lated, to the effect that the South has no personal property be-

sides its blacks. The taxable valuation of the Eastern States
compare as follows:

|  | Census, 1850. | State, 1859. |
|---|---|---|
| Maine............................ | 96,799,553 | 162,472,914 |
| Massachusetts.................... | 551,106,824 | 597,936,995 |
| New Hampshire.................. | 95,251,596 | 103,804,326 |
| Vermont........................ | 72,980,483 | 86,775,213 |
| Connecticut..................... | 119,088,672 | 211,187,683 |
| Rhode Island.................... | 77,758,974 | 111,175,174 |
| New York....................... | 715,369,028 | 1,404,907,679 |
| New Jersey...................... | 153,251,619 | 179,150,000 |
| Pennsylvania.................... | 500,275,851 | 568,770,234 |
| Total........................ | $2,381,782,690 | $3,426,180,218 |
| Increase....................... | | 1,044,398,61 |

This increase has been mostly in city values. Thus, Vermont gives the official value of lands in 1859 at $69,274,600,
and in the above census table, it was given at $63,367,227,
showing that six millions only out of an aggregate increase
of 16 millions is due to lands. As a result, the nine Northern
States give an increase of 1000 millions in city and personal
property. This increase has been in the face of the vast sums
that have been sent West for investment, and the migration of
capital with settlers to that region. The South has supplied
the capital which has accumulated at the North, and which
has endowed the West with such factitious prosperity. It is
to be borne in mind that very much of the personal property of
the North escapes taxation.

It is not alone in the valuations that the increased capital at
the North manifests itself, but in banks, ships, manufacturing,
corporate companies of all descriptions, of which the figures
can be realized. If we compare the bank returns for the present year with 1850, we find the increase in capital as follows:

*Bank Capital of the United States.*

|  | **1850.** | | **1859.** | | |
|---|---|---|---|---|---|
|  | No. | Capital. | No. | Capital corporate. | Private. |
| North.............. | 516 | $121,909,000 | 934 | $261,773,830 | $94,545,000 |
| South.............. | 182 | 77,632,000 | 399 | 104,030,994 | 10,276,369 |
| West.............. | 65 | 8,675,000 | 243 | 23,171,418 | 13,204,711 |
| Total.......... | 753 | $208,216,000 | 1,576 | $388,976,242 | $118,036,080 |

The bank capital of the Union began to take a start in 1848,
having then recovered from the breakdown of the old revulsion. The increase of the capital was mostly North and East,
following the concentration of general business. The increase
at the West was on a basis of Eastern capital, sent out with a
view to control business. The private banking capital is that
as given in the report of the Secretary of the Treasury for 1856,

page 141. That capital had mostly grown up within a few years. The increase of corporate capital at the North was, in round numbers, 140 millions, and 90 millions of private, making together 230 millions employed in a business which pays 10 per cent. net upon mostly Southern connections.

The increase of tonnage at the North has been as follows:

|  | NORTH. | SOUTH. | WEST. | *Total.* |
|---|---|---|---|---|
| 1850 | 2,653.975 | 760,841 | 140,678 | 3,535,454 |
| 1859 | 3,669,115 | 1,005,852 | 374,841 | 5,049,808 |
| Increase | 1,015,140 | 245,011 | 234,163 | 1,514,354 |

The whole tonnage has increased, it appears, 1,514,354 tons; of this two-thirds, or 1,015,140, has been North and East, representing a value of $45,000,000.

The railroads have increased North and West $700,000,000, of which nearly the whole was owned in the Eastern States. That a good portion of it was lost does not take from the fact that it was there to invest.

Manufacturing capital has increased in a very rapid ratio. Thus, the census report gave the capital in New York and Massachusetts, invested in manufactures in 1850 at $188,184,697. The state census of the two States give it at $227,042,000 in 1855, an increase of 20 per cent. in five years. The same ratio would give an increase to 1859 of $142,000,000.

These items give a Northern increase of capital as follows:

| | |
|---|---|
| Banking | $232,000,000 |
| Tonnage | 45,000,000 |
| Railroads | 500,000,000 |
| Manufacturing | 142,000,000 |
| Corporate companies | 100,000,000 |
| Total | $1,019,000,000 |

This gives a round amount of capital derived from Southern business mostly, and employed in enterprises which derive a profit from the same source. This capital should pay 10 per cent., which would give 100 millions per annum. That portion of it invested in Western railroads will fall short of that income for the reason that the Western resources will not pay the investment.

The results of these figures plainly show that while the South produced vast wealth, the Northern profits have absorbed most of it. They also show that the South begins to accumulate itself. Its personal property begins to show a high figure. Its railroads and manufactures begin not only to reimburse capital but employ labor. In short, the South has commenced to make capital work at home, and, by so doing, not only to propagate itself but to attract. In addition to its strength of position and natural resources, it is rapidly gaining wealth, and by so doing, creating a defence to the operation of Northern capital. To this growing strength the folly of the North has added desire. In an early chapter of this book we gave from Judge Johnson's charge a description of the South in 1807. Contrast that with the picture we have presented in these pages, and it will appear that the South does not occupy a position to be trifled with.

---

## CHAPTER XI

### APPORTIONMENT.

At the time of the adoption of the federal constitution the condition of slaves was very different at the South from what it has since become. At that time there was, as we have shown in a previous chapter, no large branch of industry to engage the blacks, and their future fate was matter of anxiety. The progress of the cotton culture has changed that, and the interests of millions of whites now depend upon the blacks. The opinions of statesmen of that day were formed upon existing facts; could they have seen 50 years into the future their views upon black employment would have undergone an entire change. The blacks were then prospectively a burden; they are now an absolute necessity. They then threatened American civilization; they are now its support. With multiplying numbers they have added to the national wealth. They have become the instruments of political agitation, while they have conferred wealth upon the masses.

From the moment of the formation of the Federal Union there commenced a struggle for political power which has not ceased to be directed against the Slave States. The instrument of union, while it provided for the extinction of the slave-trade, which then formed so large a portion of Northern traffic, contained also a provision for black representation in the Southern States, stipulating that that representation should not be changed until 1808, and thereafter only by a vote of three-fourths of all the States. That provision has been the groundwork of that constant Northern aggression upon Southern interests which has so successfully gained on the federal power until now it imagines the desired three-fourths is within its reach, when the South, with its interests, will be at the feet of the abolitionists. The South has stood steadily on its defence, but while the circle has narrowed in upon it, the North has not ceased to clamor against Southern aggression! Like Jemmy Twitcher, in the farce, who, having robbed a passenger, loses the plunder, and exclaims, " there must be some dishonest person in the neighborhood!" The following are passages that occur in the Constitution :

### Art. I., *Clause 3d.*

" Representatives and direct taxes shall be apportioned among the several States, which may be included within this Union, according to their respective numbers, which shall be determined by adding to the whole number of free persons, including those bound to service for a term of years, and excluding Indians not taxed, three-fifths of all other persons."

### Art. I., *Section 9, 1st Clause.*

" The migration or importation of such persons as any of the States now existing shall think proper to admit shall not be prohibited by the Congress prior to 1808 ; but a tax or duty may be imposed on such importation, not exceeding $10 for each person."

### Art. V.

" The Congress, whenever two-thirds of both houses shall deem it necessary, shall propose amendments to this Constitution ; or, on the application of the Legislatures of two-thirds of the several States shall call a convention for proposing amendments, which, in either case, shall be valid to all intents and purposes as part of this Constitution, when ratified by the Legislatures of three-fourths of the several States,

" *Provided*, that no amendment which may be made prior to the year 1808 shall in any manner affect the first and fourth clauses in the ninth section of the first article."

The original 13 States that adopted this Constitution were all Slave States with the exception of Massachusetts, which, although it then held no slaves had an interest in continuing the slave-trade, in opposition to the wishes of the Slave States. The struggle in the Convention in relation to the discontinuance of the slave-trade, was between the New England States, that desired the traffic, and Virginia and Delaware that wished no more slaves, while those Southern States that had but a few blacks desired to import them without tax. On the vote New Hampshire and Massachusetts voted to continue the trade until 1808, and Virginia and Delaware voted " nay," or for its immediate discontinuance. No sooner had the Constitution been adopted, however, than the annexation of Louisiana became a necessity, in order to give an outlet to the sea for the produce

of the West, but, notwithstanding the great advantage which
the annexation was to confer upon Massachusetts, she opposed
it to the point of threatening to dissolve the Union if it was carried out. That, after the great rebellion of Shay within her
borders, was the first disunion threat, and the motive was fear
of the political increase of Southern strength. Those fears
were like all party pretences, short-sighted, since that territory
has given more Free than Slave States to the Union. This threat
of disunion was made while yet Massachusetts was engaged in
the slave-trade, that the State had voted to prolong to 1808.
The same cry was renewed in respect of Florida, and again,
with greater violence, in the case of Missouri; to be again revived in respect of Texas; and once more, with circumstances
of greater atrocity in the case of Kansas. It is remarkable
that while Free States come in without any great struggle on
the part of the South, the safety of which is threatened by each
such accession, the admission of Slave States is the signal of so
much strife, and this resistance to a manifest right of the South
is denounced as " Southern aggression."

The gradual abolition of slavery in the old Northern States,
and the rapidity with which Eastern capital, following migration,
has settled the Western States, has given a large preponderance
to the free interest in the national councils. Of the 26 senators
that sat in the first Congress, all represented a slave interest,
more or less: with the States and territories now knocking for
admission, there are 72 senators, of whom 32 only represent the
slave interest. That interest, from being " a unit" in the Senate, has sunk to a minority of four, and yet the majority do not
cease to complain of Southern " aggression." With this rapid
decline in the Southern vote in the great " conservative body,"
of the Senate, the representation in the lower house has fallen
to one-third. How long will it be before the desired three-
fourths vote, for which a large party pant, will have been obtained, and, when obtained, what will have become of those
Southern rights which are even now denied by party leaders to
be any rights at all. In the last 30 years 11 Free States have
been prepared for the Union; a similar progress in the next 30
years and the South will have fallen into that constitutional minority which may deprive it of all reserved rights. This circle is
closing rapidly in upon it, amid a continually rising cry of abolition, pointed by bloody inroads of armed men. This is called
Southern "aggression." The apportionments have been as follows:

Representation under each Census Apportionment.

| | Before census. 13 States. | 1790. 16 States. | 1800. 17 States. | 1810. 19 States. | 1820. 24 States. | 1830. 26 States. | 1840. 26 States. | 1850. 31 States. |
|---|---|---|---|---|---|---|---|---|
| Maine | .. | .. | .. | .. | 7 | 8 | 7 | 6 |
| Massachusetts ... | 8 | 14 | 17 | 20 | 13 | 12 | 10 | 11 |
| New Hampshire.. | 3 | 4 | 5 | 6 | 6 | 5 | 4 | 3 |
| Vermont ......... | .. | 2 | 4 | 6 | 5 | 5 | 4 | 3 |
| Rhode Island .... | 1 | 2 | 2 | 2 | 2 | 2 | 2 | 2 |
| Connecticut ...... | 5 | 7 | 7 | 7 | 6 | 6 | 4 | 4 |
| New York ....... | 6 | 10 | 17 | 27 | 34 | 40 | 34 | 33 |
| New Jersey...... | 4 | 5 | 6 | 6 | 6 | 6 | 5 | 5 |
| Pennsylvania .... | 8 | 13 | 18 | 23 | 26 | 28 | 24 | 25 |
| NORTH ....... | 35 | 57 | 76 | 97 | 105 | 112 | 94 | 92 |
| Delaware ........ | 1 | 1 | 1 | 2 | 1 | 1 | 1 | 1 |
| Maryland........ | 6 | 8 | 9 | 9 | 9 | 8 | 6 | 6 |
| Virginia ......... | 10 | 19 | 22 | 23 | 22 | 21 | 15 | 13 |
| North Carolina... | 5 | 10 | 12 | 13 | 13 | 13 | 9 | 8 |
| South Carolina... | 5 | 6 | 8 | 9 | 9 | 9 | 7 | 6 |
| Georgia ......... | 3 | 2 | 4 | 6 | 7 | 9 | 8 | 8 |
| Florida .......... | .. | .. | .. | .. | .. | .. | .. | 1 |
| Louisiana........ | .. | .. | .. | 1 | 3 | 3 | 4 | 4 |
| Texas ........... | .. | .. | .. | .. | .. | .. | .. | 2 |
| Alabama ......... | .. | .. | .. | .. | 3 | 5 | 7 | 7 |
| Mississippi ...... | .. | .. | .. | .. | 1 | 2 | 4 | 5 |
| Arkansas ........ | .. | .. | .. | .. | .. | .. | 1 | 2 |
| Tennessee ....... | .. | 1 | 3 | 6 | 9 | 13 | 11 | 10 |
| Kentucky ........ | .. | 2 | 6 | 10 | 12 | 13 | 10 | 10 |
| Missouri......... | .. | .. | .. | .. | 1 | 2 | 5 | 7 |
| SOUTH ....... | 30 | 53 | 65 | 79 | 90 | 100 | 88 | 90 |
| Ohio ............ | .. | .. | 1 | 6 | 14 | 19 | 21 | 21 |
| Indiana.......... | .. | .. | .. | 1 | 3 | 7 | 10 | 11 |
| Illinois .......... | .. | .. | .. | .. | 1 | 2 | 7 | 9 |
| Michigan ........ | .. | .. | .. | .. | .. | 1 | 3 | 4 |
| Wisconsin ....... | .. | .. | .. | .. | .. | .. | .. | 3 |
| Iowa ............ | .. | .. | .. | .. | .. | .. | .. | 2 |
| California........ | .. | .. | .. | .. | .. | .. | .. | 2 |
| WEST ......... | .. | .. | 1 | 7 | 28 | 29 | 41 | 52 |
| Total........ | 65 | 110 | 142 | 183 | 213 | 242 | 223 | 234 |

There are now nearly ready to come in—Kansas, Minnesota, Oregon, Washington, Nebraska, Utah, New Mexico; while the vast immigration of the last ten years, reaching over 3,500,000 souls, will have added to the Western numbers, under the supposition that the estimate of population given for each section in another chapter on population of this book is correct, and that nearly the same number of representation is returned, the representation will be: South, 81; North, 88; West, 62; giving the South less than one-third.

With this future before it, and these manifestly hostile intentions encouraged by party votes in favor of the leaders that avow them, it certainly is wise on the part of the South to seek safety in prompt remedies. It is in vain that unscrupulous party leaders deny any design ulterior to the exclusion of slavery from new territories. That pretence ever was fraudulent, since it is nature that decides the question, and has so decided it against slavery in nine original Northern slaveholding States, and will always so decide it North. Public indignation aroused by the evident dangers evoked by this partisan object, compels a denial of abolition intentions; but this denial is too evidently a mask to deceive the mass of the people. The immigration from Europe in the past few years has inured almost entirely to the benefit of the North. The census of 1850 gave the nativities of the white population; the figures are contained in a chapter upon that subject. The immigrants and their descendants number 5,000,000 souls, or one-fifth of the entire white population, and these have swollen the Free State representation; while the population of the South, as well black as white, has progressed only by natural means. It is to be borne in mind, also, that the very prosperity of the South, growing out of large crops, and higher prices for it, operates against the political extension of the section, since it tends powerfully to concentrate the population. We have shown, under the head of cotton-culture, the remarkable extension which took place during the speculative excitement, from 1830 to 1840, in the black population. The fertile lands of the great valley were then discovered to bear more cotton at less price than the Atlantic States, and that migration of blacks took place which produced so manifest a change in the slave population in the several States by the census of 1850. In the table of black population, given in the preceding chapter, of the blacks who left the Atlantic for the new States, a considerable number, when the disasters came on, were run to Texas; when that State was reannexed, these slaves again appeared in the enumeration of 1850. The effects of hat migration are very remarkable. In Delaware and Maryand the slave population fell from 106,286 in 1830, to 92,342 in 1840, a decline of 13,944 in addition to the natural increase. The free blacks in the same time increased 10,204. The census of 1850 gave a slight increase of slaves in 1850. In the State of Virginia the slaves declined over 20,000 up to 1840, but recovered 23,000 up to 1850. In the nine years that have elapsed since the census, an immense addition has been made to the cotton crop, and also to its value. Although the crop doubled from 1830 to 1840, under the spur of the speculation of those years, it remained nearly stationary in the ten years up to 1850, since then it has again doubled; that is to say, the cotton raised in the five years ending with 1860 is 17,732,307 bales, and in the five years ending with 1850 there were raised 8,951,587, or 85,434 bales less than half; at the same time the price per lb. at one time, in 1857, ranged 18 cents. Under such circumstances, the value of cotton hands reached $2,000; while they were nearly as valuable for sugar culture. It is obvious that, under such circumstances, no one can spare blacks for the settlement of new States. On the other hand, they are concentrated on the cotton lands of the old States with great rapidity, and the census of the next year will show the effects of those influences upon the local populations. The same causes that are operating to make black servitude annually more important to the world at large, are also operating against the expansion of political power in the South. It need hardly be said that concentration of population aids powerfully in the development of wealth, giving a greater impulse to manufacturing industry. By so doing, it becomes the more important for Northern and confederate States to avoid all political aggression.

The concentration of hands in the cotton States must diminish the direct interest in the Northern Slave States; but it increases their interest in slave-labor, since they possess the elements of supplanting the Northern Free States in the supply of manufactured goods to the South.

Under these circumstances, the apportionment to take place under the eighth census, to be taken this year, will indicate a concentration of blacks; but in the last decade the arrivals of emigrants from abroad have been over 3,000,000, a large portion of whom have gone West, in company with considerable numbers from the Eastern and Middle States, drawn thither by the railroad speculation, and the West will receive a vast accession of power in the lower branch of the national government. The interest of that section is less in common with the South than is the East, since the South—if it affords an outlet by the great river for Western produce—is not of itself a large customer for it. And the Northern railroads have diminished much of the importance of the Southern water courses. The Atlantic States have sought to build up a Western interest by large railroad expenditure, and it may draw its food thence in exchange for manufactures for a season or until the West manufacture for itself. The West cannot afford it commerce, or raw materials, or an extended market. The East is, therefore, the "natural ally" of the South, and the two united would without difficulty hold their own against the West.

It is to be borne in mind that the causes which, since the famine of 1846, have given so great an impulse to immigration, have now measurably ceased to operate. The condition of Ireland is reversed, and great numbers return thither every year, while the prospect of peace and renewed prosperity in Europe have operated in the past few years to check the disposition to migrate to America, and the cutting off those supplies of population will greatly affect the North.

It results that if the mere politician sees in the course of events the chance of reaching power by riding the anti-slavery hobby, he does it at the risk of concentrating Southern wealth into a powerful nation, that will be compelled to seek the safety of its present institutions in independence.

The kind of argument which is used in support of this aggressive policy, based upon violence, is beneath contempt. The French Emperor exclaimed, "The Empire is peace;" with how much greater force is it asserted that "the Union is peace," and also the converse, that "disunion is war?" When a member of the national councils, probably after dinner, exclaims that the North is too strong to permit disunion,—in other words, that it will "compel" union, no matter how hard the conditions, he gives an example of the "meeting of extremes,"—his zeal against slavery leads him to threaten the enslavement of a whole people. The North has but one interest,—it is to side earnestly with the Union, and extinguish every public man who dares to excite sectional prejudices in order to obtain votes for his own aggrandizement.

---

# CHAPTER XII.

### CONCLUSION.

In the preceding pages we have traced briefly, in several branches, the surprising progress which the U. States have made in population and wealth during the first 60 years of their existence. We have seen that the original States have increased from a valuation of $619,977,247 in 1798, to $3,899,226,347 in 1850, or thus:

|  | 1798. | 1850. |
|---|---|---|
| Valuation | $619,977,247 | $3,899,226,347 |
| Population | 5,305,925 | 23,191,879 |
| Value per head | $117 | $168 |

The real estate has improved 45 per cent. in value per head of a population that has quadrupled. The personal estate in the same period rose to $3,834,143,378, or about the same as the real estate, making an aggregate of about $336 per head of the population. Such a rate of progression cannot indicate a wrong system. The increase of wealth has been prodigious, and it has been well distributed through the Northern States. We find, however, this fact, that while the population of the North has increased less rapidly than that of either of the other sections, its wealth has increased more rapidly.

The following table presents a summary of the leading facts set forth in the preceding chapters in relation to the production and valuation of each section, with the population and area:

|  | NORTH. | WEST. | SOUTH. | *Total.* |
|---|---|---|---|---|
| White population.... | 8,626,852 | 4,900,368 | 6,222,418 | 19,749,638 |
| *Production.* |  |  |  |  |
| White hands in agriculture............ | 823,171 | 728,127 | 849,285 | 2,400,583 |
| Area, acres......... | 102,878,080 | 917,315,240 | 538,533,120 | 1,558,926,440 |
| Product agriculture.. | $295,568,699 | $246,097,028 | $528,571,103 | $1,070,236,830 |
| Hands in manufacture | 684,761 | 122,354 | 151,944 | 959,069 |
| Cotton manufacture.. | $52,062,953 | $438,900 | $9,367,331 | $61,869,184 |
| Total " .. | 715,846,142 | 138,780,537 | 164,579,937 | 1,019,106,616 |
| Exports............. | $78,217,202 | ........ | $198,389,351 | $278,392,080 |
| Tonnage............ | 3,481,436 | 373,661 | 918,092 | 4,773,189 |
| Railroads, miles...... | 8,685 | 10,706 | 8,171 | 27,562 |
| *Property.* |  |  |  |  |
| Value of animals....'. | $173,812,690 | $112,563,851 | $253,795,330 | $538,171,871 |
| Capital in manufacture | 382,366,732 | 155,883,045 | 94,995,674 | 533,245,822 |
| Value of tonnage..... | 17,407,180 | 1,868,305 | 4,590,460 | 23,865,945 |
| "  railroads.... | 451,949,410 | 298,837,647 | 221,857,503 | 972,644,560 |
| "  bank capital.. | 186,668,462 | 16,978,130 | 97,730,579 | 301,376,071 |
| "  private " .. | 94,545,000 | 13,204,711 | 10,286,369 | 118,036,080 |
| Real estate........... | 1,835,063,613 | 619,154,287 | 1,445,008,447 | 3,899,226,347 |
| Personal estate....... | 544,718,966 | 195,054,073 | 1,385,727,523 | 2,125,440,562 |
| Total........... | $3,688,532,053 | $1,413,544,049 | $3,514,074,185 | $8,616,150,287 |

The Southern valuation includes the slaves. The Northern agricultural productions include hay, which is rather an expense than a product. The valuations of real and personal estate are those of the census returns, to which the commissioners affixed a corrected value, at $7,066,562,966. Of this the Northern proportion was $380 per head; the Southern $304;

10

and the Western $200. That part of the country which had
the least natural resources accumulated the most wealth. This
has resulted from the workings of capital in aid of manufacturing and commercial industry, favored by the laws of the federal
Union. The bounties paid to fisheries, the protective tariffs,
giving to the Northern factories a monopoly of supplying the
South and West with goods; the monopoly of the carrying trade,
and the expenditure of the government revenue mostly at the
North,—these have all resulted from the operation of the federal laws, and the laws of finance governing accumulated capital, have put the whole country under contribution to that
capital. The laws of trade have, by concentrating the markets
at the North, required a periodical Northern pilgrimage, which
has enriched the cities of the East, as Mecca is supported by
the pilgrimages of the faithful. The whole surplus production
of the country has, therefore, centred at the North, making
the rich richer, and making "capital" the sole strength of the
North, as opposed to the "labor" of the South and West.
While this has been the case, a very curious change has been
going on in the population of the Northern States, as disclosed
by the census. The poor classes of native, mostly agricultural,
population, have emigrated in hundreds of thousands to the
West and South, and as many poor foreigners have filled the
space thus vacated to carry on small trades, and perform domestic service. This change is apparent in the census returns.

| | |
|---|---:|
| Population of the North in 1790................................. | 1,968,455 |
| "        "        "        1850................................. | 8,626,851 |
| Increase................................................. | 6,658,396 |
| Native Northern emigration..................... 1,428,579 | |
| Foreigners domiciled........................... 1,292,241 | |
| Excess native emigration..................... 136,338 | |

These foreigners are mostly domestic servants and artisans.
If these were deducted from the Northern aggregate population, the value of property per head would be so much the
greater. Thus the North has been dividing into a poor foreign
population and a wealthy native population. The revenues
and profits of the latter are derived from the large productions
of the South and West, both of which contribute in a different
degree to the Northern profits. The South has, however, been
by far the most productive. As we have seen, its lands and
slaves have risen annually in value, step by step with the rising

value of their productions, and the resulting wealth is reflected in the magnificence of the North.

The North has been concentrating wealth and cheap labor, thus strengthening its position as manufacturer for the Union, and paving the way for the export of a large surplus of manufactures, when the South and West shall have made further progress in supplying themselves. It has enjoyed the entire markets of the Union as a means, so to speak, of learning its trade. It has retained the whole carrying trade of the country for its shipping. It has received a bounty in high tariffs during its weakness, to defend it from importation, and it has gradually acquired strength in experience, capital, and skill. It had before it a most brilliant future, but it has wantonly disturbed that future by encouraging the growth of a political party based wholly upon sectional aggression,—a party which proposes no issues of statesmanship for the benefit of the whole country ; it advances nothing of a domestic or foreign policy tending to national profit or protection, or to promote the general welfare in any way. It simply denounces the system of labor which has conferred such prosperity upon the North, as a "moral wrong." While it disavows any intention of interfering with servitude at the South, it encourages, in every possible way, all that tends to undermine it. It enters the common national dwelling, and scatters firebrands amid the most solemn protestations of harmless intentions. It claims the right to explode mines, without being answerable for the mischief that may result. If questioned as to the object of such conduct, it replies, that it is one of its "inalienable rights" so to act, and that certain persons who have combustible materials have had the effrontery to express fears of the consequences, and therefore it is the more bound to persist. It is for such reasoning as this that the North has for more than ten years constantly allowed itself to be irritated by incendiary speakers and writers, whose sole stock in trade is the unreasoning hate against the South that may be engendered by long-continued irritating misrepresentation.

From time to time in the history of the country the attempt has been made to acquire party strength by stirring up slumbering passions, and these attempts have always been made under the cloak of philanthropy. These attempts have generally failed, but their repetition, with greater violence, from time to time, has warped the truth in relation to the real position of the Federal government in regard to the blacks, until the monstrous doctrine has acquired strength, that one species of property, recognized by the Federal Constitution, is without protection on Federal soil! Thus, the speech of William H. Seward, Esq., in the national Senate, on the 29th of February, laying down the platform of the party of which he is the chief, remarked:

"The fathers authorized Congress to make all needful rules and regulations concerning the management and disposition of the public lands, and to admit new States. So the Constitution, while it does not disturb or affect the system of capital in slaves, existing in any State under its own laws, does, at the same time, *recognize every human being, when within any exclusive sphere of Federal jurisdiction, not as capital, but as a person.*

"What was the action of the fathers in Congress? They admitted the new States of the Southwest as capital States, because it was practically impossible to do otherwise, and by the ordinance of 1787, confirmed in 1789, they provided for the organization and admission of only labor States in the Northwest. They directed fugitives from service to be restored, not as chattels, but as persons. They awarded naturalization to immigrant free laborers, and they prohibited the trade in African labor. This disposition of the whole subject was in harmony with the condition of society, and, in the main, with the spirit of the age. The seven Northern States contentedly became labor States by their own acts. The six Southern States with equal tranquillity, and by their own determination, remained capital States."

We have italicized the lines which contain the erroneous assumption to which we have alluded. The spirit of the assertion therein contained is contradicted in the succeeding lines, which claims that Congress conferred slavery upon six States, and prohibited it in seven—in a part of which it had existed before the territory became the property of the Union. Since the only powers possessed by the Constitution are those especially delegated to it, the exercise of the power on the part of Congress to "confer" involves that of "exclusion." If it has power over any subject at all, it has the affirmative as well as the negative. It is, however, with the first assertion that we have now to deal, viz., that the Constitution recognizes blacks only as "persons." This assertion is contrary to both the law and the fact. At the time of the formation of the Federal Constitution, the law of nations recognized lawful property in African slaves throughout the civilized world. In this country, they had been so held in every part of it from its earliest settlement. No colony was without owners of black property, and none doubted the legality of the holding. It was about that date that the agitators in England began to question the humanity of the negro, and to seek to raise him to the level of the white. With this experimental idea, necessarily was born the doubt of the right to hold him as property. England was then beginning that experiment in humanizing blacks that has ended so disastrously, and which so clearly demonstrates the fallacy of the theory of black equality. It was not surprising that the generous-hearted of our own statesmen should have adopted the seductive, but untried theory, and hesitate about the rightfulness of "holding property in man." Nevertheless, the fact of the property in negroes existed, and the Constitution was framed in the recognition of it. It has since been attempted to dispute whether the Con-. stitution recognized the blacks as property, or as persons *only.* The generally received opinion, when the Constitution was adopted, was that it recognized blacks as "property" only. The ultra men of that day contended that the Constitution regarded them as something more than property, raising them to the level of "moral persons." Gradually ultra men denied that they are property at all under the Constitution. Mr. Seward and his party are of those who contend for the latter, thus reversing the judgment which was held by the men who made the Constitution. If we go back to the highest contemporaneous authority, we find Mr. Jay, in the *Federalist*, states it as follows:

" We must deny the fact that slaves are considered merely as property, and in no respect whatever as persons. The true state of the case is, that they partake of both these qualities, being considered by our laws in some respects as persons, and in other respects as property. In being compelled to labor, not for himself, but for a master; in being vendible by one master to another master; and in being subject at all times to be restrained in his liberty and chastised in his body, by the capricious will of his owner; the slave may appear to be degraded from the human rank, and classed with those irrational animals which fall under the legal denomination of property. In being protected, on the other hand, in his life and in his limbs, against the violence of all others, even the master of his labor and his liberty; and in being punishable himself for all violence committed against others; the slave is no less evidently regarded by the law as a member of the society, not as a part of the irrational creation; as a moral person, not as a mere article of property. The Federal Constitution, therefore, decides with great propriety on the case of our slaves, when it views them in the mixed character of persons and property. This is, in fact, their true character; it is the character bestowed on them by the laws under which they live, and it will not be disputed that these are the proper criterion."

This was the view of Mr. Jay in opposition to those who at that day contended that slaves were property *merely*. There is a long stride from that position to the present assertion of the "Black Republicans," that slaves are "persons *merely*." The progress of this aggression upon the South and Southern rights in property is thus very clear. The Constitutional "property" view of the black position was not left to be a barren idea; but under this view of "property" in blacks, Congress proceeded to act. A law was passed March 2, 1807, of which the 9th and 10th sections provide in substance as follows: "That the captain of any vessel of more than forty tons burden, sailing coastwise from one port of the United States to another, having on board persons of color, to be transported in order to be sold or disposed of as slaves, shall make out and subscribe duplicate manifests, describing those slaves, and shall, with the owner or master, swear that they are not held to service or labor contrary to any law of the United States, or of the State."

The 9th section goes on to provide that the Collector shall thereupon grant a *permit* to the master, authorizing him to transport these slaves to the port where they are to be unladen, and forfeits any vessel departing without the manifest.

Section 10th provides—"That the master of every vessel having on board persons of color, to sell or dispose of as slaves, shall, upon arriving at his port of destination, before *unlading* these persons, exhibit a copy of the manifest to the Collector." And the penalty for a refusal by the master of a ressel, laden as aforesaid, to deliver the manifest to the Collector, is fixed at ten thousand dollars.

The laws of the United States have thus lawfully placed the slave on board a vessel of the United States,—have provided in what manner he shall be lawfully embarked,—in what manner he shall be landed at the port of destination,—regulating the trade altogether in the manner of "property," and that on the high seas under the national flag.

The object of the law thus regulating the transportation of black property, had special reference to the safety of that property in positions where it might be imperilled, viz., on the high seas, out of the jurisdiction of the State, but under the national flag. The idea had, probably, not then been broached, that the property of American citizens could be imperilled on the soil of the common country, by persons, who, having abandoned their own similar "property," might seek to destroy that of their neighbors.

We find, in a contemporaneous history, a debate which took place Jan. 2, 1799, during the administration of John Adams, and which throws some light on the views of Northern legislators of that day upon the same subject. On the day mentioned, Mr. Waln, of Philadelphia, presented a petition, praying for "a revision of the laws of the United States relative to the slave-trade; of the act relative to fugitives from justice; and for the adoption of such measures as should in due time emancipate the whole of their brethren from their disagreeable situation."

Mr. Rutledge opposed the petition. "The gentlemen," said he, "who formerly used to advocate liberty, have retreated from their post, and committed the important trust to the care of "black patriots;" they tell the house they are in slavery: thank God they are. They say they are not represented: certainly they are not; and I trust the day will never arrive when the Congress of the United States will display a parti-colored assembly. Too much of this new-fangled French philosophy of liberty and equality has found its way among these gentlemen of our plantations, for which nothing will do but liberty."

"Harrison G. Otis, of Massachusetts, brought forward his usual eloquence on this occasion. He said that though he possessed no slaves, he saw no reason why others might not; and that the proprietors of them were the fittest persons, and not Congress, to regulate that species of property."

Mr. Thatcher, to the surprise of many, differed from his countryman, and thought the petitions for black men deserved equal consideration with those for whites."

" Mr. Brown, of Rhode Island, argued that the petition was but the contrivance of a combination of Jacobins, who had troubled Congress for many years past, and he feared never would cease. He begged, therefore, that the gentleman who put the petition on the table, might be desired to take it back again. He was truly sorry to see such a dangerous paper supported by such a worthy member of the House, and good Federalist, as Mr. Thatcher."

This incident is curious, since it shows that the " Black Patriots," of 1799—a " combination of Jacobins," who " never would cease troubling Congress"—are the Black Republicans of the present day, still troubling it. While Mr. Thatcher, " a good Federalist," was the only one advocating the " troubling," Mr. Harrison Gray Otis referred the " property" to its " proprietors." The " Federalist" party, of which Mr. Thatcher was a " good one," also passed, in the Massachusetts Legislature, the resolution to " dissolve the Union," if Louisiana should be annexed. That party has " dissolved" on the occasion of every new Slave State added to the Union since the annexation, no matter what " name" the party may have assumed for the moment. The free-territory question has ever been revived when it was thought useful to " defeat the Democrats," which seems to have been its leading principle on all occasions, and at the present moment its " sole" principle.

John Adams was a shoemaker in Braintree, Mass. When out of his time he studied law, on the advice of his uncle, a schoolmaster. He became, after the Revolution, the leader.of the monarchal party, and his leading idea was " hereditary rulers ;" and through his influence the alien and sedition laws were enacted. The former gave the executive absolute power over foreigners who arrived, and they were imprisoned and expelled for no reason but the will of the executive. The law of Congress in relation to the importation of such persons as any other States chose to admit until 1808, was held to apply only to negroes ; hence the alien law, originated by that founder of the party now known as the Black Republican party, was allowed to operate against whites.

There was but one idea at that time in the country. All the States of the Union, the Federal Constitution, the laws of Congress, the popular mind, and the theories of legislators, all acknowledged property in slaves, and, as an inevitable consequence, that the "property" was as much entitled to protection under the national flag, or on the federal soil, as any other possession. The slave-owner, with his property embarked upon the high seas, had, by express statute, the national flag, as an ægis, thrown around him, to protect him from both the foreign and domestic assailant; and yet we are told that if he walked forth on the open prairie—on the national soil, owned by the common government and regulated by its laws—that he was therein without recognition, and without protection; that his property is the prey of the spoiler; his civil rights lost in the mire of free-soilism, and his complaints the derision of those who there hold other property under laws that are nugatory for him! The doctrine is monstrous, and born only of a desperate party faction, which seeks power by any means, no matter how dangerous, disreputable, or deceitful. The territories of the government are said not to be States, but become so only when a sufficient number of persons shall have settled to entitle them to admission. The first settlers, it is said, carry into a new territory the laws of the States they have left, and their affairs are so governed until a territorial Legislature shall have devised laws that are subject to the revision of Congress. It is, then, very clear that settlers upon new territory—not being in any State, but having one before them in the future—are in their passage from one State to another, and slave property is under the special protection of Congress in such circumstances. If, when the new State shall have been formed, a majority abolish slavery in the exercise of State sovereignty, as the Northern States have done, the loss will fall upon the owner, he having passed without the protecting influence of the Federal laws.

That protection to Southern "property," recognized in the Constitution as such, when on Federal soil outside of the States, is the only offset that the South possesses to the special advantages conferred on Northern interests and industry during 70 years past. The fisheries of the North, as we have seen, received nearly $13,000,000 hard cash—two-thirds paid to Massachusetts. The Northern manufactures have been protected by a duty which has laid all Southern consumers of Northern goods under tribute to the manufacturers, and Northern shipping has had a monopoly of carrying, by virtue of laws which exclude foreign ships from the coasting trade.  In return for those special advantages, all the South has claimed is the constitutional protection to her property under the national flag, and that has been denied.  With these facts patent to the world, Mr. Seward, in his late speech, had the effrontery to ask:

" What are the excuses for these menaces?  They resolve themselves into this, That the Republican party in the North is hostile to the South.  But it already is proved to be a majority in the North; it is, therefore, practically the people of the North.  Will it not still be the same North that has forborne with you so long, and conceded to you so much?  Can you justly assume that affection, which has been so complying, can all at once change to hatred, intense and inexorable ?"

Truly, a forbearing and conceding party that has been!  In the same sense, the speaker denied that the party is sectional.  In his view of it, it certainly is not.  If the Republicans can have the whole, and govern the whole, they go in for the whole ;—there is no " sectionality" in that.  If they cannot have the whole, they will ruin the whole; and no one will perceive sectionality in that.

The Constitution also provides that slaves who escape into other States " shall, in consequence of no laws or regulations therein, be discharged from such service or labor, but shall be delivered up."  Pursuant to this, a fugitive-slave law was one of the first passed by Congress, and its operation was continued down to the adoption, by the " old Federalist party," of the English anti-slavery sentiments, on the strength of which they have become the " Black Republican" party.  By this party, armed resistance was offered to the execution of the Federal law, affording an illustration of the following clause from Washington's Farewell Address:

" The Constitution, which at any time exists till changed by an explicit and authentic act of the whole people, is sacredly obligatory upon all.  The very idea of the power and the right of the people to establish government presupposes the duty of of every individual to obey the established government.

" All obstructions to the execution of the laws; all combinations and associations, under whatever plausible character, with the real design to direct, control, counteract, or awe the regular deliberation and action of the constituted authorities, are destructive of this fundamental principle, and of fatal tendency.  They serve to organize faction, to give it an artificial and extraordinary force, to put in the place of the delegated will of the nation the will of a party, often a small but artful and enterprising minority of the community; and, according to the alternate triumphs of different parties, to make the pub-lic administration the mirror of the ill-concerted and incon-gruous projects of faction, rather than the organ of consistent and wholesome plans, digested by common councils, and modi-fied by mutual interests.

" However combinations or associations of the above de-scription may now and then answer popular ends, they are likely, in the course of time and things, to become potent engines by which cunning, ambitious, and unprincipled men will be enabled to subvert the power of the people, and to usurp for themselves the reins of government; destroying, afterwards, the very engines which had lifted them to unjust dominion."

The clear rays of Washington's sagacity thus, at a distance of 54 years, accurately photographed the " Black Republican" party. There is nothing wanting but to add the names of Seward, Sumner, and Smith, to John Brown, Beecher, and Brotherhood, to make it perfect. The party that these persons represent and illustrate is, on its face, a bald sham. It pro-fesses to respect the rights of sovereign States, and to have no intention of interfering with the institution of slavery within them. The chief of the party, in his recent speech in the National Senate, stated :

" The choice of the nation is now between the Democratic party and the Republican party. Its principles and policy are, therefore, justly and even necessarily examined. I know of only one policy which it has adopted or avowed, namely, the saving of the Territories of the United States, if possible, by constitutional and lawful means, from being homes for slavery and polygamy."

This " one policy adopted" is, it appears, to save Territories from the institution of slavery. The last word in the quotation indicates the late mission of Mr. Seward's editor to Utah. In relation to the States the speaker remarked :

" But we do not seek to force, or even to intrude, our system on you. We are excluded justly, wisely, and contentedly from all political power and responsibility in your capital States. You are sovereigns on the subject of slavery within your own borders, as we are on the same subject within our borders. It is well and wisely so arranged. Use your authority to maintain what system you please. We are not distrustful of the result. We have wisely, as we think, exercised ours to protect and perfect the manhood of the members of the State. The whole sovereignty upon domestic concerns within the Union is divided between us by unmistakable boundaries. You have your fifteen distinct parts; we eighteen parts, equally distinct. Each must be maintained in order that the whole may be preserved. If ours shall be assailed, within or without, by any enemy, or for any cause, and we shall have need, we shall expect you to defend it. If yours shall be so assailed, in the emergency, no matter what the cause or the pretext, or who the foe, we shall defend your sovereignty as the equivalent of our own. We cannot, indeed, accept your system of capital or its ethics. That would be to surrender and subvert our own, which we esteem to be better. Besides, if we could, what need for any division into States at all? You are equally at liberty to reject our system and its ethics, and to maintain the superiority of your own by all the forces of persuasion and argument. We must, indeed, mutually discuss both systems. All the world discusses all systems. Especially must we discuss them, since we have to decide as a nation which of the two we ought to ingraft on the new and future States growing up in the great public domain. Discussion, then, being unavoidable, what could be more wise than to conduct it with mutual toleration and in a fraternal spirit?"

The question of slavery in Territories settles itself according to the adaptation of the soil to slave-labor. This is not a matter of sentiment or surmise, it is simply a matter of experience and history. The whole of the Northern Free States were once "the homes of slavery." They all possessed that "property," and they all gradually abandoned it as of no practical value. This process is now going on in the Northern Slave States. We have seen in the table, page 120, that the free negroes in Delaware were as 1 to 2 of the slaves in 1790, and as 9 to 1 in 1850. In Maryland the free blacks were to the slaves, in 1790, as 1 to 13; and in 1850 they were as 1 to 1$\frac{1}{4}$. In Virginia they rose from 1 to 20 to 1 to 8$\frac{1}{2}$. Nine States holding slaves in 1709 abolished the institution within 30 years of that date. The reason for doing so was not philanthropic nor yet political, but simply a matter of dollars and cents. Slave-labor in that region was not worth having. This economical principle it is which governs slavery in the Territories. Slavery will not go on to any of the present unappropriated Territory of the nation, for the reason that it would not be profitable to go there. If it should do so it would be certain to lose. Because the future States would abolish the institution on account of its inutility; and would, like Ohio, Illinois, Indiana, and Minnesota, forbid blacks from coming in at all, either bond or free. These are fixed and well-known principles ; and when a party of political hucksters profess only " one policy," that of keeping slavery out by virtue of their acts, they profess only a bald sham, which is an insult to the intelligence of the people whose votes they seek. As well might a party of political traders point to the influx and efflux of the tide, and pretend that their efforts alone prevent the farm-lands of the Atlantic from being drowned at each recurring flood. Barefaced as would be such an assumption, it is not more baseless than the pretence that Kansas was " saved to freedom" by Brown and Beecher. There is no man of intelligence who does not know that if Kansas had been made a Slave State, and any number of slaves had been carried into it, that a very short time only would elapse before those slaves would have been emancipated by State laws, and consequently "freedom" would have gained instead of losing. If, then, we are to believe the assertion of the Black Republican leader, the " one policy" only " of which he knows" is a gross deception. It has no practical force or meaning beyond its use, as a means of irritating the popular mind, in order to turn votes to the party, on the strength of that exasperation ; yet he denominates this sham " the great national issue between free labor and capital labor for the territories," that parties are " conducting to its proper solution."

Notwithstanding these disclaimers of the leader in the part of " moderator," seeking to retain those partisans who see more danger than profit in the gratuitous agitation of this deceptive issue, the active partisans are earnest in their deifications of John Brown, and virulent in their hatred of the South.

Mr. Seward himself seems to have been as unfortunate in his partnership with John Brown as he was with the Auburn rumseller during the Temperance campaign in New York. In the latter case he put $2000 capital into partnership to sell "paints, oils," &c., but his zealous, money-making " young partner" construed the " &c." into champagne and " fine old brandies." Mr. Seward, in his published apology, elicited by public surprise, stated that he had been overreached by his partner in drawing the papers, and could not now help himself. History does not record whether he pocketed the profits on the champagne and brandies, but the chances are that he did. The North Carolina teacher, and shrewd New York lawyer and apostle of temperance, was turned into a rumseller by the will of a journeyman painter. In the Free-soil business he was not more fortunate. He went into business with John Brown, to deal in freedom, &c., in Kansas. John Brown, however, having got possession of his stock in trade, construed the " &c." into invading Virginia, to rob and slaughter the whites, and stampede the negroes. Mr. Seward is again in a dilemma with his " young partner." John Brown's strong doctrine is as objectionable as the Auburn partner's strong drink, and he is compelled to repudiate John Brown to satisfy the temperate people, although the partnership continues by contract, and the profits will accrue in due time to the poor, victimized " sleeping partner."

The system of irritation against the South has long been a staple for Eastern agitation. Under the laws of the United States blacks are not citizens. It is only of late years that the attempt has been made to enforce that attribute of citizenship upon them. The Western States, on their formation, nearly all of them as we have seen, enacted laws excluding blacks from their territories, and their right to do so has never been disputed, although, as citizens, the blacks could not legally have been excluded. The Southern States have done the same thing in many cases, and the coast States, where vessels navigate between the North and the South, found it necessary to restrain such free blacks as came from the North in the capacity of seamen, while in Southern ports. Thus, under the law passed by Ohio, a vessel from Buffalo with a free negro in it, would be subjected to $500 fine, and other punishment. A vessel arriving at Charleston, S. C., from Boston, with a free negro in it, would only be required to restrain the negro of his liberty until the vessel sailed.

The Free State law was much more severe than the Slave State law, and neither treated the black as a citizen. Massachusetts, however, never took any notice of the conduct of the Western States, but picked a quarrel with South Carolina because they restrained a " Massachusetts citizen" of his liberty. Every art was used in Boston to inflame the public mind against the "infamous" conduct of South Carolina, and Mr. Hoar was sent thither as a commissioner from Massachusetts, to bully South Carolina into repealing their laws, without success. The United States courts have long decided that blacks are not citizens, and it was as well known before Mr. Hoar's mission as afterwards. The effect was, however, to sustain excitement for party purposes, and with success. Mr. Sumner owes his political rise simply to those factious irritations, and it was to pander to those puerile and baseless passions, causelessly excited, that he made that famous speech, defamatory of South Carolina, which drew on him the wrath of Preston Brooks. The people of South Carolina no more enacted those laws for regulating the blacks out of hostility to Massachusetts, than Illinois and Indiana did when they enacted more severe laws of the same nature. She exercised her sovereign right of regulating her affairs in her own way, and the attempt of Massachusetts to coerce her into relinquishing her sovereign rights may be taken, possibly, for one of those concessions and forbearances which the "Black Republican" leader boasts of in the national Senate. A party that rests only on the fruition of such animosities, so industriously sown among different classes of the people during so many years, and avowing but "one policy," which is to concentrate these animosities on so transparent a flam as the saving territory to freedom by law, can have but one real object, that is, official spoils, at all and every hazard.

It is not alone the unfavorable nature of territorial soil which checks that expansion of black labor, because there are now vast tracts of lands in Slave States altogether unoccupied. It is that the black force is altogether inadequate to the work before it. The civilized world is pressing upon that small force of blacks with an ever-increasing demand for that material which they alone can produce. Under that demand the price of the product rises, and the value of the hand swells annually in amount. As a consequence every straggler is turned into the fields, to add ten more bales to the annual crop. If we turn back to the chapter on the cotton culture we find the following facts:

| | Crop, bales. | No. slaves. | Slaves per bale. |
|---|---|---|---|
| 1800 | 35,000 | 857,095 | 24 |
| 1820 | 509,158 | 1,524,580 | 3 |
| 1830 | 870,415 | 2,005,471 | $2\frac{1}{4}$ |
| 1840 | 2,177,532 | 2,486,226 | $1\frac{1}{8}$ |
| 1850 | 2,796,796 | 3,204,051 | $1\frac{1}{8}$ |
| 1860 | 4,500,000 | 4,000,000 | $\frac{9}{10}$ |

Thus the demand for cotton has gone on to increase from one bale for 24 blacks, to 26 bales for 24 blacks, and the price rises on this demand. The concentration of hands upon that labor is immense. In all directions of the South the hands are moving to a common point—the cotton-fields. In a recent publication by John C. Abbott, Esq., describing a voyage from Cuba, through New Orleans to New York, he remarks:

"When the De Soto was made fast to the levee, the wide and extended plateau was thronged with laborers, but they were nearly all Germans or Irish. Rarely could I see a dark skin. It was the same in the streets as we drove through them. Upon speaking of this to a very intelligent gentleman, he observed that the slaves were becoming so exceedingly profitable upon the plantations that large numbers had been sold from the city for that purpose."

It is not the cotton alone that demands the slave-labor, but sugar, tobacco, and other interests require growing numbers of hands, for which there is no source of supply but natural increase. It is not, therefore, a matter of surprise that the blacks should be taken from the non-productive employments of the cities, and made to furnish the present profitable productions. The North exhibits a contrast to this—while the cities are over-run with poor who find no employment, the West is destitute of hands for harvest. It is in vain that the papers preach to the " free laborers" the importance and benefits of farm labor. They cling to the cities, crowd tenement houses, and raise numbers of pauper children, which in New York, to some extent, are collected in benevolent institutions, sent West, and "bound out" to farmers for some years. Thus, on a small scale goes on at the North what is found so generally necessary at the South.

The concentration of the blacks upon plantations leaves a vacancy in the cities that is now being supplied, to some extent, with Irish and Germans. It is obvious, however, that with the rising value of the black hands, and the necessity of their continued industry, under the imperative demands of the civilized world, that there is little room for the occupation of new States, least of all such as those of Kansas, and others not adapted to the cotton culture. It may probably require three times the number of hands that now exist to cultivate the available cotton lands in the present States, and this supply, at the rate of progress now going on, will not be reached in 70 years, by natural means, while the demand upon them for produce will, in all probability, grow faster than their own numbers. In other words, their value will continue to rise. In this view, there is no chance of extended removals to new States. It is true, at this moment a considerable removal is going on from Florida to the cotton lands of the valley; but it is not important in a general view. The migration that took place formerly into new lands was when the employment of blacks was not so profitable as now, and the richer lands of the Mississippi afforded greater inducements. That will not be repeated, since the richest lands are occupied, and lack of hands only prevents a more extended cultivation of them. These general facts show conclusively how absurd it is to pretend that the planters, with their blacks so lucratively employed, would abandon these occupations to migrate into a new State, where there are no cotton lands, and which are not adapted to slave labor, for the sole purpose of an ephemeral recognition of slavery under the prospective State laws. Yet this is the *ignis fatuus* held up by the Black Republican agitators, to bias the popular mind. This puerile chimera is the "one policy" for which the North is driven to forego its position, its profits, and prosperity. It is goaded by specious falsehoods into distrust and hatred of the South, which asks simply to have its independent rights respected, while it supplies materials, business, and wealth to the North.

Among the great privileges that the North has enjoyed at the expense of the South has been the operation of the protective tariff revenues. The South, with the full knowledge of their injurious operation, consented to their imposition from purely patriotic motives, as a sacrifice laid upon the national altar. It has ever been watchful of the progress of the Union, and alternately leaned to the side of the Federation when it was too weak, and to that of the States when it was too strong. The Constitution of the Federal States provided that the Federal Government, while it had the right to levy direct taxes upon all the property of the country for its own use, also conferred upon it the exclusive right to levy taxes upon imports. This right has been the surest bond of union. The taxes laid under it were originally for revenue purposes only. The manufactures of the country were unimportant, and New England interests being commercial, free trade was the rule, and very low duties were imposed. It followed, as a matter of course, that that resource of revenue failed altogether in times of embargo and war, while these circumstances gave an impulse to manufactures. At the peace of 1815, the government was $120,000,000 in debt; its revenues were small; its credit not great, and the effort to raise money by direct taxation brought it in conflict with the States in many respects. Instead of employing its own tax-gatherers, it apportioned the amount upon the States, and it was then at their mercy to pay or not; there were no means of enforcing payment. In this state of affairs the government became very weak, and was in danger of falling to pieces. It was then that Mr. Calhoun came forward and devised a tariff, which not only gave large revenues to the government, making it independent of the States, and enabling it to pay off its debt—$10,000,000 per annum—but gave great protection to manufactures. He devised what was called the *minimum* system, by which merchandise was to pay *ad valorem* down to a certain point, below which the duty should not fall. Thus, cottons were to pay 20 per cent. duty as long as the duty amounted to more than six cents per yard; but the duty was not to be less than six cents. This was the great boon to New England (which repaid South Carolina subsequently by picking a quarrel with her on the negro question) manufacturers, as well as a great and indispensable aid to the Federal government, but a great sacrifice to the South, where the consumers of goods were to pay the duty—nevertheless, it was a tribute to patriotism; but Mr. Seward numbers it among the "concessions" of the North to the South. Mr. Calhoun received unmeasured abuse for his pains from the North, where the interests were then navigation, and Daniel Webster was the great apostle of free trade. A very few years served to make those two statesmen change places. Under Mr. Calhoun's tariff, the New England manufacturers prospered rapidly; that interest came to predominate over the commercial interest, and became clamorous for more protection. Daniel Webster accordingly became a protectionist in 1824, and the tariff was raised. Success stimulated cupidity, and the "black tariff" of 1828 marked the growth of abuse. The power of the Eastern manufacturers had become prodigious; the Federal debt was nearly paid off; the finances redundant, and power was rapidly concentrated at the expense of the States. The tendency of the Federation, which had been centrifugal in 1815, had become alarmingly centripetal in 1830. It was then that Mr. Calhoun again stepped forth. He stated that the South had cheerfully paid the enormous burden of duties on imports when Northern manufacturers were young, and the government weak; they had continued to pay them sixteen years; the manufacturers had become rich, the government strong—so strong that State rights were being merged into its overshadowing power; he therefore demanded a recognition of State rights, and an amelioration of those burdens that the South had so long borne. To the gallant resistance of South Carolina, under his lead, the country owes the compromise tariff of 1832 by Henry Clay. It was thus that Mr. Calhoun supported the government when it was too weak, and opposed it when it was too strong.

The manufactures at the North had become firmly established under the high duties, and did not flourish the less under the reduction, the more so that prices rose steadily under the financial inflation of the country. By the compromise of Mr. Clay, the duties were to undergo biennial reduction, until a common level of 20 per cent. should be reached on all goods in 1842. Before that year financial revulsion made more revenue necessary for the welfare of the Union, and the South again assented to an increase in import duties, making another of Mr. Seward's "concessions of the South."

The idea of "concessions" to the South, seems to have been born of a most extraordinary degree of effrontery on the part of political agitators. As we have seen, from universal slave owning and slave trading, with a general recognition of blacks as "property," and property only, there has been a gradual aggression upon that institution. The blacks were first claimed as persons as well as property, then as persons only, then as citizens of a State, and finally as citizens of the United States. Their condition of slavery was gradually abolished at the North, within the States that owned them, and then their presence on the common soil of the Union was denied, and the abolition of the institution at the seat of the Federal Government was clamored for. All the territory is now claimed as exempt from slavery, and the abolition of slavery by force in the States where it has always existed, is so far favored by a class, as to require the most earnest denials from the leaders of the Republican party that it is part of their platform. In face of this denial, however, the writers of the party favor the meas-

ure, and applaud the overt acts of the John Browns among
zealous adherents. While "ideas" have been thus increasing,
by aggression upon Southern rights the political power of the
South has been greatly curtailed, and that process of curtail-
ment is now going on in the double ratio of the expansion of
the Free States and the concentration of the Slave States, as
a consequence of the enhanced value of the blacks. Every aggression made upon Southern rights and equality before the
law, has been accompanied by louder pretences of "concessions" to the South. The mere existence of the present party,
based upon hostility to the institutions of that section, is an ir-
refragable proof of the extent to which Northern aggresssion
is carried. The extent to which partisan feeling has been
carried, manifests itself in the attempts that have been made
to deprive new States of some of those sovereign rights which
were reserved to the States on the formation of the government. Thus, the power over slavery was distinctly reserved to
the several States, each within its own territory. Any State
had the power to abolish or continue, or establish slavery at its
own will and pleasure, and the Northern States generally exercised the right to abolish. When Missouri presented herself
for admission into the Union, party spirit, running very high,
sought to deprive her of that sovereign right enjoyed by all
other States, and to admit her only as a vassal to the old States,
by compelling her to forego her right to slavery. That was a
long stride towards consolidation of power in the Federal Government. All the parties to the Constitution were free and independent; each enjoyed full sovereignty, except in regard to
those powers delegated to the government formed by the Constitution. The government was a sort of joint-stock company,
into which political capital was contributed by each State, and
it possessed no more capital, or power, than had been so contributed. When a new State presented itself for admission, a
new partner to the concern, it was required to throw away one
of its political powers, without conferring it upon the Federal
Government. The Constitution says, "all powers not conferred
upon the Federal Government are reserved to the States."
Missouri was required to forego its sovereignty over slavery,
and, by so doing, become inferior in sovereign powers to the
other States. That act of abnegation would not, however, confer the abandoned power upon the Federal Government. It
would make the State weaker, and the Federation no stronger.

This attempt was resisted, and abandoned, and the abandonment was called a " concession" to the South. If Congress had a right to call upon one new State to forfeit a reserved power in respect of slavery, it might demand the abandonment of any other, and new States might thus be stripped of all reserved powers.

The mode of Northern " concession" shows itself in the disposition of the Territory of Louisiana, on the occasion of the admission of Missouri into the Union. That territory was all slave territory. The North demanded a division of it, so that the northern half should become free. The South assented. New territory being afterwards acquired, the South proposed a division again, and the North refused the South any share of it. This is called a " concession" of the North.

While the institution of the South has been thus pressed by Northern agitators, it was necessary that they should set up some pretence to account for the manifest injustice of their course. Accordingly, we find the leader of the Black Republican party framing the following theory :

" In the field of federal politics, slavery, deriving unlooked-for advantages from commercial changes, and energies unforseen from the facilities of combination between members of the slaveholding class, and between that class and other property classes, early rallied, and has at length made a stand, not merely to retain its original defensive position, but to extend its sway throughout the whole Union. It is certain that the slave-holding class of American citizens indulge this high ambition, and that they derive encouragement for it from the rapid and effective political successes which they have already obtained. The plan of operation is this: By continued appliances of patronage, and threats of disunion, they will keep a majority favorable to these designs in the Senate, where each State has an equal representation. Through that majority they will defeat, as they best can, the admission of Free States, and secure the admission of Slave States. Under the protection of the Judiciary, they will, on the principle of the Dred Scott case, carry slavery into all the territories of the United States now existing and hereafter to be organized. By the action of the President and the Senate, using the treaty-making power, they will annex foreign slaveholding States. In a favorable conjuncture they will induce Congress to repeal the act of 1808, which prohibits the foreign slave-trade, and so they will import from Africa, at the cost of only $20 a head, slaves enough to fill up the interior of the continent. Thus, relatively increasing the number of Slave States, they will allow no amendment to the Constitution prejudicial to their interest; and so, having permanently established their power, they expect the Federal Judiciary to nullify all State laws which shall interfere with internal or foreign commerce in slaves. When the Free States shall be sufficiently demoralized to tolerate these designs, they reasonably conclude that slavery will be accepted by those States themselves."

The reader might laugh at the barefaced effrontery that put such statements as these before an assemblage of men accustomed to think for themselves, if it were not for the gravity of the designs disguised under them. We have seen how rapidly Free States have been admitted, while every Slave State encountered fierce opposition at the threshold, until the latter have fallen into a hopeless minority. The world knows that slavery goes only where it is profitable, yet we are told that the owners will carry slaves where they will be valueless. We are told that the owners of blacks worth $2000 each will degrade the value to $20, for the purpose of sending them where they will be of no value; and finally, that the States which have already possessed and abolished slavery as of no value, will be induced to resume it! Such is the fog raised in order to cloak the treasonable aggression which is meditated. The idea of importing, at $20 per head, slaves enough to fill up the interior of the continent, is certainly a great stretch of a very sanguine imagination, and one attractive to ship-owners.

The above remarks were made by Mr. Seward at Rochester, Oct. 25, 1858. In the same speech he announced the "irrepressible conflict." That announcement we may compare with a paragraph in his speech in the United States Senate, Feb. 29, 1860.

| *October*, 1858. | *February*, 1860. |
|---|---|
| It is an irrepressible conflict between opposing and enduring forces, and it means that the United States must and will, sooner or later, become either entirely a slaveholding nation, or entirely a free-labor nation. | "The whole sovereignty upon domestic concerns within the Union is divided between us by unmistakable boundaries;" "you have your fifteen distinct parts; we eighteen. parts, equally distinct. Each must be maintained, in order that the whole may be preserved." |

There is a very remarkable change in the views here entertained.

The great question that now agitates the old world is the supply of labor for the colonies. The fact is rapidly developing itself, that future commerce, if it increase at all, must depend, not on the exchange of goods between manufacturing nations, but on the exchange of goods by manufacturing nations with those which produce raw materials and tropical products. Coffee, sugar, cotton, cocoa, which are articles of tropical production, have become very necessary for the comfort of the inhabitants of temperate climates and manufacturing countries. These articles have hitherto been produced by slave-labor. The operation of production was disturbed by the experiment of emancipation. At the moment the demand for those articles was receiving its greatest development, the production was stopped by the emancipation of the cultivators. This was done because it was firmly believed that the free black would work. That belief was erroneous. The utmost efforts have since been made to " supply labor." For this purpose the Coolie trade has been mostly resorted to; but, conducted under a system more atrocious than the African slave-trade, it is quite inadequate to the object. It has succeeded, in the British West India Islands, only in maintaining a certain extent of production. In the Mauritius, the facilities for procuring Coolies have been great, and 142,534 are there employed, but the supply is quite insufficient. This is the case to a much greater extent in the West Indies, where the distance of transport increases the difficulty. England has obtained but about 50,000 Coolies for her colonies, and the supply drags. She has used every effort to increase the supply of blacks, and to do so, sends to the plantations the slaves she captures from other nations. The numbers, however, increase but slowly, and the stimulus of will to work is wanting.

The future of commerce is therefore clouded by the prospect that the tropical materials and products, which must compose the equivalents for goods sold, will not be forthcoming, and the civilized white people of Europe, while they will have no market for their goods, will be deprived of those articles which they have come to consider as necessary. A bountiful Providence has endowed those sunny climes with a soil of the utmost fertility, and has created beings whose constitutions are adapted to its development. He has not endowed them with intelligence, but they remain in their native Africa to-day what they were at the date of the deluge, an unprogressive and savage race of cannibals. The white has emerged from the pastoral state, and risen gradually to the highest development of the human intellect. Providence has not endowed him with the physical capacity to develop the riches of those tropical climes. It has endowed him, however, with the intelligence to appreciate them, and has pointed out to him the means of making them subservient, not only to the white, but to all other races of men. The African, a docile and capable worker, was placed in his hands. He educated him in the path of industry, made him useful to humanity, turned him from the worship of idols to the knowledge of the true God, and raised him from the grade of an animal to the semblance of manhood. The 4,000,000 blacks and their descendants now in the United States, have been raised from the cannibal and troglodyte state to a condition far above that of many white men. This has not been done by their own volition, but through the instrumentality of the slave-trade, ministering to the wants of humanity under the direction of Divine Providence. The system of slavery, and the condition of the slave—moral, religious, and physical— is continually on the advance in the United States, but that advance is due only to the rigorous law of industry, which must be compelled by white intellect. To say that the condition of black servitude is wrong, because some vices and evils attend it, is to condemn humanity and the whole scale of creation, for no part of it is without what appears to feeble human observation as exceptionable. That the black is a dependent race, to be taken care of, was never doubted at the date of the formation of the government. The experiment of making labor optional with them has been made, and has failed. The United States, except Spain, are the only nation that has not made this fatal mistake. France and England are now fearful that she may. They acknowledge their mistake. They are incumbered with pauper blacks, and are doubtful of the future. The course of the United States upon this matter was clearly put by Charles O'Conor, Esq., in his address at the Union Meeting, New York, Dec. 19, 1859 :

" As a white nation, we made our Constitution and laws, vesting all political rights in that race. They, and they alone, constituted, in every political sense, the American people. (Applause.) As to the negro, why, we allowed him to live under the shadow and protection of our laws. We gave him, as we were bound to give him, protection against wrong and outrage; but we denied to him political rights, or the power to govern. We left him, for so long a period as the community in which he dwelt should so order, in the condition of a bondman. (Applause.) Now, gentlemen, to that condition the negro is assigned by nature. Experience shows that his race cannot prosper—that they become extinct in any cold, or in any very temperate clime; but in the warm, the extremely warm regions, his race can be perpetuated, and with proper guardianship, may prosper. He has ample strength, and is competent to labor, but nature denies to him either the intellect to govern or the willingness to work. Both were denied him. That same power which deprived him of the will to labor, gave him, in our country, as a recompense, a master to coerce that duty, and convert him into a useful and valuable servant. (Applause.) I maintain that it is not injustice to leave the negro in the condition in which nature placed him, and for which alone he is adapted. Fitted only for a state of pupilage, our slave system gives him a master to govern him and to supply his deficiencies: in this there is no injustice. Neither is it unjust in the master to compel him to labor, and thereby afford to that master a just compensation in return for the care and talent employed in governing him. In this way alone is the negro enabled to render himself useful to himself and to the society in which he is placed.

"These are the principles, gentlemen, which the extreme measures of abolitionism compel us to enforce. This is the ground that we must take, or abandon our cherished Union. We must no longer favor political leaders who talk about negro slavery being an evil; nor must we advance the indefensible doctrine that negro slavery is a thing which, although pernicious, is to be tolerated merely because we have made a bargain to tolerate it. We must turn away from the teachings of fanaticism. We must look at negro slavery as it is, remembering that the voice of inspiration, as found in the sacred volume, nowhere condemns the bondage of those who are fit only for bondage. Yielding to the clear decree of nature, and the dictates of sound philosophy, we must pronounce that institution just, benign, lawful, and proper. The Constitution established by the fathers of our Republic, which recognized it, must be maintained. And that both may stand together, we must maintain that neither the institution itself, nor the Constitution which upholds it, is wicked or unjust; but that each is sound and wise, and entitled to our fullest support.

"I have maintained the justice of slavery; I have maintained it, because I hold that the negro is decreed by nature to a state of pupilage under the dominion of the wiser white man, in every clime where God and nature meant the negro should live at all. (Applause.) I say a state of pupilage;

and, that I may be rightly understood, I say that it is the duty of the white man to treat him kindly—that it is the interest of the white man to treat him kindly. (Applause.) And further, it is my belief, that if the white man, in the States where slavery exists, is not interfered with by the fanatics who are now creating these disturbances, whatever laws, whatever improvements, whatever variations in the conduct of society are necessary for the purpose of enforcing in every instance the dictates of interest and humanity, as between the white man and the black, will be faithfully and fairly carried out in the progress of that improvement in all these things in which we are engaged. It is not pretended that the master has a right to slay his slave; it is not pretended that he has a right to be guilty of harshness and inhumanity to his slave. The laws of all the Southern States forbid that: we have not the right here at the North to be guilty of cruelty toward a horse. It is an indictable offence to commit such cruelty. The same laws exist in the South, and if there is any failure in enforcing them to the fullest extent, it is due to this external force which is pressing upon the Southern States, and compels them to abstain perhaps from many acts beneficent toward the negro which otherwise would be performed. (Applause.) In truth, in fact, in deed, the white man in the slaveholding States has no more authority, by the law of the land, over his slave, than our laws allow to a father over his minor children. He can no more violate humanity with respect to them, than a father in any of the free States of this Union can exercise acts violative of humanity toward his own son under the age of twenty-one. So far as the law is concerned, you own your boys, and have a right to their services until they are twenty-one. You can make them work for you; you have the right to hire out their services and take their earnings; you have the right to chastise them with judgment and reason if they violate your commands; and they are entirely without political rights. Not one of them, at the age of twenty years and eleven months even, can go to the polls and give a vote. Therefore, gentlemen, before the law, there is but one difference between the free white man of twenty years of age in the Northern States, and the negro bondman in the Southern States. The white man is to be emancipated at twenty-one, because his God-given intellect entitles him to emancipation and fits him for the duties to devolve upon him. The negro, to be sure, is a bondman for life. He may be sold from one master to another, but where is the ill in that?—one may be as good as another. If there be laws with respect to the mode of sale, which by separating man and wife do occasionally lead to that which shocks humanity, and may be said to violate all propriety and all conscience—if such things are done, let the South alone and they

will correct the evil. Let our brethren of the South take care
of their own domestic institutions, and they will do it. (Applause.) They will so govern themselves as to suppress acts of
this description, if they are occasionally committed, as perhaps
they are, and we must all admit that they are contrary to just
conceptions of right and humanity."

This just view appeals to the understanding of every intelligent man. There are none who do not admit that, in every
point of view, the black is better off in his servile state in
America than in his savage state in Africa. To deny this is to
deny all the merits of civilization, since the civilized man loses
a large portion of his personal liberty in submitting to the restraints and conventionalities that are necessary to the peace
and well-being of communities. If, then, the condition of the
black thus far has been progressive, what may not be expected
from a continued operation of the same influence, when his
value has so much enhanced? This question reduces itself to
a mere matter of dollars and cents. At the North, a horse of
$30 value has bestowed upon him a certain degree of care be-
cause of even that value; but when the price of the animal
rises to 5 and 10 thousand dollars, the care he receives becomes
princely. He has expensive stables and special attendance.
His owner becomes anxious for his health and safety, and looks
after the faithfulness of those who have him in charge. Up to
1808, the New England traders would sell slaves in the South
at £30, $135, each. At a succession sale in West Baton Rouge,
a few days since, the following enormous prices were paid for
common field-hands:—One female negro and four young,
$5,650; one male, $4,400; do. do., $3,475; do. do., $3,400;
do. do., $3,305; do. do., $3,200. In Selma, Alabama, a hand
24 years old brought $2,245, a female $3,205, another hand
$2,050. These prices do not indicate merely that the hand is
worth so much more because his services to humanity have
risen in that proportion, but they indicate that he has so much
greater hold upon the consideration of his master. That not
only his material well-being will be better cared for, but all
cruelty, moral and physical, that might affect his health or diminish his usefulness, will be more strictly prohibited ; that the
powers of overseers will be restrained ; that his moral culture,
as conducive to his physical usefulness, will be cared for, and
the path thus laid open to his higest mental and material development. This is the process now going on under direction

of divine Providence, and the black, like the white Northern minor, is legally required to exert himself in the furtherance of the great end in view.   This process is attended with immense benefits to the white race at large and the American Union in particular.   Every part of it enjoys, as we have seen in foregoing chapters, the highest degree of prosperity, and all that is required to prolong and heighten that favorable condition is to preserve harmony, to bear and forbear, and to second Providence in its manifest designs for the welfare of his creatures. If those blacks produced great wealth under white tutelage, and in return for the great blessings bestowed upon them, it is shared by all parts of the Union in a degree; in return, each lends its aid in protecting and fostering a dependent race and promoting its improvement.   The buyers of slave-grown produce are accused, in some cases, of encouraging, by so doing, what some persons believe to be a sin; but they are also, by those purchases, making the value of the slave greater, and thus compelling an amelioration of his condition.   If, on the other hand, he should be made free, his freedom, as the world too well knows, would consist only in the unrestrained practice of vices, a neglect of industry, an abandonment of all hope of improvement, a turning of his back upon civilization, and a resolute return to the brute condition.

The theory of the agitators is that the South will not, in any event, seriously resist the hostile action of the North, no matter how much they may be oppressed; that they will still cling to the Union; that the patriotism they have heretofore so uniformly shown will still induce them to stand by a Union become valueless, since it deprives them of the right to property they have so long enjoyed.   The question with them is not, however, one of mere political ascendency; it is one of existence.   If the cotton-fields, sugar plantations, and tobacco lands are deprived of hands—for that is the ultimate object of the agitating party—of what value will the lands or their surroundings be to those owners?   It will then be too late for them to resist, for they will already have been despoiled.   It is this necessity for timely resistance that begets the danger.   The only mode in which the North can realize the approach of that danger we have endeavored to set forth in the preceding pages, when showing the dependence of all industry upon the productive South.   The preliminary measures have already been taken in most of the Southern States to promote direct trade, and curtail purchases at the North. The first pressure resulting from these measures must fall upon Northern artisans, in the shape of lower wages and diminished work. The non-intercourse, carried to any extent, will naturally produce depression at the North and a rise of prices at the South. If the latter is sustained by any vigorous State legislation, it will give a great impetus to manufactures, which will drain men and capital into the Northern Slave States. The depreciation of property which would follow at the North is matter for serious contemplation, and it well behooves those interested to guard against it.

While the dangers and disadvantages that attend this sorrowful issue are so great, what are the advantages that attend its success ? Suppose the agitators reach the power—they now profess to have but " one policy," and that a negative one. Is it worth while to convulse the world in order to give offices to those who seek them under a sham pretence ; who assert that they oppose slavery in opposition to the law of the land, under the dictates of a " higher law," and who, in making that assertion, profess treason to the " higher law," in favor of States' rights ? Is it not better to stand by the Constitution and the laws, and avoid such issues as are based only on passions factiously excited, and to brand with infamy the man who seeks office at the risk of disunion, anarchy, and servile war ?

# BIBLIOGRAPHY

I THOMAS PRENTICE KETTELL'S PUBLISHED WORKS

1 Books

*Constitutional Reform: In a Series of Articles . . . Upon Constitutional Guarantees in Political Government.* New York: n.p., 1846.
*Eighty Years' Progress of the United States.* By Eminent Literary Men. Hartford: L. Stebbins, 1869. (Kettell was the author of pages 132-225 and 274-434.)
*History of the Great Rebellion.* New York: N. C. Miller, 1862; Worcester: L. Stebbins, 1863.
*History of the Great Rebellion.* 2 vols. Hartford: L. Stebbins, 1865.
*The History of the War Debt of England; the History of the War Debt of the United States, and the Two Compared.* New York: Society for the Diffusion of Knowledge, 1866.
*Southern Wealth and Northern Profits, as Exhibited in Statistical Facts and Official Figures: Showing the Necessity of Union to the Future Prosperity and Welfare of the Republic.* New York: George W. and John A. Wood, 1860.
*Vollständige Geschichte der grossen amerikanischen Rebellion.* Illustrated. Hartford: L. Stebbins, 1866.

2 Articles in Periodicals

a In J.D.B. Debow, *Commercial Review of the South and West* (or *DeBow's Review*)
"The Commercial Growth and Greatness of New York," V (June, 1848), 30-44.
"Currency and Banks," IX (October, 1850), 412-416.
"The Future of the South," XXI (September, 1856), 308-323.
"Industry of the South," XII (February, 1852), 169-181.
"The Money of Commerce, I," VI (October, 1848), 243-264.
"Progress of American Commerce, Agriculture, and Manufactures, I," IV (September, 1847), 85-95.
"Progress of American and Foreign Commerce, Agriculture, and Manufactures, II," IV (November, 1847), 326-337.
"Stability of the Union," VIII (April, 1850), 348-363.
b In *Hunt's Merchants' Magazine*
"British Commercial Policy," XII (June, 1845), 538-549.
"The Commercial Treaties of the United States: With Reference to the Progress of Commercial Freedom," XVII (October, 1847), 339-357.
"Debts and Finances of the States of the Union: With Reference to Their General Condition and Prosperity." Chapter II. "New England States. Maine and Massachusetts," XVII (December, 1847), 577-587.

175

Chapter III, "Middle States. New York," XVII (March, 1848), 243-255.

Chapter IV, "Middle States. Pennsylvania," XX (March, 1849), 256-259.

Chapter V, "Middle States. Maryland," XX (May, 1849), 481-493.

Chapter VI, "Western States. Indiana," XXI (August, 1849), 148-163.

Chapter VII, "Western States. Ohio," XXI (October, 1849), 389-410.

Chapter VIII, "Western States. Michigan," XXII (February, 1850), 131-145.

Chapter IX, "Western States. Illinois," XXVII (December, 1852), 659-671.

Chapter X, "Western States. 2nd Illinois," XXXVIII (March, 1858), 275-286.

Chapter XI, "Western States. Missouri," XXXVIII (April, 1858), 438-444.

Chapter XII, "Western States. Wisconsin," XXXIX (July, 1858), 62-71.

"A Hamburg Merchant in His Counting House," XV (August, 1846), 177-181.

"State Debts of Europe and America," XVII (November, 1847), 466-480.

c In J.D.B. DeBow, *The Industrial Resources, Etc., of the Southern and Western States*, 3 vols. New Orleans: DeBow's Review, 1852, 1853.

"The Future of the South," III (1853), 37-45.

"New York," II (1853), 154-164.

"Southern Industry," III (1853), 45-53.

"Union—Its Stability," III (1853), 357-367.

d In "Strength of Union—Magic of Cooperation," in *The Southern Trade. An Epitome of Commerce North and South, Movements of Exports, Etc., with a Directory of Prominent New York Houses Interested in Southern Trade*. No. 2. New York (May, 1860). Published semi-annually by E. K. Cooley, 66 Cedar Street, New York.

"The Strength of Union," 5-32.

e In *The United States and Democratic Review*

"The Methodist Church Property Case, United States Circuit Court, Southern District of New York, N.Y. 1851," XXIX (October, 1851), 382-383.

"The Podesta's Daughter," XXVIII (May, 1851), 417-429.

"The South," XXVIII (February, 1851), 139-147.

"Stability of the Union," XXVII (June, 1850), 1-16.

3 Newspaper Articles

"Money Articles," New York *Herald*, 1837-1843.

"Printice" weekly article, Washington *Union*, July 7-September 21, 1849.

II CONTEMPORARY ARTICLES AND REVIEWS OF
*Southern Wealth and Northern Profits*

DeBow, James Dunwoody Brownson. "Southern Wealth and Northern Profits." A Review Article of T. P. Kettell, *Southern Wealth and Northern Profits, DeBow's Review of the South and West,* XXIX (July, 1860), 197-215.
Hunt, Freeman. "The Editor to His Friends and Patrons," *Hunt's Merchants' Magazine and Commercial Review,* XXI (July, 1849), 143-144.
[Powell, Samuel]. *Notes on "Southern Wealth and Northern Profits."* Philadelphia: C. Sherman and Son, Printers, 1861.
"'Review' of *Southern Wealth and Northern Profits,*" *Southern Literary Messenger,* XXXII (February, 1861), 159-160.
"Thomas Prentice Kettell," *Hunt's Merchants' Magazine and Commercial Review,* XX (June, 1849), 618-627.


III SECONDARY SOURCES

Albion, Robert Greenhalgh. *The Rise of the New York Port, 1815-1860.* New York: Charles Scribner's Sons, 1939.
Chandler, Alfred D., Jr., *Henry Varnum Poor: Business Editor, Analyst, and Reformer.* Cambridge: Harvard University Press, 1956.
Foner, Philip Sheldon. *Business and Slavery. The New York Merchants and the Irrepressible Conflict.* Chapel Hill: The University of North Carolina Press, 1941.
Russel, Robert Royal. *Economic Aspects of Southern Sectionalism, 1840-1861.* Urbana: University of Illinois Press, 1923.
Skipper, Ottis Clark, *J. D. B. DeBow: Magazinist of the Old South.* Athens: University of Georgia Press, 1958.

# INDEX